CAUGHT IN THE ACT

CAUGHT IN THE ACT

A MEMOIR

SHANE JENEK AKA
COURTNEY ACT

PANTERA
PRESS

The information in this book is published in good faith and for general information purposes only. Although the author and publisher believe at the time of going to press that the information is correct, they do not assume and hereby disclaim any liability to any party for any loss, damage or disruption caused by errors or omissions, whether they result from negligence, accident or any other cause. In the interests of protecting privacy, some names and other details have been changed.

Every effort has been made to trace copyright holders and to obtain their permission for the use of copyright material. The publisher apologises for any errors or omissions and would be grateful if notified of any corrections that should be incorporated in future reprints or editions of this book.

First published in 2021 by Pantera Press Pty Limited
www.PanteraPress.com

The quote on page 288 is from the essay 'Poetry Is Not a Luxury', from: Audre Lorde, *The Master's Tools Will Never Dismantle the Master's House*, London, Penguin, 2018

Please send all permission queries to:
Pantera Press, P.O. Box 1989, Neutral Bay, NSW, Australia 2089 or info@PanteraPress.com

A Cataloguing-in-Publication entry for this work is available from the National Library of Australia.

ISBN 978-0-6454129-0-1 (Hardback)
ISBN 978-0-6452401-7-7 (eBook)

Cover Designer: Alissa Dinallo
Cover Photo: Mitch Fong
Publisher: Lex Hirst
Project Editor: Tom Langshaw
Editor: Kate O'Donnell
Proofreader: Anna Blackie
Typesetting: Kirby Jones
Photo Page Layout: Elysia Clapin
Printed and bound in Australia by McPherson's Printing Group

The paper this book is printed on is certified against the Forest Stewardship Council® Standards. McPherson's Printing Group holds FSC® chain of custody certification SA-COC-005379. FSC® promotes environmentally responsible, socially beneficial and economically viable management of the world's forests.

This book is dedicated to 14-year-old me, and to every 14-year-old out there. (For those of you reading this: first of all, this book is way too racy for you, but more importantly, don't listen to the people who say, 'You can't change the world, you can only change yourself.')

To Colleen, who introduced me to Rocky Horror, *Bob Downe and k.d. lang: I'll fondly remember your homemade pasta and Christmas pudding, but most of all I will remember how much you loved and believed in us. May you rest in peace.*

To Mum and Dad. I love you.

Contents

Opening Act

I would always burst out crying when I watched the opening scene of one of my favourite movies, *Grace of My Heart*, a straight-to-VHS box-office flop. Edna, a young singer–songwriter, is trying on outfits for an upcoming performance. Her overbearing mother, after picking out what her daughter is wearing, says to the sales assistant, 'We'll take the dress she has on.'

'Mother,' Edna says, 'I can't sing in a dress that doesn't fit. Look at it.'

'The dress fits the occasion; it's you who doesn't fit.'

That line was a punch in the guts. I never felt like I fit the occasion either, and not *just* because of the clothes I was wearing. I didn't have an overbearing mother, but I did grow up in an overbearing world – one that constantly told me I had to dress a certain way, act a certain way, even feel a certain way, and none of that lined up with who I was. The clothes I tried on made sense from the outside but, from around the age of 11, a low-lying rumble began: I didn't feel comfortable on the inside. I always felt like I was wearing someone else's clothes – as with Edna, the dress fit the occasion and it was me who didn't fit. I always assumed that was a weakness, but it turned out to be my greatest strength.

I suspect this will be a familiar experience for many people who have picked up this book – that you've been made to feel as though you don't fit. But it's not you and it's not us; it's the system that doesn't fit. In *Caught in the Act* I share my journey towards resolving my questions about gender, sexuality and identity, and through my stories I hope to give you a glimpse of different possibilities.

And listen… I got stories. These pages are a first-hand anthropological study that reads at times like sexed-up Tumblr fanfic (you're welcome). You could even say I've dedicated my body to science; for decades now I've been out in the field, having sex with people from a broad spectrum of sexualities and genders, changing the world one straight-identifying man at a time, boldly going where no mouth-breathing mammal has gone before.

Though I have been caught in the act quite a bit in my life, this book is not all raunchy smut, I assure you. In these pages you'll read of the wholesome love of my parents; my adolescent angst as I grew up in Brisbane in the 80s and 90s; the thrill of the Sydney drag scene at the turn of the millennium; getting lost in drug abuse in my late teens; fumbling around in the dark, trying to shed some light on my gender identity; losing so many reality TV shows and finally winning one. Oh, and there's lots of *Drag Race* tea for you thirsty bitches too – but it's hot, so be careful it doesn't scald your mouth when it passes your lips (consider that the literary version of a death drop).

The prologue of a memoir is basically like the caption on an Instagram video that says, 'Omg! Make sure you keep watching till the end!' But unlike so many of those clickbait videos, as you make your way from cover to cover you'll be heartwarmed, entertained, scandalised and titillated – at least, that's my hope. My other hope is that in reading this book you might see your own flaws reflected back through mine and still find the compassion to hold yourself, and me, in high esteem.

Act I

1

From before I can remember, my big sister, Kim, would put me in fancy dress for Halloween. A clown (though not as glamorous as Bianca Del Rio), a bumblebee, even Crocodile Dundee. What could be cuter than a four-year-old reciting the lines my big sis taught me: 'That's not a knife, this is a knife' and 'Barramundi's a bloody big fish!' We'd gallivant around the neighbourhood trick-or-treating.

We lived at 76 Kennedy Street, Brighton, a coastal suburb right up the northern end of Meanjin (Brisbane). For non-Australian readers, Brisbane is on Country whose custodians are the Turrbal and Jagera First Nations peoples. It's the third largest city in Australia and the capital of Queensland (yes, I was born in *Queens*land). Hot, tropical and conservative, it's basically the Florida of Australia.

Our home was an oasis on an otherwise dull street. When Mum and Dad bought the house in 1980 for $21,500, it was stock-standard suburban. Chainwire fence, buffalo grass, and a Hills hoist clothesline in the back of a single-storey Queenslander-style house, set up on pillars to allow air flow underneath. By the early 2000s, seven-foot wooden fences bordered our rainforest-like yard, which was filled with giant palms, lush lilly pillies and all manner of towering Australian native trees. Organically landscaped undergrowth covered every patch – not a blade of grass remained. There were banksias, bottlebrushes and wattles; fragrant florals like gardenias, jonquils and jasmine. It was less of a backyard and more of an ecosystem that Mum and Dad had built and planted themselves.

Automatic gates led down a pebble driveway to our double carport. In the entertaining area down the back – under a shadecloth pergola – was a big wooden table and an old cast-iron stove repurposed into a classic Australian barbie (barbecue, not the doll). We even had a palm-lined kidney-shaped in-ground swimming pool, the height of 80s suburban success. It might sound like a big place but it was all crammed into 600 square metres, guarded by my best friend, Honey, our German shepherd.

While Brighton was a working-class suburb, we were living the great Australian dream.

Dad was an only child and came to Australia with his mum and stepdad by ship from Offenbach, Germany, in the late 1950s. His mum is best described as 'very German': calling her a clean freak is an understatement. Four years old, sitting at her kitchen table, I'd put the fork down from my last bite.

'Hands up!' she would say.

It was like being apprehended by law enforcement. She wiped the table, my face and hands, and pulled out a hand-powered carpet-sweeper: no crumb could make a quick getaway. Only then was I allowed to leave the table.

Dad was a naturopath and acupuncturist. It mightn't sound too uncommon these days in the trendy metropolises of the world, but on the northside of Brisbane in the 80s it was pretty out there. Dad had been in a bad car accident in the 70s: his seatbelt snapped and he flew through the windshield, fracturing his skull and severing ligaments in his hand and knee. Mum said he was read the last rites and sent home with a bottle of aspirin. Dad's Polish stepfather (and my surname-sake) took him to a naturopath and acupuncturist, who mended him back to health. Inspired, Dad did an apprenticeship then two degrees: bachelors of naturopathy and Chinese medicine. Mum and Dad opened Brighton Natural Therapies Clinic in 1987. They worked from 8 am to 9 pm, five days a week, for all of my childhood, but I never felt like they were absent.

Dad has had his iconic moustache most of his life – he gloats that while in grade 10 at high school, the headmaster gave him an ultimatum: 'Shave off your moustache or don't come back to school.' He didn't go back to school. I've never seen my dad without it and I actually don't know what I'd do if he ever shaved it off.

The giant moustache aside, Dad's always been quite a character. He was never really like the other dads. Most Australian fathers seemed rigid and barely capable of speech, let alone affection. My dad, Gilberto (Gill for short), was free, fun and always let me know I was loved. He was enthusiastic and had a genuine interest in me and the world.

When I was 11 and having a hard time at school, Dad concocted a plan he was sure would make me 'cool'. Back in his day, Dad was a rebel who had pierced ears, long red hair and the aforementioned moustache. Unfortunately the things that made boys cool in the 70s weren't as effective in the 90s. Taking me to the Stefan Hair Salon at Toombul Shopping Centre to get my ear pierced didn't really help: 1) Boys weren't allowed to wear earrings at school, so I wore a bandaid over the gold stud in my ear, and 2) Earrings were the antithesis of cool for boys in my circles! They were for girls, and any proclivity towards feminine presentation attracted the jeers of my peers.

According to a kid in my grade, wearing an earring in a specific ear was a known marker of being gay. I didn't know what 'being gay' meant, but it seemed worse than being a girl; if I was reading the signals right, it was about the most degrading thing a boy could be. No one really knew which ear was the 'gay ear', so my piercing left a big question mark hanging over my sexuality (whatever *that* was).

My mum, Annette, emigrated from Copenhagen, Denmark, with her parents and brother around the same time as Dad, not that they met till much later. On the ship over Mum got sick and they quarantined her in the mortuary with the dead bodies; she recalls being a very scared three-year-old locked in a cold, dark place for a long time. There are many other shitty stories from her childhood; they break my heart when I hear them. One day, she came home from school and her parents had moved house without bothering to tell her. She sat out the front crying until well after dark, when they finally came and picked her up. Mum was determined her kids wouldn't have an upbringing like that.

Throughout my childhood I assigned my mum the same status as a superhero. To me, He-Man, She-Ra and the ThunderCats, stars of my favourite 80s cartoons, were revered symbols of safety, loyalty and strength. That's how I saw my mum. I knew she always had my back. I burst into tears when I wrote that last sentence! Sitting on my chair, hugging myself, with healing tears streaming down my face. Mum made sure I knew I was cherished, whether it was with words, her hugs and kisses, or the 'I love you' notes she'd slip into my lunchbox with my beetroot and liverwurst sandwiches on pumpernickel bread (I thought this was a normal Aussie sandwich, but Mum says it's a Danish thing). She always believed in me, and simply knowing my mum loved me got me through some tough moments. I always knew my parents loved me unconditionally. I doubt I'll ever be able to fully appreciate what a huge impact that has had on my life, and how unique and privileged my situation is. I love you, Mum and Dad. Thank you.

Mum always wore a white power-suit to work – at first as a beauty therapist and nail technician, then as the manager of the clinic with Dad. It was like her superhero outfit: a white cotton blazer with shoulder pads, a white camisole, white trousers and always a heel (in the 80s – by the 90s she was in a sensible white flat). Her shoulder-length blonde hair would be beautifully roller-set, her long maroon acrylic nails always perfect, and she wore a simple day face of glowing skin, mascara, eyeliner, lip liner and a deep maroon lipstick that was always immaculate.

It feels kinda trite to be commenting on my mum's appearance, but I remember so vividly sitting on the bathroom floor watching her put her hair in rollers each morning, in awe of her dedication to glamour. From Mum I learnt about skincare from a young age, whether it was to follow a healthy diet and drink lots of water, or about cleansing, exfoliating and moisturising. When it was time to put on makeup for shows at Fame, the theatre school I went to, my mum came and gave all us kids a tutorial – she was the original beauty influencer. I can still smell the sweet damp of a sea sponge and Max Factor pancake in Bisque Ivory. Mum taught us to use blush on the apples of our cheeks, but also a dash on the temples and tip of the nose, something I still do to this day when I'm getting in drag, and I think of Mum every time. She's such a kind, warm and loving woman who always made me feel safe and protected.

I have two half-sisters: Heidi, Dad's daughter from a previous marriage, and Kim, Mum's daughter from a previous marriage. Heidi is nine years older than me, lived with her mum and family, and we saw her during the holidays. Kim is ten years older than me and we grew up together at Kennedy Street. Mum and Dad are happily married and I'm their only child together. During Kim's childhood, Mum and Dad were 'Aussie battlers', working hard to make things happen; after I was born they moved into the 'Australian success story' phase as small business owners, and it's safe to say that I was spoilt. Kim left home when she was seventeen and I was seven, so she was always a cool older sister who I'd see on weekends to do fun things with.

The night she moved out, after several beers in the backyard with his mates Dad decided to knock out the common wall between Kim's bedroom and the kitchen. Really open the space up and create a formal dining room, or 'good room' as it's known in parts of Australia. Knocking out a wall isn't a small task and requires a team of professional builders with an insight into architecture and carpentry... or Dad and a couple of mates after a few tinnies.

My first taste of fame and fortune was when I was five and Mum entered me into the Tiny Tots pageant. I'm not sure what the judging criteria were, but I cartwheeled into a room at Currumbin Bird Sanctuary, a small zoo with more than just birds, and had a chat with some people who sat behind a desk. Then I got to hang out with the kangaroos and feed the rainbow lorikeets, which was exciting. After I passed the judges' questions portion of the pageant, I was off to the finals at Dreamworld. This theme park on the Gold Coast was the ultimate children's destination: there were rides and waterslides, and the mascot was a giant koala character called Kenny. In the 80s, international air travel wasn't widely affordable and the Gold Coast was Australia's most renowned holiday spot. Only an hour's drive from Brisbane, with its hotels, restaurants, a casino and nightlife nestled along glamorous white-sand beaches, it felt like another world. The final of the Tiny Tot pageant was all business: a sea of children dressed to impress, lined up on a metal grandstand. Mum had bought me a new outfit for the occasion: bright baby-blue trousers and a matching jacket, a baby-blue and white horizontal-striped polo, and white canvas shoes.

'And the winner of Mr Tiny Tot 1987 is... Shane Jenek! Congratulations! Shane Jenek? Shane, where are you? Come on down.'

I was daydreaming about the Rocky Hollow Log Ride and had to be gently nudged back to reality by the girl next to me. I was shepherded to the front, where a sash was placed over my head. People were cheering – I could see my mum in the crowd waving and smiling. It seemed like a big deal, and I enjoyed all of the adults making a fuss as Miss Tiny Tot and I stood at the front of the stage and posed for a photo.

Someone asked if we could hold hands but I wasn't interested at all. Then a photographer asked if we'd kiss. Was he nuts? Someone pushed our heads together and next thing I was face to face, lip to lip, with the white-haired girl next to me. Unimpressed, I scrunched my face up: it was embarrassing being forced to kiss a stranger. Then the photo was all over the front pages of the *Gold Coast Bulletin* and our local newspaper, the *Bayside Star*. Family members sent telegrams (emails hadn't been invented yet) congratulating me on the win and on my new girlfriend. Maybe the forced kiss was my first PR scandal, implicating Miss Tiny Tot as my very first beard?

One year I had my heart set on getting a She-Ra action figurine for Christmas. She was my favourite superhero. I watched her cartoon each day before school and collected the toy figurines: I had He-Man, Skeletor and Man-at-Arms – all men. Yes, I enjoyed running my little fingers over the rippling muscles on their hard plastic bodies, but I really wanted She-Ra. She was so beautiful, feminine and strong. The day she held aloft her magic sword and said, 'For the honour of Grayskull!', I was in love.

'Shaneo, what's wrong?' That Christmas morning Dad had found me behind the couch in the living room crying.

'This is the worst Christmas ever,' I blubbered as if there'd been a global cataclysm.

'Shaneo, why? What's happened?'

'All. I. Wanted. Was. She-Ra!' Hyperventilating between each word.

'Oh, Shaneo, we tried, but she was sold out… Let's go to the Boxing Day sales tomorrow and see what we can find.'

'I love you, Daddy.'

This wasn't a public tantrum designed to get what I want: it was a private moment of grief that Dad accidentally witnessed. The next day it was off to Kmart, a big discount store, to brave the sales and bring home She-Ra. But she was sold out, like Dad said. I was melancholic, despondent.

'What about this one, Shaneo?' Dad was holding She-Ra's horse, Swift Wind, in his hand. My eyes lit up. It wasn't She-Ra, but her white flying unicorn with his pink, blue and yellow wings would fill the void. Straightaway I wanted to open the box.

'Ah, Shaneo. Wait till we get home, please.'

'But, Dad! Why?'

'We'll be home in 20 minutes; you can open it up then.'

Dad's lessons in delayed gratification were challenging to understand. Something else I didn't yet understand was how lucky I was to have a dad who didn't subtly or forcefully suggest a 'boy's toy' instead. The idea that She-Ra (and Swift Wind) might be considered girls' toys – therefore not for me – didn't enter his mind. He didn't blink. Which is the perfect response. Here come those healing tears again. My dad, my primary male role model and benchmark for masculinity, never expected me to fit in a box. He just loved me.

Then I put on some tap shoes. I loved music class at school and I was always singing and dancing around the house, so Mum asked if I wanted to go to lessons. Saturday mornings were for jazz, tap and drama. I made a friend in tap class called Julian Origliasso, and after a couple of months our teacher, Mr Wood, invited us to join him busking. If Tiny Tots was my first time in front of an audience, my first time performing was tap dancing on a couple of bits of Masonite at the Riverside Markets in Brisbane. We wore black trousers and shirts with sequined braces and only had one routine, but it worked with any song. For that two minutes and 52 seconds, everything from rehearsals was focused into one continuous moment. People smiled and clapped and threw coins into the hat we put out. I knew exactly what I had to do and who I was in relation to the world. That rectangle of Masonite felt sacred, and I instantly loved being on stage.

2

At primary school I was happy. I loved learning. But if things didn't move quickly enough I'd strike up a conversation or tune in to a far more interesting event taking place in my head. My report cards always had top marks, but in grade two the comments started: *He can be disorganised and restless at times.* In grade three it was, *Shane chats too much. He is easily distracted.*

In grade four I really disengaged, but it wasn't out of boredom: I encountered one of my first alpha-male authority figures. I didn't like my teacher, Mr Walker. The class was made up of 26 students, each of us unique: 26 different heights, 26 different hair colours, 26 different individual expressions. The only obvious characteristic that delineated us was that half wore shorts and half wore skirts. The variation in uniforms seemed to have something to do with what was between our legs. Mr Walker was insistent that people with penises should act differently from people with vaginas. For the life of me, I couldn't see why: wasn't genitalia dished out at birth in a kind of lottery that determined how you peed, and that was roughly all there was to it? But because I (in particular) wasn't upholding some sort of unspoken agreement regarding these behavioural distinctions, I seemed to incur his displeasure.

What was I doing wrong? Playing hopscotch and skipping rope with the girls at lunchtime was fun! What's not to approve of? I didn't know what he expected of me, only that I felt *less than* in his eyes. I wasn't *right*. Mr Walker's disapproval reminded me of my Uncle Mick's disapproval: 'Shane, quit walking on your tiptoes like a sissy!' Whatever a sissy was, if Uncle Mick's demeanour was anything to go by, it was something I didn't want to be.

Up until this point, all I'd registered in the playground was a mélange of gender identity. Now an invisible divide had emerged and I didn't feel I fit on either side. Despite my being small, gentle and delicate with a high-pitched girl's voice, the adults had decided I was a man. A label I was never able to make fit. After much persistent begging on my part, Mum spoke to the school and I was moved into the other grade four class. As always, I knew that Mum had my back.

Right as things were becoming binary at school, I switched to a new dance school called the Fame Talent Agency and Theatre Company. It was a safe haven where the new rules didn't apply. Fame ran weekly singing, dancing and drama classes all over Brisbane, and the closest one to us was on Wednesdays after school at the Strathpine Community Centre. Our family and Julian's had become good friends and he and I, along with his younger twin sisters, Lisa and Jessica, started going to Fame. Because my parents worked late during the week their mum, Colleen, would take us all to the classes.

When I think about Fame I'm flooded with happy memories of laughter, friendships and freedom. Even though Fame classes were only a few hours a week, they were the highlight of my life for the years I went there. More than that, at those classes I found refuge from an outside world that was increasingly insistent I pick a side. At Fame I was never told, nor did I ever feel, I had to 'butch it up'. There were practical categorisations: when we sang I sat with the sopranos (all girls), and because Julian and I were the only boys, in performances we'd be placed next to each other or else we'd bookend a row of girls. But that didn't lead to microaggressions like it did in Mr Walker's class.

Picture it: Strathpine, a small working-class suburb, 1991 – the first songs we learnt at Fame were 'Step Back in Time' by Kylie Minogue and 'Venus' by Bananarama. That Stock Aitken Waterman sandwich was a joy to my nine-year-old ears long before I knew who the Brit hit-makers were. Thirty years later I still remember our choreography, the occasional slip of a piece of the parquetry floor beneath my feet as I danced, and the desire to be noticed and affirmed by our teachers, Jodie Maller and Crystal Taylor.

Aside from my mum, Jodie and Crystal were the two most beautiful people I'd ever come across – otherworldly princesses of kindness on loan from a fairytale. They emanated joy and support, and always made me feel special. It could have been because I was one of two boys in a gaggle of girls – but no, I was pretty sure they made everyone in that class feel special.

As well as dancing, singing and a whole lot of laughter between the stark white plasterboard walls of the Strathpine Community Centre, I also remember learning to meditate. I didn't know what it was at the time, but one day Jodie and Crystal asked us all to lie down on the floor, close our eyes and relax. They turned off the overhead fluorescent lighting and told us to breathe in and out through the nose.

'Imagine you're lying on the grass on a warm summer's day. Your body is an ice cube and the sun's rays are shining down; feel your body melt into the grass. Feel your toes start to tingle and melt away. Now your ankles are melting into water...'

The room of 40 primary school kids hushed to complete stillness and silence. An extraordinary feat. I felt all my muscles relax and my body go tingly. I couldn't tell the difference between my nose and my toes, my fingers and my ears.

'It's so hot now that the sun is evaporating you up into the air and carrying you away on a cool summer's breeze.' The sensations of my body and the sounds of their voices were the only things in the world that existed. The guided meditation dissolved the construct of time. All over my body I could feel the most delicate version of pins and needles. Jodie and Crystal told us to bring our attention back into our bodies and focus again on the physical room. I heard the light switch flick, and as the electric current flowed into the fine glass fluorescent tubes above, so below my body lit up and started to glow. I opened my eyes slowly and my pupils constricted as I re-emerged into the room. I felt so calm and focused – as if I had travelled somewhere without ever leaving my body.

This exercise reminded me of how my mum would always calm me if I ever got upset or hurt or just needed to focus. Like the time I got my hand stuck to the element on the inside of the fridge, which differed from the time I got my tongue stuck on it. On a tropical, humid Brisbane day, in a time before air conditioning, the metal refrigerator element looked cold and frosty, like a lemonade ice block. The mercury was climbing up to 40, so I decided to pull a chair up to our Kelvinator 480L and give it a lick. My tongue instantly got stuck and in shock I pulled away quickly, leaving behind tastebuds and blood. I spoke with a lisp for a few days, but it healed quickly.

The next summer, I was not quite tall enough to reach the freezer and decided I wanted some ice. I got a knife and began to scrape the frost from the metal element. Noticing how the butt of my hand caught when I accidentally brushed it, I decided to see what would happen if I placed my whole palm on the element. My hand stuck instantly and I couldn't pull it away. I screamed for my mum. She was in the backyard watering the garden, but a combination of my high-pitched squeal and her supersonic mum-hearing alerted her to my distress. Like Cheetara from the ThunderCats she ran at superhuman speed down the driveway, up the back stairs, through the back door, past the bathroom and into the kitchen, where the layer of skin touching the fridge had become solid. Using her acrylic nails as talons she sliced my hand from the fridge, carried me to the sink and ran tap water over my frozen little paw. I was screaming and crying.

'Breathe, Shaney. Take some deep breaths with me. In through your nose, out through your mouth.' She was unable to pacify me at first but didn't give up. 'Come on. Deep breath in, one, and out. Good boy.'

'IT HURTS, MUM!'

'Another deep breath in, two, and out. Breath in, three…' She guided me all the way to eight breaths. My hand was still frozen, but I wasn't hyperventilating at least. Not sure what damage I'd done, she bundled me up and we headed to the hospital. After weeks of going to school bandaged up and having to write with my left hand, my palm healed. Only a tiny invisible bump remains today, which doesn't remind me of the trauma but rather of how my mum was always there to take care of me.

My first year at Fame, the junior musical was *Monster Mash Bash*, a full-length show starring kids from the school's different locations around Brisbane. I played a werewolf in the chorus and had my first encounter with spirit gum, later a staple in my drag career. Every time I glue my lace-front wig on and get a whiff of the spirit gum, I'm transported to the upstairs dressing rooms at Fame. I'm nine years old and a den mum is pulling tufts of hair from a plastic bag and gluing them all over my face to transform me into one of many little werewolves. I wouldn't recommend plying a child's face with spirit gum: it will probably leave an unsightly graze across their top lip like a burn from huffing amyl nitrate, but I assure you I wasn't sniffing poppers – yet. (I also definitely wouldn't recommend using spirit gum as eyelash glue, but I'd have to wait ten years to learn that lesson the hard way.)

There were at least 150 kids in the junior musical – gangs of werewolves, ghosts and Dr Frankensteins buzzing with enthusiasm, fuelled by cans of soft drink and chocolate bars (Passiona, a passionfruit-flavored soft drink, and Fry's Turkish Delight, a rose-flavoured jelly rectangle covered in chocolate, were my faves). The theatre was kinda ugly – an old besser-brick warehouse in Bowen Hills, an inner-north industrial suburb of Brisbane, with bench seating that raked at a sharp angle all the way to the ceiling. It was intended to accommodate only 280, but 300 family members saying, 'Can you squish down a bit?' would cram into every last inch to watch their cherubs on stage. The director of Fame, Mr Kennett, described the space as 'intimate'. This was a further stretch of the suspended disbelief that audiences are asked to bring to the theatre – but when the overhead low-watt institutional lighting snapped to black and the filaments of the stage lights warmed up, the magic that occurred on that stage made up for it all. For eight years, I spent every school holiday in a Fame production in that theatre or on a Westfield shopping centre stage somewhere around Brisbane.

Anyone at Fame under the age of 12 could be chosen to be in the Show Team, a group selected as the best from all the open-call groups around the city. I was on track to join the Show Team when I was cast to play a mouse in a holiday pantomime of *Cinderella*. I don't know what most kids did on school holidays, but mine were spent treading the boards two shows a day wearing a grey Lycra catsuit… or rather, a mouse-suit. Jodie Maller played Cinderella and the musical director of Fame, Brian Emerson, played Gertrude Guzzle-Gutzer (Mrs GG, for short), the wicked stepmother – my first brush with drag. It was in the tradition of the pantomime that the 'dame' role was always played by a man, and Brian was so good at the role that he stole the show. It was grotesque, comedic and over the top, and completely celebrated and accepted in a family environment.

Each day of the school holidays, I got to live immersive fantasies on stage. I loved the songs and stories, the friendships, the discipline of rehearsals, the reward of doing a great show, the laughter, applause and thrill of a live audience. I loved all of the costumes, hair, makeup and creativity. I even broke out my Derwent colouring pencils one day and sketched up some unsolicited charts as suggestions for Mrs GG's makeup.

I loved after the show when Mr Kennett gave us notes. The cast would sit on the motley green-carpeted bench seats while he told us all the things that were right and wrong with the performance. He was a short, round, marvellous man who taught me theatre craft. Many people worked extremely hard to make the magic that was Fame happen, but the vision started with Mr Kennett. He'd often get overexcited and squeal like a kid. Sometimes he'd yell, but I always sensed his love for us and his love for the craft. He even imparted showbiz superstitions and etiquette – like never to say the name of the Scottish play, no whistling backstage, and that peacock feathers were bad luck on stage.

When I turned 11, I moved from Strathpine Juniors to the Show Team, and from my state school to St Paul's Anglican school. Mum and Dad had booked me into St Paul's for high school and figured I might as well settle in for my last years of primary and get acquainted with the set-up. Unfortunately I hated it almost instantly. Until then, I'd been with the same kids since pre-school – we'd grown up together; any changes had happened so incrementally that they were just accepted (despite Mr Walker's best efforts). St Paul's was a battlefield where new binaries were apparent – public/private, poor/rich, secular/religious. The kids were unfamiliar and mean, the school campus was vast and cold, and there was a big emphasis on sport and an even bigger emphasis on religion.

I'd never been to church and the whole concept of religion seemed creepy to me. I didn't understand what their cloud daddy was all about; he seemed like a bit of a vengeful prick tbh. On Fridays we had to go to chapel, sit through a church service, and hear dark stories about how this old, supposedly white, dude sent his only son to be murdered on my behalf because a woman made from the rib of some guy in a garden got tricked into eating an apple by a lisping snake. I mean... come on? What a violent ideology to indoctrinate kids into! I always sat up the back by myself and never spoke any of the words from the prayer or hymn books. I was scared of supernatural beings and what wicked spells they might conjure if I uttered their words.

Instead I'd tear out the translucent pages of my green prayer book and practise making origami, an idea from Japanese class. I loved that you could take a plain piece of paper and turn it into something special. Not that I was particularly good at it – all I could make was one of those paper fortune-tellers when I'd rather have made paper cranes and butterflies and tortoises.

Thanks to a YouTube tutorial, I've just made my first ever paper crane. It brought me so much simple joy; I've put it on my bookshelf with some other prized possessions. It was a lovely circle back to an incomplete childhood experience. Some of my favourite moments as an adult are remembering how to be a child again. I'm nearly 40 and the older I get, the more I love reclaiming the artefacts of my youth, many of which I was never allowed to fully enjoy at the time simply because I was born with a penis. There are so many expectations placed on us and I've found that adult life has been about recognising those expectations, acknowledging them, and working out if they serve me. Often they don't, and I now get to reimagine how I want the story to go. An expectation some people might have of me is that I shouldn't go around folding paper into butterflies – because I'm a boy or because I'm an adult. But really there are no rules. I'd have dazzled the other kids at St Paul's with my Japanese paper-folding skills if only I'd had an online tutorial back then.

Alas, I wasn't yet skilled in the tactics of diversion: I was simply a target who hadn't learnt to draw attention away from the more vulnerable aspects of myself and so I was bullied, verbally at first, and then physically. And it wasn't just the students: there was another alpha-male teacher at St Paul's. It wasn't as bad for me as I know it is for many queer kids, but it was still a horrible experience. I was chased and had rocks thrown at my head; I was spat at; I was shoved into a hand dryer in the locker rooms, which left a bleeding gash on the back of my head.

It wasn't always the big things – in life it's the little things that can get to you the most and are the hardest to understand.

When someone throws a rock at your head it's pretty clear. But all the microaggressions, the looks, the exclusion, the 'straight as default' expectations are small acts of violence that can never be understood by a child, and compound over years and years. I couldn't understand why I was being singled out, and I don't think the aggressors even knew. All we knew was that there were two categories: boys and girls. And I didn't fit properly into either.

Between the bullies and apathetic teachers, I was miserable. I begged Mum and Dad to send me back to public school. All my friends from primary school would be going to Sandgate District State High: that's what I wanted. But they asked me to stick it out at St Paul's for another year.

In my bedroom, I put 'Without You' by Mariah Carey and 'Again' by Janet Jackson on repeat. Eleven years old, crying into my pillow, wishing I could die. I made some limited attempts to end my life: I tried holding my breath and suffocating myself under a pillow and in the bathtub. I sat on the first-floor windowsill of our home, considering jumping, but I knew that, at best, I'd only break a limb, which wouldn't alleviate any of my pain. My attempts weren't serious, but the fact is I was experiencing suicidal ideation at 11 years old. I had loving parents, a great home life; I had friends at Fame, where I got to express myself freely – and I *still* wanted to kill myself. That's how despicable and violent the heterosexist world can be for a young queer kid.

If you want to kill yourself too, it's OK – you absolutely shouldn't do it, but there is nothing wrong with you for feeling like you want to. Wanting to cease existing when your existence is constantly threatened and invalidated, and even greeted with violence, is a normal reaction. Suicidal thoughts are valid, but please don't act on them. There are people out there who get it, and who will care about you. I care about you. There is someone to talk to: even if you don't exactly know what you want to talk about, just having someone willing to listen can be helpful. In the back of this book, there's a list of websites and phone numbers you can text or call. Never hesitate to reach out. You are loved.

3

Australia in the 90s wasn't a completely desolate wasteland of heteronormativity. There were glimmers of a different reality – of hope – that I would mentally bookmark, without fully understanding what they meant. When I was 11, I found all the older boys at Fame gathered around a cassette. I asked what it was, and they seemed unsure if they were allowed to say, handing me the plastic case without explanation. The song was RuPaul's 'Supermodel'. It was clear that the excitement they were feeling was also a secret.

There were also whispers from that same group about the Sydney Gay and Lesbian Mardi Gras Parade being broadcast on the ABC. That Sunday, I stealthily recorded it on the VCR in my bedroom and played it later when Mum and Dad thought I was asleep. My TV didn't have a remote control so I stood right next to it, watching with the volume turned down in case someone came past and I had to switch it off. Mardi Gras looked like a Fame musical. There were people in colourful costumes dancing in the street and having a good time. There was such freedom and fun to it – I didn't know why this was a secret, but I understood I had to be covert.

When I was 12, the video of Madonna's Girlie Show Tour elicited a bodily function that, until then, I hadn't been aware of. As the number 'Deeper and Deeper' evolved into an orgy scene, Madonna gyrated between two dancers. The two men, with their hands and mouths all over Madonna, reached across and started sexually touching each other. Huh! I hadn't known that was possible. I felt movement in my underwear and stopped to rewind and play that scene over and over, stretching the Mylar tape and warping the sound. I watched in awe as human bodies of all genders and colours writhed on stage and simulated sex in crushed velvet. This kicked off my sexual awakening (though I fell back to sleep moments later).

No one ever explicitly explained anything about queerness; no one really even alluded to it, not directly at least. I could see the trees blowing, but no one told me what wind was. There was no concept in my mind of what being gay, lesbian, bi or trans was. I didn't know two men or two women could like each other. I didn't know boys could be 'feminine' and girls could be 'masculine'. There was no reference point in the world around me for who I was if I wasn't the default. Growing up queer in the 80s and 90s was like searching for pieces of a jigsaw puzzle I didn't know existed while everyone was trying to hide them.

If only someone had told me. Laid it out in simple terms. I wish there'd been honest and frank conversations going on as well as visible queer people in the world and on TV. I can't begin to explain what a significant difference that would have made, or what a difference increased visibility since then has made for queer kids today. Growing up in a world of queer invisibility was so isolating. The strange part is I didn't know I was isolated – I didn't know I was learning shame, or to hide who I was for safety: it came instinctively for survival. Every now and again I wonder if I've retrofitted shame where it didn't exist. Then I remember: shame is a deposit made for a future debt, and it accumulates over time with compound interest.

When we weren't rehearsing at Fame, the Origliassos and I would be hanging out at their place. Julian and I would play *Zelda* on Super Nintendo, and Lisa and Jessica would do whatever girls their age did – us boys didn't pay them much mind. I really loved getting to be a part of their family and I loved the priority their parents, Colleen and Joseph, placed on entertainment. They were encouraging parents – Julian, Jessica and Lisa had microphones and stands, a PA, and even some lights to rehearse their numbers with – and I got to reap the benefits of that. They saw potential for their kids, and me, to be stars, and I always sensed Colleen's belief in me and my talent. A few friends from Fame performed in talent quests at shopping centres and RSLs, a kind of community centre for veterans and their families where the community is also welcome. The Origliassos stood out as they were super polished and had matching costumes.

My first comp was at Deception Bay Shopping Centre and I performed a freestyle dance solo to 'If' by Janet Jackson dressed in red cross-colour jeans, a white Bonds undershirt and a set of striped braces. Although I didn't win, I got a highly commended award. Dancers never won talent quests so at the next one I sang. Mum and I had a killer coat made to go with the 'Joseph and his Amazing Technicolor Dreamcoat Megamix', and I entered the Hyperdome Talent Quest – which I won. Then I won the Suncorp Variety Crackerjack Carnival Talent Quest singing my rendition of 'Don't Rain on My Parade', despite being told by one of the judges at the heats to 'choose more appropriate songs for a boy' (I showed him!). Then the Origliassos asked if I wanted to start performing with Lisa and Jessica as the Yabba Dabba Doo Young Entertainers. I was so excited to be a part of their troupe. We got bookings at Blue

Light Discos, a police initiative for under-18s, and Lions Club meetings, and of course continued on the talent quest circuit.

Colleen Origliasso, or Mother Two as I called her, sat us all down and aired *The Rocky Horror Picture Show* with the sex scenes edited out. Probably still too adult for a couple of 12-year-olds and two nine-year-olds, but we were going to do a *Rocky Horror* performance and it was important we were familiar with the source material. We'd sung 'Time Warp' in the *Monster Mash Bash* at Fame, but that was a far cry from getting to see Dr Frank N. Furter, Brad, Janet, Riff Raff, Columbia and Magenta in all their celluloid glory. Now this might come as a shock, but I played Brad, not Frank. Years later, after *Drag Race*, I got to play Dr Frank N. Furter when dental issues forced Adore to pull out and I got the last-minute call to play alongside Bianca as Magenta. I've never been happier about anyone's root canal problems. But this 90s Brisbane rendition was sort of like my first ever drag show: we lip-synced along to the dialogue from the movie but sang the songs live. We performed it at the Bracken Ridge Community Hall at a benefit to raise money for someone who'd had a car accident – this was what people did before GoFundMe. Strangely, the perfectly formed Adonis, Rocky, barely enters my recollection.

Colleen was always delivering key bits of pop culture we'd have otherwise missed. She loved The Divinyls and Baz Luhrmann, and had a burning passion for John Travolta. Despite being a married woman and k.d. lang being an out lesbian, Colleen loved k.d. in her early country-music days and even when she released an album called *Drag*. It was a joy when we all went together to see k.d. in concert; getting to appreciate an artist through someone else's eyes is such an exciting thing, and k.d. didn't disappoint. With her smooth voice and confident swagger, she was mesmerising: I understood why Colleen admired her. Colleen was the only adult I knew who passionately loved pop culture. It was never what was *cool*, though: her tastes were left of centre, often on the edges. She was so sure about the things she enjoyed that it encouraged us to fall in love with them too, and also find our own slightly off-centre things to love.

Lisa, Jessica and I were closer now we were a bit older and performing together. I'd been a part of their family since they were four and loved them as if they were my little sisters. They were twins born on Christmas Day and were the cutest pair. I imagine the sweetness of their younger years led to the rebellious image they had in 2004 when they formed The Veronicas. By then I'd been living in Sydney for a few years and was stunned by the sight of them: these sexy, grungy, red-lipped girls. When they topped the Australian pop charts with their song '4ever', I was proud and inspired to see my childhood friends become a bona fide success. Initially I was nervous around them because of their fame. But I quickly realised they were still the kids I'd dressed in bright colours and sung 'Love Shack' with.

One day at their place Lisa, Jessica and I were rehearsing a medley of Aussie rock classics – we'd changed the words of the AC/DC classic to 'It's a long way to the shop if you wanna sausage roll' – when Colleen called me upstairs.

'Shaney, quick, come look at this!' On the TV was *Good Morning Australia* with Bert Newton, and his special guest was Bob Downe: a flamboyant man dressed in a polyester safari suit with a blond wig, swirling around the set in the most peculiar of ways.

'Isn't he wonderful?'

It shocked me that a man could act like that, and on television no less, but before I was able to fully connect, the shame crept in. I became aware *I* had been singled out to watch this. Why had Colleen only called *me* upstairs? I was spooked. The logical reaction would have been to see that Colleen was an ally, letting me know she saw me and approved. But I didn't see myself yet, so instead I was defensive.

Maybe Colleen had cottoned on because of the rumours she'd heard about my party trick. Packs of Fame kids often had sleepovers on the weekends and school holidays; nothing was better than sleeping on a makeshift bed on the floor with a group of your best friends. One night at a sleepover at the Cains' house, for some reason I came out of the bathroom naked with my junk tucked between my legs and declared, 'Look! I'm a *girl*!' I didn't realise the youngest Cain family member, five-year-old Franny, was in the room. She saw me, screamed and started crying. In shock, I lost control of my rudimentary tuck and exposed myself; it became Fame folklore. When word reached Mrs Cain I was unofficially off her sleepover guest list. Thankfully, I'd discovered tuck tape by the time I lost my skirt on live TV heading into the *Celebrity Big Brother* house in 2018.

The art of tucking is like origami in reverse, taking a penis and balls and turning them into a flat surface. When cold, scared or ejaculating, your testicles (if you have some) retreat up inside your body, so when tucking you gently push them back up there and pull what's left (the scrotum and penis) between your legs. There are regional differences with what to do next: in Sydney we'd purchase a tucking G-string, with a one-way stretch that holds it all in place, from the House of Priscilla on Oxford Street. In the US a similar garment is called a gaff and can be made out of a pantyhose waistband and a cut-up tube sock. These days, to achieve a tight and sturdy tuck I use a delicate paper surgical tape from a pharmacy to mummify my scrotum and penis into one stump, and then three pieces of clear vinyl PVC two-inch-wide tape that I get from the hardware shop. One piece goes from front to back, and the other two from one side at the front to the other side at the back. I turned my teenage party trick into a profession!

In 1994 the world was gifted *The Adventures of Priscilla, Queen of the Desert*. The movie was a cultural phenomenon and a hit at the box office in Australia; it won an Oscar and two BAFTAs and received a string of other nominations. Three drag queens on a bus trip to the middle of Australia! I was in awe of the characters, the heart and of course the costumes. It was all anyone at Fame could talk about. Dad remembers us watching it as a family and me, then 12 years old, running through the house with a scarf trailing behind me after Felicia's iconic scene sitting on top of the bus lip-syncing to 'Sempre libera (Free Forever)' from *La Traviata*. My loins were also captivated by a hunky Guy Pearce in a pair of plaid overalls painting the bus purple – 'It's not purple, it's lavender.' He was muscular, strong and handsome, but didn't seem trapped by his masculinity like most men did. He transcended it, embodying flamboyance and theatrics in a way men weren't 'supposed' to. But what did all that mean exactly?

That said, I in no way imagined I'd one day make my career as a drag queen. I loved the freedom and frivolity of the characters in *Priscilla*, and the film was the first mainstream 'gay' thing I'd seen, so there was something subconsciously validating about that. I definitely identified with the non-traditional masculinity of the characters and I'd say it also introduced the concept of the trans experience into my brain. *Priscilla* became a touchstone, but nowhere in my mind did it give me an 'a-ha!' moment pertaining to drag or my own sexuality.

That December I went on a bus tour of my own with Fame in a show called *The Spirit of Christmas*. In *Priscilla*, Mitzi, Felicia and Bernadette unplug their curling wands and head to Lasseters Hotel and Casino in Alice Springs, but our busload of 40 Famers were driven 13 hours north of Brisbane to the Pilbeam Theatre in Rockhampton. On the bus we watched *Priscilla* and I listened to the soundtrack on my Discman. The final night of the tour we had a cast party in Toowoomba and, as was tradition, put on a show for each other.

My friend Scotty and I decided to do a number. Scotty was a friend but also my sometime nemesis – though I doubt he ever knew he'd knocked me off my perch as the favourite boy at Fame when he came onto the scene.

Scotty had packed some wigs from his dress-up box at home, so we borrowed bikinis from the girls and applied a smear of lipstick and a lick of mascara. We lip-synced 'I Don't Care if the Sun Don't Shine' by Patti Page from the *Priscilla* soundtrack, and Shanice and Scottina became a legend of that tour.

The whole performance happened by accident. I didn't set out to perform in drag; it wasn't a deep, burning desire, just something that happened naturally. It does seem odd how transgressive it was perceived as when a boy dressed up as a girl, a boy who'd previously dressed up as a bumblebee, a werewolf and a mouse; at least I was dressing as the same species! But I take pride all these years later in the fact that my first drag performance was at 12 years old. Makes me feel extra queer. I wear it as a badge of honour.

Growing up, I didn't have many aunts, uncles or grandparents in my life, but Fame filled those gaps. In my Fame family everyone knew everyone's business and everyone cared. Whether it was carpooling (probably not called that back then), rehearsals, the dressing room between shows or sleepovers whenever possible, there was a strong sense of community, support and love. All of us were growing up together as people and as performers. We weren't at Fame because we had to be: we were all there because we loved it. It kept us out of trouble and was free babysitting during the school holidays for our families. Everyone won.

I admit I've dusted off some rough edges in the name of nostalgia, but it really was a joyous, important and informative time of my life. I'd miss that feeling of family when I left Fame to focus on my senior years at school, and when I moved to Sydney at 18 I left most of those friendships behind. But a couple of years ago, some 25 years later, I contacted a few Fame friends and invited them to be in the audience of a *Dancing with the Stars* live show. I was heartened by how familiar we all were. Like no time had passed. Not a shred of awkwardness – we knew the key things about each other, the underpinnings of the people we'd become. As an adult, in nearly every similar situation, being faced with other people's assessments of who we once were can feel oppressive, but because Fame was a foundation of freedom and authenticity there was never anything to feel oppressed by.

4

It was time for high school. Mum and Dad could see their little boy's light was starting to dim at St Paul's: my grades were slipping too. I begged relentlessly to go to Sandgate High and eventually just flat out refused to go to St Paul's. Against their better judgement and wishes, Mum and Dad relented.

It wasn't quite the return to the remembered utopia of the publicly funded school system I'd hoped for, but it was a noticeable reprieve. Grade eight, the first year of high school in Queensland, *everyone* was new and adjusting. Kids from different primary schools in the area were conglomerating for secondary education. The old hierarchies were destroyed and new ones were being built, and the social order was demonstrated by where you sat at lunchtime. The artsy students sat near F block; there was a large group near the music block; the popular girls sat outside A block; and the popular boys sat under the A-block walkway. I sat by the library and spent most of my lunch hours working as a library monitor. I've since learnt that queer kids all over the world have historically claimed sanctuary in the school library at lunchtimes. It was a safe place, away from the sports field: no jock would go there. Generally though, I floated between social circles at school, always feeling on the edge.

High school is saved in my brain as a horrible experience, yet I recall only a few specific dreadful incidents and a lot of fond memories. What was horrible were the different layers of struggle of being queer in the 90s. There were the abovementioned flashes of queer pop culture, but nothing regular or normal or aspirational. Mostly when queer people were talked about in pop culture or in the world around me it was with disgust or as a punchline. All of this, coupled with general high school angst and the sudden addition of hormones to our bodies, cast a shadow over a lot of high school. I didn't understand who I was. I didn't know I was in the closet because I didn't have any understanding of what 'the closet' was. I guess the closet doesn't just hide your identity from others; it can also hide it from yourself. I knew I had feelings for boys, but those feelings were unacknowledged because I didn't know they were possible.

I don't want to flash forward too much, but I didn't realise I liked boys until I moved to Sydney when I was 18. And I wasn't aware I'd suffered with the shame of being queer until I read *The Velvet Rage* sometime in my mid-20s. That book finally gave me the language and tools to understand how growing up gay in a straight-as-default world we learn very early on that who we are is to be hidden and 'we fear that there is something about us that made us unlovable'. So while the individual moments at high school didn't necessarily feel painful, they contributed to an underlying shame about who I was.

One sunny lunchtime I found myself running along the edge of the playground where it met the local bushlands. Strong ironbark trees blurred as I whizzed by. I was running as fast as my legs would carry me – being chased by some bullies. It wasn't a familiar experience at Sandgate High, but that's not why this memory stands out. Randomly, a tall, handsome, blond senior stopped me dead in my tracks. I don't know where he came from, or how I had so much of a headstart on the bullies that any of this had time to transpire.

'Are those kids bullying you?'

'Yes,' I answered coyly.

'Get behind me and just agree with what I say.'

Really I had no choice. Next thing, the boys chasing me were right there. Whereas this senior had spoken in a polite and conversational volume to me, he turned to the bullies and let them have it: 'ARE YOU BULLYING MY LITTLE BROTHER?!' My knight in grey Stubbies was outraged.

The posse were slack-jawed.

'You bother him again and I'll rearrange your faces. Ya hear me? NOW GET OUT OF HERE!'

I was slack-jawed too. Enamoured. Speechless. I didn't know why this senior who didn't know me had done that. He just stepped in and saved the day. But that was when I learnt about allyship. This senior had reached across the threshold to help me. He was an upstander instead of a bystander. I never knew who he was but I've thought about that moment many times throughout my life. Those little acts of kindness go a long way.

At school I went out of my way to be different. Perhaps I could have been a wallflower, assimilating and drawing as little attention to myself as possible, but I took the opposite path. Being different wasn't a real choice though; it was irrepressible. The things I loved were always different – I don't know if I loved them because they were different or if I was different because I loved them. Where all the other kids had soft zip-up pencil cases, I had a hard clipped-together one. They used biros and I went for the far superior liquid-ink Uniball (I still write with a Uniball). I had a manicure kit in my pencil case and would sit there filing my nails in Business Principles class. One day, the teacher told me to stop, but I didn't really like her so, as she stood tapping her foot waiting, I took as long as possible packing away my cuticle oil, orange stick and favourite Vaseline Intensive Care hand cream. Some hand creams left you feeling greasy; others didn't moisturise enough; but this pink tube of wonder was my Goldilocks of 90s suburban hand cream. Not something most teenage boys probably think about I suppose, but I was the child of a beauty therapist and nail technician and had dreams of becoming a hand model! Most likely a ladies' hand model.

Driving into school one morning I was complaining to Mum that I wanted to stop biting my nails. I didn't bite them down to the nubs but I certainly didn't have the perfect manicure I desired.

Mum suggested, 'Just stop then.'

Which sounds like a redundant piece of advice, but it cut through. She was right. If I wanted to stop biting my nails, all I had to do was stop. And I did. It gave me a real sense of empowerment, knowing I had this control over my own mind.

My choices all made perfect sense to me – they were practical, functional and I liked them – but as I said, I think my desire to be different was also a factor. Part of it was a defence mechanism – I knew I was different from all the other boys, and there was no hiding it, so I sought ways to really articulate that. Instead of repeating the same mistakes I'd made at St Paul's, I learnt how to give the popular boys superficial things to focus on to keep them from seeing the vulnerable part of me, which I knew was different in really unacceptable ways.

Take the humble backpack. I didn't like it: I had so many heavy books to carry around, and putting them on my back seemed silly when the practical solution of a roller bag existed. We didn't have lockers we could leave our books in, so I brought a carry-on style roller bag to school. I have no idea if this is a thing anywhere – maybe kids use them for school now? It was certainly absurd back then. Roller bags were barely a thing in air travel, let alone in high school.

'Can you pick up B105FM on that thing?'

This was a kid at school referring to a local radio station and my braces headgear – basically a fabric jockstrap on my head with a silver metal bull bar protruding out the front. I only had to wear it for eight hours while I slept, but I chose to wear it to school as well. Even my mum tried to stop me: 'Shaney, you know you only have to wear your headgear at night.'

'Yeah Mum, I know. But Dr Patrikios said I would get it off sooner if I wore it as often as possible.' My defiance was rooted in pragmatism: I was honestly grateful to have orthodontics hanging off my face. Before braces I couldn't close my mouth over my bucked front teeth, and if I was ever going to be famous like my idol, Leonardo DiCaprio, I would definitely need a Hollywood smile.

Despite the bullies, I was pretty well liked at school. I exuded confidence, and to the outside world it seemed like I gave no fucks about what anyone thought. And I guess I didn't, to an extent, or I'd have assimilated. But there was one group who always took issue with my existence – the popular boys who sat at A block. They weren't all horrible, but their group was the source of constant low-level, and sometimes medium-level, bullying.

When my therapist and I talk about adult behaviours or repetitive patterns, often the memory that flashes into my mind is standing looking at where the boys sit at A block and asking, 'Why don't you like me?' I couldn't understand why they were disgusted by my existence. I was bullied for what I can see now was my air of femininity. Even though I was called 'faggot' and 'poofter', I wasn't having sex with anyone and wasn't really aware of my sexual attraction to boys. I knew these words were slurs and not anything I wanted to be. I wasn't aggressive. Or tall, or strong. I wasn't good at sports. I wasn't toeing the party line and all the boys let me know so. They'd try to shame me into being a man. I definitely felt shamed, but I never felt like a man. I was incapable of pretending to be what they were: if gender is a spectrum I was much closer to the middle.

What confused me most was my sense that they were performing their identities too. I saw how they puffed out their chests in confrontation, played up when the girls were around, and bowed down to male authority figures. They were trying every bit as hard as I was to 'be a man' – I just had further to travel. And yet the things I loved doing were more important to me than their approval. I had my parents' approval, I had approval from the kids at Fame, and most of the kids in my grade seemed to like me – just not the popular boys at school or most men.

My first computer was an Atari 1040ST. It was pretty fancy: its files could be saved on a 3.5-inch floppy disk with a storage capacity of 1.44MB. That's less than half of a single photo taken on your iPhone today. We didn't have the internet yet; I'd dial local phone numbers to log in to a Bulletin Board Service and hear that iconic sound through my 9600BPS modem: *Pshhhkk kkkkrrrrkakingkakingkakingtshchchchchchchchcch*ding*ding*ding*

When I was 14, we were connected to the actual internet and got a new modem. It was before Google so you couldn't search the net – you just had to know the web address you wanted to go to. A school friend told me about a porn site. The computer was in my bedroom, so I sat there in an office wheelie chair and typed in the address. The page was white with green text, and as I scrolled through the headings *The Birdcage* caught my eye. A movie of that name starring Robin Williams had recently come out; it was set in a drag club in South Beach, Florida. The link description was *The web's best pages of gay material.*

I rolled my chair forwards and clicked on the link, and a list of filenames loaded up. I selected the first one and an image started to load. In those days it would take a couple of minutes to load a photograph as it would appear slowly, line by line. First the man's hair, eyes, nose, mouth, neck, shoulders… My crotch started stirring, so I got up and locked my bedroom door. As his chest loaded, I was fully aroused and started masturbating. The image didn't even get to load his junk before I'd ejaculated all over the plastic office chair mat on the floor. I closed the website, got a tissue and disposed of the evidence.

The real revolution was IRC, or Internet Relay Chat, which allowed you to connect with people all over the world. I'd log on to the DALNet Server and hang out in the #14and15yearold chatroom. Someone would ask a/s/l (age/sex/location) and everyone in the room would sound off. I was 13/m/Brisbane. My handle was Xman – I was obsessed with X-Men comic books, collector cards and the cartoon series.

IRC was this strange world beyond the superficial where no one had a face or a backstory and there were no expectations of anyone – they were whoever they said they were, and I was whoever I said I was. No text logs of those conversations survived, but I tried on different ages, genders and other identities, playing around in a fantasy land to see where it got me. There was a user called Stormy who I thought was cool and would chat to a lot, and even though they'd have stated their gender when someone asked a/s/l, I can't remember whether they said M or F because it wasn't a relevant part of their identity to me. No one cared if my hips swished when I walked. They cared about what was in my head.

While I was Xman online, in 1996 I became a Spice Girl at school. My obsession with the world's most successful girl group led to the forming of a new girl group at Sandgate High. Kimberly, Kate, Morgan, Belinda, Hailey and I shared a passion for the Spice Girls that transcended playground politics. Figuring the best way to be different was to be exceptional, I became exceptional at being a Spice Girls fan. I learnt everything there was to know about them: their full names and birthdates, their lyrics, their B sides. Mum and Dad let me buy anything and everything Spice Girls, including the dolls. Now the envy of every red-blooded girl in school, I went from library monitor to popular girl sitting with the others at A block.

In the Spice Girls, with their 'girl power' slogan, I saw five girls defying what society said they should be, and it gave me strength. Although I wasn't a girl, I felt liberated to defy what society said *I* should be. Women might still have been struggling for equality, but the Spice Girls refused to wait: they demanded it. Although I wasn't even aware of what misogyny was back then, I now recognise the force that oppresses women as the same force that was oppressing me. I was being told that being feminine, creative, expressive, flamboyant and emotional made me 'less than' what a boy or man should be.

The Spice Girls got me through high school: they were cooler than any bully in the playground. On a family weekend away to Melbourne I bought a pair of four-inch Buffalo Boots like the Spice Girls wore. As Mum and I got out of a taxi at the hotel with the giant shoebox, the bellboy said, 'Thank you, ladies.' I turned the same colour as my red Saba lambswool turtleneck jumper. How embarrassing to be called a girl in front of my mum.

Back up in our hotel room I tried to use the groundbreaking technology of phone banking to transfer some money from my savings account to my keycard.

'I'm sorry, ma'am. This account says it belongs to Mr Jenek.'

'Yes, this is Mr Jenek.'

'I'm sorry, ma'am. I don't think you understand what I'm saying.' She must have thought she'd muted her mic 'cause then I heard her say, 'You'll never believe this. There's a woman on the phone trying to access an account for a Mr.'

'I can hear you! I'm putting my mum on!' I replied in hurt and frustration.

Then Mum took the Bakelite handset and stretched the curly cord to her ear. I squished up beside her so I could hear too.

'Hello, this is Mrs Jenek, Shane's mother. Shane is not a she; he is Mr Jenek. He's just young.'

Still not using the mute button, the phone banking woman then said to her colleague, 'Get this: now she says she's put her mother on the phone but it's just the same person doing a voice!'

Twice in one hour. First my appearance was on the wrong side of the binary, now my voice. I felt my face heat up with embarrassment again. I'd failed at the most essential task I had – being a boy. And in front of my mum no less! Well… I did look and sound like a girl, so what I perceived as an attack was simply society operating as usual. There was no language available to Mum or me to acknowledge that it was OK I was a feminine boy. To Mum, I was her little Shane. She wasn't judging and comparing my masculine development against some arbitrary yardstick; she just cared that I was happy and felt loved. Mum defended my identity by correcting the bellboy and the phone banking lady, but this reinforced the necessity of my adherence to the correct side of the binary. Maybe there was something wrong with me.

After I spent a week exclusively speaking in a Spice Girl accent and wearing my Buffalo Boots to school, Ms Quartermaine, my English teacher, bailed me up in the playground with some advice. This wasn't a teacher telling me what to do, she was speaking to me human to human. 'Shane, I love your shoes, and I get it. I get the statement you're making. I'm not saying you shouldn't make it or that you can't wear those shoes to school, but I just want to point out that these boys are so anally retentive they're not going to get it. And maybe not wearing those shoes to school would make your life easier.' Once she said the word 'anally' I started chuckling; I didn't know what she'd meant but I've always chuckled at dick and bum humour.

I valued Ms Quartermaine broaching the subject – more than any other teacher ever bothered to do. Her advice was enlightened for 1996, but essentially I was being asked to change my behaviour to placate the bullies. An effective strategy to mitigate my bullying, but really backward when you think about justice. Still, I did stop wearing the shoes to school. They were like a red flag to a bully. I didn't care – I loved those shoes – but I'd made my point (they were also really heavy and painful to wear all day).

Lisa, Jessica and I had made a talent quest friend called Beccy, and the four of us formed a Spice Girls tribute band under the moniker Mixed Spice. We all loved the Spice Girls and loved each other. I had a crush on Beccy and followed her around like a puppy dog, but she never took my advances seriously. Over time, she and I became like brother and sister, but we made a pact that we'd get married if we were both still single at 30. We were… but by then agreed circumstances had changed. My mum and dad had hoped Beccy and I would fall in love and give them beautiful grandkids, but that wasn't to be.

On 31 May 1998 I was in grade 11 and had to take the day off school: Geri had left the Spice Girls and I was heartbroken. The previous two years of Spicemania had given me so much strength and Geri was my queen. Needing to grieve in the digital age, I taught myself to code HyperText Markup Language (HTML) so I could start a Geocities page and memorialise the greatest girl band of my lifetime. When I recently googled 'Geocities' and saw the pages had been deleted, I was mad.

My ambition was to be a Spice Girl when I grew up. I never presumed that would happen, or dreamt I'd get a video message from Geri when I won *Celebrity Big Brother*, or sing '2 Become 1' with Melanie C, live on stage in NYC at World Pride, or that 22 years later I'd see them live on stage at Wembley Stadium (sans Victoria)! I was inspired by their punk energy and ability to be true to themselves in a world that told them they couldn't. That empowered me.

Move over Barbie; teens and tweens now had five archetypes they could embody instead of just one. Myers and Briggs have been doing it wrong all these years. Instead of INTP all you needed to know was someone's GSSBP (Ginger, Scary, Sporty, Baby, Posh) – their identity within the Spice Girls taxonomy – and you would get much greater insights into someone's personality. If it was OK for the Spice Girls to be different then it was OK for me to be different too.

In grade 12 I had *SPICEBOY 99* embossed on my senior jersey. As the 90s came to a close, I strutted across the bitumen playground at school in my Buffalo Boots, roller bag in tow, with this homage to my teenage saviours emblazoned across my back.

Now that I was one of the popular girls, I had to walk past the boys at A block to get to my lunch spot. The jeers evolved from gay slurs to accusations I was trying to steal their girlfriends. I mean… which one is it, boys? Am I a poof? Or am I kissing the girls? I can't be both! But… they were right. I did like boys so I guess I was a faggot, but I also had crushes on their girlfriends. I had distinct crushes at different times on each of my five best friends in school, and even managed to make out with two of them! What a weasel. That's another reason I got by: I *was* attracted to girls – not grossed out by them, like many gays are, so it wasn't like I was denying the entirety of my sexuality.

The girls weren't the only ones who took my fancy though; I had unacknowledged crushes on the boys too. The male school captain, Ezra Dale, was dreamy, with his snaggle-toothed smile and golden surfer curls. But there was one boy in particular – Ritchie Samson. He was so hot – a gymnast with the body to prove it: he had actual muscles – the only boy who did. Ritchie had taut, tanned skin, shoulders that were broad from doing backflips and calves strong from leaping into the air. Two buxom pecs rested atop an assortment of ripples and bumps, framed by V-lines that led down to his crotch. His brown hair was floppy on his head and sparse in the middle of his chest.

Above all he had this cheeky smile and he always used it. The other boys didn't smile, but Ritchie? Forever grinning. He was one of the boys at A block, but because he'd come to Sandgate midway through high school he seemed to socially float on the outside. Ritchie was the only A-block boy who ever spoke to me like an equal; he engaged with me, smiled at me, looked me in the eye. But no matter how much I pined for him, or any boy back then, it was only ever in my mind. I was never able to express my feelings out loud to friends, to my parents, and definitely not to the objects of my affection. Ritchie was never going to be capable of loving me back.

That unrequited schoolyard crush set the stage for my love life. The deepest romantic and sexual feelings of my formative years were never acknowledged – they stayed a secret even from myself. Yes, I knew I had these feelings, but without a social context to understand what it all meant, those experiences got stored as mild traumas instead of as stepping stones towards healthy adult lust and love. The core human expression of my desire was stunted – there was no place for it to exist in the world I lived in – so it was added to the box of unresolved issues in the attic of my mind.

While deep down I longed for the innocent first love of a boy, I focused my external efforts on girls. My earliest success story in the dating department was Chloe Jones, my first girlfriend and my first kiss. We were 15, both had braces and both went to Fame. The first time our lips touched, I was confused by her tongue going into my mouth. I hadn't known that was part of kissing: I'd assumed it was an exclusively lip-focused activity. Our braces sporadically clanging together is a 90s mood.

Under my bed lay a solid collection of dirty dishes with Weet-Bix and soy milk dried to them and a Vegemite jar filled with olive oil. I'd siphon it off from the bottle in the kitchen hoping Mum wouldn't notice and use it to assist my 'nocturnal emissions'. I'd fantasise about different people and scenarios – the Spice Girls, Sarah Michelle Gellar (and Ryan Phillippe) in *Cruel Intentions*. Girls from school, boys from A block, Marky Mark, Antonio Sabàto Jr, Leonardo DiCaprio, the men in Dad's *Muscle & Fitness* magazines. Oh, men really did seem to turn me on. Worried my mum could read my mind, and figuring my thoughts would be loudest when I ejaculated, I'd switch to thinking about a girl when I came. I didn't want Mum's ESP detecting my secret.

After school, before Mum and Dad finished work, I had plenty of time to myself. One evening after twirling the white curtains of our rumpus room into stunning red-carpet gown creations in the mirror I decided to explore my bum, specifically the hole part. I tried a shampoo bottle but it was too scratchy, then a carrot from the fridge but it was too cold, and finally settled on a banana. For some reason, I put it in a condom. I went into the shower and tried to put it up my butt, but it wouldn't budge: too much friction. I smeared on some tea-tree body wash and tried again. Squatting on the terracotta tiles with the glass walls steaming up, I slowly slid the tip of the banana inside me. It wasn't really sexual – more of a science experiment.

With a couple of inches of banana inside me, my sphincter proved too strong for the structural integrity of the fruit and it took a bite. Now I had a quarter of a banana inside a condom, inside my butthole, and the tea-tree soap was starting to sting. Try as I might, I couldn't seem to get it out. After an hour tugging at the condom, popping in a finger or two trying to ease it out, I started to freak out. How could I explain to Mum that I had a banana in a condom stuck up my bum? Would she have to help me? This was too much – I had to get it out. With a couple of fingers, one final tug and a push, the banana slingshot out of my arse and I lay on the shower floor exhausted.

On most weekends in grade 11, someone whose parents were out of town would throw a house party.

'Shaneo, are you going out tom-catting tonight? Find yourself a girlfriend?' said Dad. When anyone asked this question it was like a punch in the guts, but when it was Dad, it was worse. The question would bring on panic that I was about to be caught out.

That was on my mind when, 16 years old at one of those parties, under a powder-coated metal carport over an oil-stained slab of concrete I took a drastic step… After finishing off a Lemon Ruski, a lemon-flavoured vodka drink in a can, I discarded the empty then fished around in the icy water of a blue cool box for another one. Settling on a West Coast Cooler, my hand stinging with the cold, I grabbed the bottle opener and popped the cap. Then I noticed someone looking my way – Savannah Danvers, an attractive blonde girl who reputedly lacked qualms about sex before marriage. Which retrospectively is a healthy approach, but that's not how she was described around the playground. I flashed her my newly metal-free smile and walked over to say hello. We started kissing, sloppy tongues exchanging saliva in our mouths and enamel sporadically clanging into enamel.

Everyone else in my grade was losing their virginity and I decided I needed to see what it was all about. My make-out session with Savannah was getting hot and heavy, then she stopped and said, 'I'm not going to have sex with you. I only have sex with my boyfriends.'

The jig was up.

'Can I be your boyfriend?' I asked, demurely.

'OK,' she said nonchalantly, as if she'd just accepted a glass of water.

A week later, we found ourselves in my bed between walls plastered with Spice Girls and Leonardo DiCaprio posters. The olive oil in the Vegemite jar under my bed was the only virgin left in the room by the end of the night. A week after that, we did it on a front lawn at another underage-drinking house party. A few days later we broke up. It had been a heady two weeks, and I'd be lying if I said I didn't use Savannah for sex. I found her attractive, but I'd been eager to have sex because I needed to prove something. Not sure to who. Myself? The girls? The A-block boys? I was desperate for a piece of the puzzle to start making sense.

For the grade 12 formal my date was the school captain. The female one, Kimberly, not Ezra; she was one of my Spice Girls sisters. She let me design her dress – an obvious clue that I missed – and wore a beautiful black velvet bodice with an ivory duchesse silk satin skirt (I was insistent on silk and not polyester). I bought myself a pinstriped suit from an Italian menswear designer called Elio Moda. Completely unlike the rental tuxedos, it was a mid-thigh three-button single-breasted jacket with stovepipe pants. I added black patent-leather shoes, a black shirt and a satin-finish royal-blue tie. My frosted tips went perfectly with Kimberly's barrel curls.

At our valedictory dinner I sang 'Copacabana' by Barry Manilow (HELLO!), but I rewrote it as a parody about our school:

> Her name was Nola,
> She was a teacher,
> Then she came to Sandgate High,
> Back in 1995…
> At the Ana Anabacapoc,
> That's Copacabana spelt backwards…

During the night I acquired a white frangipani behind my ear and won the 'Most likely to become rich and famous' peer-voted award. Australian daytime TV icon Kerri-Anne Kennerley had gone to Sandgate High and there was a photo of her up in the lobby of the office. I always dreamt of having my portrait up there one day next to KAK's, but as yet I believe it's just her and tennis player Wendy Turnbull.

Through my senior years I'd struggled to work out what to do after I finished high school. Going to university held prestige, and shame surrounded any other choice. The part of me that needed to be the best (the smartest) chose my subjects for me: straight maths and science – Biology,

Chemistry, Physics, Maths B, Maths C – and English. Ever since grade six, I'd wanted to be a surgeon. Or a lawyer... my mood changed depending on whether I was watching *E.R.* or *Ally McBeal* on TV. That's when I realised I wanted to be an actor.

And who was I kidding? I love science and maths, but those subjects were way harder than I was willing to work in grade 11. Most of my energy went into surviving the social aspect of high school, so I didn't have enough headspace for algebra and the acceleration rate of gravity at the Earth's surface (9.8 metres/second). For the second semester I switched out of Maths C, Physics and Chemistry to the more sensible choices of Dance, Drama and Economics. I still wasn't focused: I was used to doing well without trying too hard, but those lazy A grades disappeared. I was fine in Dance and Drama, in Biology and English I did OK, and I passed Maths B and Economics, but not with the usual high marks.

In Queensland the metric to gauge entry into tertiary education is called an Overall Position or OP. It's a score out of 25 where 1 is the best and 25 is the worst. I was aiming for a 4 but was expecting something higher (as in... not as good). I'd have to wait months to find out how I had done.

But now school was out forever and that meant Schoolies Week on the Gold Coast. Thousands of kids would converge on Surfers Paradise for a week of drinking and debauchery to celebrate the end of final exams and mark our pathway into adulthood. I was only two months off being 18, so Mum and Dad allowed me two bottles of alcohol to take with me. I chose a bottle of vodka and a bottle of Kahlúa, and bought cartons of soy milk so I could make Soy White Russians (as if White Russians at Schoolies weren't gay enough, given I was the son of a naturopath dairy wasn't a part of my food pyramid).

The girls and I rented hotel rooms in the same complex as the boys from A block. I was a little nervous to fraternise with them out of school with no teachers around to ensure my safety, but there was a weird easing of tension. I became a ping-pong ball in a social game between the boys and girls to determine whose side I'd end up on by the end of the week. The boys apparently decided to bring me into their fold, so one night there was lots of drinking and pulling bucket bongs from the spa bath. The next evening the boys, all proud, proclaimed to the girls, 'Nah, Shaneo is one of us now. He was up all night getting drunk and stoned with us!'

'Well, guess who did my makeup before we came out tonight?'

'Ahhh fuck! Shaneo! Noooeeeee!'

Even though the boys were devastated when I crossed back over, it was different now: I didn't threaten them, they just saw it as some fun. But this battle of the binary would play out inside my mind for the next 14 years as I tried to work out whose side I was on. The boys'? Or the girls'?

New Year's Eve arrived, the millennium ticked over, and my university entrance score came. It wasn't what I hoped for. I can't tell you my OP because I have genuinely blocked it out. My plan – in tatters thanks to my score – had been to go to NIDA, the National Institute of Dramatic Arts, and it was well known they rarely accepted people straight out of high school anyway: they wanted first-year students to have some real-world experience. So I bundled this in with my poor OP and saved face by saying I was taking 12 months off so I could get into NIDA the next year.

I found myself on the threshold of adulthood empty-handed. My future appeared hazy and my sense of failure was intense. It had nothing to do with Mum and Dad, who didn't make a fuss or say I'd underperformed academically. But I'd internalised the pressure and expectation, and felt as if I'd ruined my life. I was 17 and it was all over – yet it hadn't even begun.

Act II

5

When the taxi pulled up on Oxford Street – within hours of my arrival in Sydney – I didn't realise I was about to plant my foot down in my new home. I was 18, it was the year 2000, and Sydney's Golden Gay Mile was buzzing. Taylor Square was clogged with cars and people crammed the footpath. The traffic signal turned red and the collective glow from the brakelights cast a scarlet hue across the faces of people waiting to get into the bars. At the Californian Café patrons seated at tables sipped caramel lattes through straws – I later found out the locals knew the beverage as a Queen's Coffee. The newsagent two doors down Blu-Tacked covers of *DNA Magazine*, featuring the perfect forms of buff men, in its window. Between the newsagent and the café was the Stonewall Hotel, a staple of the Sydney scene but still relatively new. Its three-storey sandstone façade, lit with a coloured wash, beckoned me inside. As I shut the taxi door my heart rate ramped up to 120 beats per minute – matching the tempo of Kylie's 'Spinning Around', which blasted through the archways of Stonewall's entrance.

I hesitated, then turned to my friend Stephanie from Fame, who was putting me up for the week.

'That's not one of those gay bars, is it?' I asked.

'Yeah, you'll love it. Trust me,' said Stephanie.

I wondered why she'd take me to a place of such depravity. Didn't she know I was straight? Thankfully Stephanie knew me better than I did.

Prior to Stonewall, my only nightlife experiences had been going to straight bars in Brisbane with the girls from school. Bars like City Rowers, official home to the Queensland Reds rugby team. Everyone there drank Bundaberg Rum and Coke, but I drank vodka and orange. This has to be important data for anthropological studies on whether being gay is nature or nurture: I was inherently drawn to white spirits. Turns out – to make a sweeping stereotyping generalisation – gay men don't drink brown spirits. I knew rum and rugby clubs weren't for me. One week the girls had suggested we catch a taxi to the valley and go to The Beat – a well-known gay bar. It was loud and filled with cigarette smoke and the only light source was UV tubes. All the patrons were wearing raver pants in neon colours, with mesh tops and reflector patches glowing in the black light. The ultra-fast techno music pounded in my brain. We did one lap and didn't stay for a drink. Nope. Didn't belong there either.

Another Brisbane friend of Stephanie's, Dimitri, had been staying with her; it was his last night and my first night. Dimitri probably assumed the same about me as I assumed about him, which was that the other was a flaming homosexual. He reminded me of one of the boys from Fame and we felt pretty comfortable around each other. I showed my very necessary ID to the bouncer to prove I was of Australian legal age and headed through the doors. Immediately I was in awe. *This is what gay is?* A whole bar full of people dancing and having fun to Bardot, S Club 7, Kylie, Vanessa Amorosi, Steps, Savage Garden and Madonna? All my favourite music! The vibe was thrilling and the place was packed. We manoeuvred our way up the narrow staircase to the third level, where we could get a drink from the bar and there was some space on the dance floor. The vibe of Stonewall was different from any bar I'd been to before: people, men, were dancing and letting loose; in fact I was dancing in a group of men and one woman, when usually I was the only guy on the dance floor. The men were wearing different clothes from what those in straight clubs wore and, more than these superficial differences, there was an atmosphere of celebration and freedom. I wasn't feeling threatened by big, aggressive straight men. I wasn't checking my behaviour, looking over my shoulder, waiting to be mocked or intimidated. I was so relieved. I could just dance and have fun without fear of retribution.

A couple of drinks in and a cute boy grooved up against me: my first ever real-world sexual contact with another human male! My heart was now racing much faster than the blasting pop beats – I'd never had someone express sexuality towards me with such ease before. He grinded up on my butt in a cheeky way and blood started flowing to my crotch. I felt exhilarated and aroused. For a moment. Then I realised Stephanie and Dimitri might see, so I quickly pulled away. I whispered to the guy to meet me downstairs and told the others I was going to the toilet. I ran down the stairs to the second level to find him waiting. I felt safer away from the eyes of those who knew me. This experience was new and I needed it to be mine – I needed to explore in private.

The boy and I made our way across to the far corner by the DJ booth and sat down on the sticky black leather couch punctured with cigarette burns. Before I even had a chance to ask his name, his mouth was firmly planted on mine. Our lips locked passionately as an entire lifetime of denied sexuality was unleashed in a single moment. Something innate and intrinsic that had lain just below the surface for the past 18 years was being acknowledged for the first time. All along I'd been 'speaking straight as a second language' with a very heavy queer accent, completely unaware I was translating in my head the whole time. His kiss triggered a synaptic connection in my brain that remembered the truth of my identity. My native tongue.

His lips were so soft and gentle, and through his kiss I felt connected to all the boys who danced within those walls. Something made sense. It felt so good. Something I'd never experienced that felt utterly familiar, and people who were strangers felt closer than my friends. We shared a bond. I'd found somewhere I belonged, somewhere I could be myself, all of myself.

In science class at school we learnt that you tested a hypothesis with practical experiments. I'd just disproven the hypothesis of the A-block boys that to be a 'faggot', 'poofter', 'queer' or 'homo' was the most contemptible and disgusting thing to be. How could something that felt so beautiful, so intense, so honest, cause such disgust? I now had empirical evidence that being a faggot was far more beautiful than anything I'd experienced thus far. The boy at Stonewall and I sat there connected at the mouth as if we were one organism, two halves that had finally found each other, desperately trying to put ourselves together again. One of his hands grasped my neck, the other the small of my back, and he pulled me in tighter.

Then came a tap on my shoulder, though I could feel both of his hands on my body. I felt another tap. I pried myself from his lips and turned to look. It was Stephanie. Shit!

'Hey, sorry to interrupt. We're going to go soon. Do you want to come with us?'

I stood up quickly. She didn't look displeased, but what was she going to say in private? Was she disgusted? Would she even let me stay at hers now she'd seen me kissing a boy?

'Um… yeah… I'll come with you guys. Is that OK?' Despite never wanting this moment to end, I didn't even know where Stephanie lived or how to get around a big new city like Sydney.

She leant in closer and whispered, 'Was that your first boy kiss?'

I winced like a puppy about to get hit with the newspaper. 'Yes.'

'Congratulations! I'll leave you to it. Meet us out the front in ten minutes.'

Congratulations? Stephanie *celebrated* the fact I was kissing a boy? In that brief moment, my sexuality was positively reinforced and I'm so grateful. It set the tone.

I sat back down with the boy for the long kiss goodbye, tore myself away, dashed down the stairs, and jumped into a cab to head back to Stephanie's. I never got his name or his number, but my journey had begun.

Back at Stephanie's house it was time for sleep. She and her boyfriend lived in a share house, so Dimitri and I slept on the floor at the foot of their bed. Dimitri was nice enough, although I didn't really fancy him. Fair to say he's what I'd now call a sister, not a lover. But I was still reeling from my first kiss and found myself lying in a dark room next to him. The lights went out and my hands drifted across to Dimitri's body. His hand nervously grabbed onto my arm and pulled me closer as we quietly did it on the floor while Stephanie and her boyfriend slept. It was nothing like the kiss. There wasn't any passion – it was more perfunctory. Negotiating the logistics of putting my penis into his butthole was… awkward. I assumed

Dimitri was an old hand at sex and that I was the newbie, but he seemed tentative.

'Is this OK?' I asked him.

'Yes,' he whispered back. 'I've just never been with a guy before.' Despite us both presenting to the world as quintessentially gay, we each operated with a massive dose of denial and identified as straight. My first kiss with a boy at Stonewall, and then Dimitri and I lost our boy virginities to each other on the floor of a Pyrmont terrace house.

This trip to Sydney was initially about discovering whether I wanted to study acting or musical theatre in 2001. My plan was to attend an open day at NIDA, then fly across the country to Perth for the open day at WAAPA, the Western Australian Academy of Performing Arts. I never made it to Perth, and I never made it to NIDA either. I was too busy going to Stonewall and having a sexual revolution. I was only in Sydney for a week – I needed to make up for lost time.

No one else wanted to go out the next night, but there was no way I could keep away. I went back to Oxford Street and checked out a different gay bar called Palms. It was down a set of dark stairs – a room that flashed with disco lights under a low ceiling. I stood off to the side by myself, drinking my vodka orange, gazing around in anticipation. A tall German guy who said his name was Rommy came up and started chatting to me. I felt an instant flutter of excitement. He had a smiley, flirty vibe and I thought he was handsome. We started making out and his kiss was warm and sloppy; he had big, soft lips and I liked it. We kept chatting but through his accent and over the music I wasn't entirely sure of everything he was saying, so we finished our drinks and walked up the stairs to the street. We strolled towards Taylor Square and he asked if I wanted to come back to the Bat & Ball Hotel, where he was staying.

In his room he didn't turn on the light, but his sun-kissed skin glowed as his fine blond body hair caught the light from the street lamp outside the window. As I stood up to get my jeans off, I glanced back at Rommy lying on the bed – I'd never seen a man naked in real life. He was beautiful, like a life model in film noir lighting. I ran my hands over his muscled torso like I would my He-Man action figurines as a kid. Unlike the night before, we didn't have to be quiet or discreet and, with my body atop his, we pressed against each other and he kissed my neck as if eating the most delicious dessert ever. I let out yelps of ecstasy and gyrated my crotch into his body. Our passion mixed with body heat and we started to sweat, lubricating our bodies, sliding on top of each other as we let out carnal groans and grunts. Sweaty love-making is one of my favourite sensations.

I fell asleep in his arms and awoke snuggled against him when morning started illuminating the room. I just let out a little groan of ecstasy thinking about how beautiful that night was – intimate, sexual, passionate, kind. After the kiss at Stonewall and the fumble in the dark with Dimitri, this felt like my first… *holistic* sexual experience. I said goodbye feeling giddy from the pleasure in the brand-new day. Then I remembered: *Oh crap! I didn't get his number.*

The next night I went out by myself to the Oxford Hotel. Stephanie told me I should start my night with a cocktail they made called the Oxford Smash. I went up to the bar on the second level, Gilligan's, ordered one and drank it. The highball glass was filled with gin, Chambord liqueur and cranberry and pineapple juices mixed with Champagne and two melon balls. My hands and feet felt warm; the drink's effect was immediate. I went to the bathroom to pee and a man came and stood next to me at the urinal. I'd stood at urinals next to men many times before and never had anything remotely interesting occurred, but, now that I was aware of the possibilities, it was exciting. I glanced over with only my eyes and, heart thumping, slowly turned my head towards the man standing next to me. He was looking right at me. He motioned his head to the side, and I knew to follow him into the stall. The man and I started kissing; he undid his pants and I pulled mine to my ankles, took off my shirt and hung it on the door hook. We started going for it and he sat down on the toilet seat. Not really sure what to do or how this worked, I turned around and tried to sit down on his penis, but he stopped me suddenly:

'Not without a condom!'

'Why?' I asked. 'I'm not going to get pregnant.'

'How old are you?'

'Eighteen,' I replied.

Without explanation the guy stood, did up his pants, and left the cubicle.

The Oxford Smash was in full effect now. Undeterred, I wandered out of the stall and back out to the urinal. Another man walked in and the process repeated. I can't really tell you anything about either of the guys, except that they both had penises. All I can see when I try to recall is their waist down, like how the faces of adults in a Tom and Jerry cartoon are always portrayed as being above the line of sight of the viewer. The guy sat down on the toilet with his pants undone and his erection standing full mast. But as I got down on my knees

I felt a sharp, cold shock hit the back of my head. *WHAT WAS THAT?!* My body froze as my senses went into a panic. Disoriented, it took a moment to realise I'd been doused: I was wet, and ice and water lay on the floor. There was banging on the door.

'All right: out of there, you two,' came a loud and intimidating voice.

My heart was galloping.

'Just a minute...' said the guy casually as he did up his trouser buttons. Wondering what was going on, I did the same and followed him out of the cubicle. Waiting at the door was one of the cocktail waiters. Grabbing me by my shirt collar he said, 'Come with me! Downstairs.'

Was I being thrown out? Why had he thrown a Champagne bucket of ice water over me? What about the other guy?

We walked out the side door and were standing on Oxford Street.

'All right, what's your name and where are you from?'

'Sh-Sh-Shane,' I stammered. 'From Brisbane.'

'You can't do stuff like that!' His tone wasn't angry, more concerned. 'You have to wear a condom!'

'Why? I'm not going to get pregnant.'

'Because of HIV.'

My head swam. 'I don't know what that is.'

'Don't you remember the Grim Reaper ads?' he said, referring to Australia's shocking 80s TV advert about AIDS.

I shrugged. 'Maybe.'

'Oh god! OK. Let me tell you a few things.'

He sat me down on a big concrete pylon in the middle of Taylor Square and patiently explained the birds and the... birds. I was so naïve. Sex education at school was strictly heterosex based – all we learnt was that you wear a condom when having sex if you don't want to have a baby. We didn't even get taught how to put a condom on. It was years before I learnt about the whole pinching-the-tip part. He pulled a couple of condoms out of his pocket, put them in my hand and told me I had to 'wear a condom when having sex, no excuses'.

I thanked him and he said I could have his number if I had any questions. This time I was prepared, in case I had another Rommy experience: from the pocket of my bright yellow Helly Hansen knock-off puffer jacket I pulled out a small mint-green notebook and pen. Mobile phones could only store ten phone numbers back then, and it was a lengthy process adding them. He wrote his name and number in my book – Luke Nero. I only ever saw my guardian angel again once or twice from across the street. I didn't get to tell him how important that chat had been.

For the rest of my stay I explored Oxford Street – by night the Midnight Shift, the Lizard Lounge, the Flinders and the Beresford, and by day the House of Priscilla, Aussie Boys, The Pop Shop, Pile Up, Betty's Soup Kitchen, Sax Leather, the Pleasure Chest, Café 191 and Pepa Mejia. I cancelled my trip to Perth and went home to pack up my things and hatch a plan. Resuming my old closeted way of life in Brisbane was unimaginable; I couldn't take the new me back home. He just wouldn't fit. I knew I had to move to Sydney somehow.

6

Returning to Brisbane felt like trying to put toothpaste back in the tube. Every sentence that came out of my mouth was prefaced with 'In Sydney…' and then came a nervous mental check: had I revealed my recently discovered proclivities? I couldn't tell anyone about my new life: nobody would understand. In my Brisbane experience there was no conversation about or visibility of queer people, but Sydney, at least the part I'd seen, was a whole new world.

Sat on the black leather three-seater couch in our very 90s living room I turned on Channel V. I always loved watching the latest music videos and seeing which songs were at the top of the charts, dreaming of the day when I'd see my name up there. In between videos the host, Andrew G (now Osher Günsberg), talked about a nationwide reporter search. This seemed too good to be true: I could totally be a music TV host! When I was in Sydney I'd been to the Channel V live studio and stood out the front watching them film the daily live TV show *By Demand*. Up came the dates of the Brisbane auditions and my little heart broke: they'd happened while I was in Sydney. But the Sydney auditions were happening the following week!

I got on the phone to Qantas, booked a flight and called Stephanie and asked if I could stay again. She was happy to have me, but only for a couple of nights. Fair enough. The pub down the road from her, the Dunkirk on Harris, had a bed-and-breakfast upstairs. When I was back in Sydney I went and spoke with the bar manager, who showed me to a dark and dingy room with a bed, a downwind view of the Pyrmont Fish Market and a communal bathroom. 'Thanks, I'll take it,' I said, then I lugged my bags up the stairs and settled in: the next day was the Channel V open call at Fox Studios.

Determined I was going to be the new host, I arrived early and did my best to make a good impression. I made it to the final group, went home and waited eagerly for 'the call'. Later that week it came! The production manager, Peter, got on the phone and delivered the bad news: I didn't get the role – that went to Yumi Stynes and James Mathison. But I was young and hungry and *had* to move to Sydney, so I asked Peter if any other roles were going. Anything at all? He'd been the one to audition me: he could see my enthusiasm, he said, and as a matter of fact someone was going on holidays for three weeks and they needed a fill-in. That was all I needed.

'Mum, Dad! I'm moving to Sydney,' I called as I walked through the back door of Kennedy Street.

'That's nice, dear,' came the reply.

My suitcase was empty, 'cause I'd left the contents with Stephanie. Now I had a week to work out what I'd fill it with for my new life.

The day before my flight I was in my bedroom, and there was stuff everywhere. Cleaning my room was never a simple process for me; things would get very messy before they got clean. I craved organisation but wasn't good at maintaining it.

'You tidying your room, Shaney?' Mum was taken aback at the piles of stuff everywhere.

'No, I'm packing.'

'What for?'

'I'm moving to Sydney.'

'What? I thought you were kidding!' Mum's voice held a note of dismay.

'I didn't get the reporter search role, but I got offered a role as the production assistant and who knows what it could lead to.'

'Shouldn't you, Daddy and I all have a chat about this?'

'It's TV, Mum! Jobs like this don't come along every day. I have to jump on it.'

I sat down and tried to make it right with Mum. To me it seemed so obvious: I'd literally been training my whole life for a career in the entertainment industry. Every holiday pantomime, every shopping centre talent quest, every rehearsal, every singing lesson was leading to this opportunity.

When I arrived in Sydney my résumé read:

Foxtel – door-to-door cable TV salesperson – two months
Jimmy's on the Mall – waiter – two months

And now I was adding *Channel V – production assistant – three weeks.*

Production assistant is an entry-level job, which for me meant answering the phones when viewers called during the live show, taking their requests and picking people to put on air to chat to the hosts. It wasn't rocket surgery, which was good because one of the stops on the bus journey from work was Stonewall. Every time, I'd tell myself to go straight home, but the hydraulic bus door opening beckoned me to Oxford Street and I'd leap to my feet and scram. That dank little room in Pyrmont could wait; I had a life to live.

Stonewall's social hierarchy was revealing itself. Ricca Paris, the promotions manager and matriarch, was a tall, glamorous Samoan trans woman who stood at the end of the bar on the third level holding court. She was always in a gorgeous dress, with beautiful makeup and her hair pulled up with a big afro puff on top. Your proximity to Ricca determined your social standing, so every night I spent at Stonewall I'd inch closer to her and her crew. It was like A block at school, except welcoming and exciting. Ricca was the coolest, and whenever I spoke to her she was lovely and warm. I figured I'd just have one drink at Stonewall, maybe two, then go home to bed. Best laid plans and all that, because when I woke up the next morning not sure where I was or whose bed I was in, I'd have to figure out how to make my outfit look different so when I went into work no one would notice I hadn't been home.

At MaleBox at Stonewall, a tall, blond and handsome boy named Paul took my fancy. He was from the Central Coast – new to Sydney too. Another thing we had in common was the pressing topic of coming out to our parents. Mine were coming to Sydney to visit in a few weeks, and it felt scary. Emotions seemed to work faster back then: we met on Wednesday night and by Friday night I was in love with Paul and asked him to be my boyfriend. He said he had feelings for me! *But* he'd just met a guy called Lee who he had feelings for too, and asked if he could have a couple of days to think about it. Seemed upfront and reasonable.

In the interim the three of us – me, Paul, Lee – and two other boys we'd met, Eddie and Linus, checked out Caesars

Bar, in a suburb a few kilometres from Oxford Street that was aptly called Camperdown. By Sunday, Paul had decided on Lee, which hurt. But being in a group of new gay boys exploring our options was fun. Despite my disappointment, all five of us continued being friends, with the two of them dating.

Back at work at Channel V on Monday I got chatting to Osher. He and his then girlfriend, Cymone, were from Brisbane and had visited my dad's clinic. They knew all about Fame because it was across the road from B105, the radio station where they'd both worked as drivers of Black Thunders, branded SUVs that would drive around the city handing out giveaways. When Osher gathered I was searching for somewhere to live, he suggested I check out the *Sydney Star Observer*, the gay newspaper, saying it might provide me with leads. It was a simple but memorable gesture. Osher was the first straight guy who engaged with me on a personal level, showed an interest in my wellbeing, knew something about the gay world and was perfectly comfortable discussing it. The mention of anything gay usually caused straight men to squirm or be disgusted. Long before it was cool, Osher was a queer ally.

In the rental section of the *SSO* I found an ad for a place near Taylor Square – the epicentre of Gay Sydney. When I turned up to see it, an old lady on a bicycle with lots of bags arrived and let me in. It was on the ground floor: 1/405 Bourke Street. Less a studio apartment and more a broom closet with plumbing, its whole floor space was 2.5 metres wide and 4 metres long. The bed was an old fold-out couch that had been hand-covered with some red stretch fabric and a staple gun, but the fabric had peeled back and brittle old foam would rub off when you sat on it, causing a choking hazard. When folded out into the bed, you could open the front door just enough to squeeze through, then you'd have to roll across it to get to the rest of the apartment. Built into the opposite wall was a battered wooden shelving unit with a mark where the metal bed frame would butt up against it. Along the same wall as the shelves was the kitchenette, and on the opposite side was a tiny bathroom with a shower, sink and toilet. When you stood up from the toilet you were standing at the sink and when you took one step left of the sink you were in the shower. Out of the rusty metal bars on the windows of the kitchen and bathroom was Little Bourke Street, a back alley littered with dirty syringes. It was objectively a $200/week dump, and I couldn't have been happier for it to be mine.

When Mum and Dad visited I was proud and excited to show off my new home, although the people shooting up outside my window didn't make for a great first impression. Mum and Dad later told me that after leaving my place they walked to Hyde Park and cried. They couldn't understand why their little boy had exchanged the comfort of Kennedy Street for this rat's nest of a dog's box in the seedy part of town. What had they done that was so horribly wrong that would drive me out of home and into this? It made no sense to them whatsoever, but it made perfect sense to me. I was living in Sydney. In Darlinghurst! Welcome to the gaybourhood!

My mint-green notebook was filling up with the names and numbers of people I was meeting. This wasn't a little black book of people I'd slept with (though there were a few in there), this was about connecting with people I'd met out. I'd go to Stonewall by myself, order a drink then strike up a conversation with a stranger. If I felt some sort of connection I'd pull out my book and ask them if they'd write in it.

Paul introduced me to a couple called Nic and Ben. Ben was the same age as me and had a nine-to-five job with a big telecommunications company; Nic, a lawyer, was a few years older. Despite their proximity in age to me, they were leaps and bounds ahead in life experience. They were smart, successful, had a nice car, lived in a nice apartment and seemed to have it all together. I enjoyed spending time with them because although we talked about all the usual things, like which boys we thought were cute and the latest Kylie music video, they also introduced me to adult topics like politics and human rights. Nic and Ben became my primary caregivers, next of kin on medical forms, and a stabilising presence in a world full of change. Being in their company made me feel more valid as a young queer person. Whenever I had a question, they were always there to offer sound, reasoned advice. As well as the regular nights out clubbing we'd go to art galleries, political protests and fancy restaurants (where they'd kindly pay for dinner: it wasn't in my budget).

Something else I loved was that Nic and Ben were in an open relationship – I'd never heard of such a thing before. They were in love with each other but could sleep with other people if they wanted. They were honest with each other and seemingly suffered no jealousy or dramas. The whole arrangement appeared to work well – I was inspired. There was something so punk about defying the monogamy of the heteronormative world. It seemed being gay meant we didn't have these conventional relationship models to follow and were free to form our own.

7

'That's Portia Turbo. She used to be thin,' Stephanie said as she pointed to a statuesque showgirl wearing a silver-sequined skullcap with plumes of ostrich feathers shooting out the top. Her painted face had thin black eyebrows that framed arching black-and-white sockets and the two biggest sets of eyelashes I'd ever seen. The sparkle of her large red glittery lips competed with the disco ball spinning above us. Her silver-sequined high-cut corset had a sweetheart bust line, and as she raised her hands to hit the final pose her nipple popped out the top. This stunned me – not because it was a woman's breast. On the contrary, it was a man's flat chest. There was a short circuit in my brain as what I knew to be man and woman overlapped on stage before me. Portia, if you hadn't already guessed, was a drag queen. And while I knew she wasn't a woman, the sight of an incongruous mammary interrupted my suspension of disbelief.

Stephanie and I were squeezed against the bar at the Albury Hotel – the pub that inspired the movie *Priscilla* – watching my first ever drag show. It was perennially crowded; there'd always be locals and backpackers spilling out onto the street. They came to see the shows: at 11 pm, 12 am and 1 am, seven nights a week. Drag queens were touchable celebrities in those days – before they started gracing our TV screens and became *actual* celebrities. Being queer meant you didn't see people like you on telly, so the drag queens, backup dancers and bartenders of the gay scene became the next best thing.

They were clearly defined characters who spoke to different audience members in different ways. Mogadonna, one of my faves, was a glamorous badass who'd perform Pat Benatar, Joan Jett and The Divinyls. She'd get progressively more drunk throughout the night, and part of the joy of watching her perform was wondering if she'd make it to the end of the show. Trudi Valentine was the sensible queen: you could rely on her to know her words and choreography and be put together. Amelia Airhead-Smith was the blonde bombshell. It amazed me when one night her mum was in the audience. I'd never thought of my Sydney and Brisbane lives commingling – and I wasn't even a drag queen. To see Amelia's mum there in support of her planted a seed of real hope.

Another standout was Maude Boate, a creative genius and master costume maker, inventor of the foam headdresses that became synonymous with the *Priscilla* style of drag. Mitzi Macintosh was the queen of the inner west: she ran the Imperial Hotel over in Erskineville. There was a rivalry between the Oxford Street queens and the inner west ones, and people kept mostly to their own turf. Other queens on the scene at that time were Wyness Mongrel-Bitch, Chelsea Bun, Tess Tickle, Hillary Eternity, Polly Petrie, Penny Tration, Farren Heit, Barbara Bubbles and the late Bust-Op and Atlanta Georgia.

Then there was Vanity Faire. She was the youngest and newest on the scene, and was causing a commotion among the seasoned queens because of her beauty. Whereas the others' style was more theatrically 'draggy', Vanity dipped into the artform of female illusion. With my mouth agape, I watched her lip-sync 'If You Could Read My Mind'. Wearing a black-and-white gown, she pivoted on the spot like a ballerina in a jewellery box. There was something otherworldly about the way she moved and drew me into the story she was telling with the lyrics of that song. As for her looks, when I was around her I couldn't help but stare. By day she worked as a wig stylist at The Individual Wig on Oxford Street, so her hair was always stunning. But she had a flair for costumes and makeup too. Whereas all the other queens used Kryolan NW4 Panstick, giving them a bulletproof corpse-like complexion, Vanity used four different shades of Dermablend to highlight and contour the three-dimensional surface of her face. When she opened her mouth to lip-sync, she shone brighter than her cheek highlight (which was very shiny) and transported the audience far from the sticky floors and grubby walls of an Oxford Street gay bar to a world of fantasy. I was enamoured by all of the drag queens of Sydney, but there was something magic about Vanity.

Meeting Vanity is saved in my memory like a scene from a movie.

1. INT: Stonewall Hotel, Second Level

SHANE is standing by the DJ booth next to the black leather couch where he had his first kiss with a boy just a few months earlier. He is still wearing his giant yellow puffer jacket, army-green PVC pants and black leather boots. He's building up courage to say hello to VANITY, who is on the opposite side of the room facing the window, sipping her drink. She is dressed like schoolgirl Britney Spears from the

'… Baby One More Time' video. There are other people in the bar, but as far as Shane is aware, Vanity is the only person in the room.

Shane's voice is very high pitched. He is stammering.

SHANE

Hi! I - I - I'm Shane!

Vanity turns around, is confused when there is no one standing behind her, then she looks down and sees Shane, who is just very short.

VANITY

Oh. Hi. Vanity Faire.

SHANE

I'm Shane. Oh I said that already. I think you're amazing.

VANITY

Oh. Thanks.

Shane smiles awkwardly at Vanity. Vanity takes a slurp of her empty drink, not really interested.

SHANE

Do you want another drink?

VANITY

Sure.

Sometimes the most banal conversation leads to the most important friendship you will ever make.

In the same way that I quickly developed a fascination for watching drag queens at work, I found myself drawn irresistibly to them socially. I started dating a boy called Camp Johnny who had a day job in a call centre and did drag socially, going by the name Destiny Calling. I had a date with Destiny – well, Johnny – at the Courthouse Hotel on Taylor Square to meet his friends. It was a fun night and turned out to be an introduction to many people I still know today. Sydney drag queens Penny Tration; Atlanta Georgia, who dubbed me 'Destiny's Child'; Mogadonna, who I loved watching at the Albury; a cis woman called Tracy, better known as 'Madam'; and a trans woman named Sarah, a former showgirl who had a regular job working in the high rollers' room at the casino. Sarah was the first trans woman I'd met who 'passed', meaning that in everyday life people assumed she was a cis woman. There was also a beautiful Fijian trans woman at the dinner called Katherine, who was very calm and nurturing. At the end of the dinner I found myself in conversation with her and Johnny.

'Camp Johnny tells me you've only just come out?' She spoke in a slow and regal tone as if she were royalty.

'Oh well, I'd say I'm bisexual. I still like girls.'

Johnny interrupted. 'Pfft, you're gay, doll.'

'But I—'

'We all say we're bi at first, darl. It's an easier pill to swallow. But trust me. You're gay. You want another drink?'

Katherine and I shook our heads and Johnny got up to go to the bar.

'It's all just very new right now, Katherine. Everything keeps changing. I definitely like boys, but I don't *not* like girls, so that's why bisex—'

Her eyes closed dramatically then she raised her hand to stop me speaking. 'I've had a vision, darling. One day you will be a beautiful woman who'll lead our community to greater heights.'

I laughed nervously and gulped. 'I'm sorry? Me? A woman? I don't know if that makes sense.'

'Tut, tut, darling. I've seen it.' She was certain about her psychic prediction and wouldn't hear otherwise. Well, I reasoned, if Katherine had had a vision of the future in which I was a woman… who was I to argue?

After dinner Johnny and I walked back to the Bourke Street Broom Closet to consummate our relationship. I'd certainly hooked up with different guys but mostly it was just blowjobs and wanking, or I fucked them; no one had ever successfully put their penis in my butt. But it looked like that's what Camp Johnny was about to do 'cause he was rolling a condom onto his penis.

'Here, I'll lie down and you sit on top; I find that's the most comfortable way.'

I straddled him and tried to navigate it in.

'You'll need lube, doll.'

He grabbed a bottle out of his bag, slathered up his penis and I wriggled, trying to squeeze the tip of him inside me. As soon as my sphincter was breached I was overcome with an uncontrollable pain that was like falling on your coccyx or perineum, that special lasting sort of pain like falling on a bike crossbar, only sharper.

'Owwww! It burns!' I jumped off him and off the bed.

'It's supposed to! Oh, hop off and let me get on you.'

We swapped positions and Johnny slid down on me in rapture. It felt good to me, but it was obvious it felt better for him. Pretty soon he was bouncing up and down in an intoxicated frenzy, which built to a vocal climax as he rolled off the bed and onto the floor, shuddering in euphoria. Wow. Apparently something good happens once you work through the pain.

Although it only lasted a month or so, Camp Johnny was my first official boyfriend. Despite the fact I hadn't started drag yet, eventually we realised we were more suited as sisters than boyfriends. But we continued to hang out and he invited me to the Drag Industry Variety Awards, or DIVAs, at Sydney Town Hall.

This was – and is – Sydney drag's 'night of nights'. The Oscars of drag (if you will). We even arrived in a stretch limousine. The only thing I'd been to that even came close to being this fancy was my high school formal, so it seemed fitting I should wear my Elio Moda suit. But that wasn't enough: I couldn't just wear the same suit. I was different now and I needed to show that, so I bought a pink tie and got a can of Fudge spray-on hair colour in pink and took to my streaked blond hair.

The sheer volume of drag queens, and how stunning everyone looked, was jaw-dropping. Floor-length gowns, structural up-dos, and over-the-top looks that had been months in the works. It was the night where all of the showgirls past, present and future would turn it out to show off and celebrate the vibrant Sydney drag scene. Vanity won DIVA Rising Star that year and led a show performing a Christina Aguilera mashup, and Destiny looked like a 70s dream with Farrah Fawcett flicks and a Peter Morrissey outfit that was straight off the rack. Which was scandalous because of the cost, and because drag queens wore costumes, not fashion. The whole night was so chic and glamorous… and legitimate. Not a closet in sight.

Meanwhile, I was still hustling on dreams of becoming 'famous'. Despite planning to go to uni for acting, what I really wanted was to be a popstar like Madonna or the Spice Girls. They spoke to me in a way that I wanted to speak to people. They told me through their defiance of 'the acceptable' that being different was OK and, in fact, could be celebrated. There was no clear route to popstardom though, so I thought I'd try other pathways like modelling and acting, and hope the answers might prevail.

Armed with new headshots, I paid visits to different agents, and even got booked as a catalogue model for a surf brand. Unintentionally I ended up looking like the gay best friend on the shoot because the other boys dwarfed me with their height and muscles. It didn't seem feasible that I could be the romantic interest of any of the girls. Then Ricca Paris asked me to be in a Stonewall advertisement for their Revolution '69 party. The vibe was hippy flower child, which seemed cool. I turned up to the shoot ready to play the masculine lead, a heartthrob perhaps. They put a long blond centre-part wig on me with a headband and I felt like a hippy rocker.

But then I saw the full-page colour ad on the outside of the gay paper. I couldn't tell which of the two available genders I was supposed to be. Seeing the image and not recognising myself as a man (or even woman) was troubling and, worse, it was plastered all over Stonewall. There was something very uncomfortable about looking at this androgynous photographic vision of myself. Whereas drag queens were being feminine, which made sense, this image of me wasn't masculine or feminine – or it was both at the same time. I'd never seen anything like that and it instantly brought on a feeling of shame. I'd failed at being a man. This 'modelling job' wouldn't be added to my portfolio. But it was a small setback. It wasn't going to deter me from my quest for fame.

My first drug of any sort was a Panadol at age 16 for a headache, so it was unexpected that I'd find myself, at 18, crammed into a toilet cubicle downstairs at Arq with seven people doing drugs. To be clear, I wasn't doing the drugs, I was just there for the social aspect. It was fun being seven in a space traditionally reserved for one. Out on the dance floor everything was so hectic and overstimulating, the lights were flashing and the music was so loud you could barely hear what anyone was saying, but in the cubicle it was a little private party just for me and my friends. You could see everyone's faces and hear their voices, and it was the time of the night where you could regroup and connect. They'd do ecstasy and lines of speed, though I never saw it – I just heard their sniffs and saw their swallows.

Until one night (technically morning) a few months into my gay clubbing career, when in one of those cubicle parties Linus said, 'Can you hold this for me?'

I put out my hand and he placed a small blue tablet with an @ symbol on it. 'What's that?'

'It's ecstasy.'

'*That's* ecstasy?!' I guess I hadn't really known what ecstasy was. It was more of a demonised concept than a real-world object. I knew it was bad. I knew it was a drug. But when I saw that cute little blue pill in my palm I wondered what all the fuss was about. It looked so harmless.

'Can I try it?'

'Sure. Just have half though.'

Forty-five minutes later I was bounding like a big red kangaroo across the dance floor at Arq. I couldn't contain my joy and elation. It did what it said on the tin – I was in ecstasy. Walking was no longer an option; my only mode of transport was giant leaps into the air. I could feel every part of my body. My internal organs and extremities. My skin tingled, my eyeballs rolled back in my head, my sphincter clenched – it was like I'd been plugged in.

Once the initial rush tapered off and I could verbally communicate again, I wanted to tell everyone how much I loved them. I was overwhelmed with a profound sense of love. All of my senses were turned up to full volume. How did half of that little blue pill contain that whole experience?

Every weekend was an opportunity to party on Oxford Street, but the special events like Mardi Gras, Hand in Hand and Pride were at Fox Studios. The big event on the October long weekend was called Sleaze Ball, a sister party and fundraiser for the iconic Sydney Gay and Lesbian Mardi Gras. My first October long weekend in Sydney I didn't go to Sleaze, but I did get a ticket to Frisky, one of the satellite parties, which took place at the Metro Theatre the following night. Everyone was talking about this event – a few thousand queers and a smattering of allies dancing all night to trance music in laser light.

Having only recently arrived at my new identity, I was keen to look the part. A golden tan was a must, so I scheduled an appropriate number of trips to the tanning bed (we weren't aware of the dangers back then). I booked a fresh haircut. But what to wear? The friends I asked told me everyone went as camp as possible, so I went all out. I bought a blue mesh top with black velvet trim around the neck and sleeves with a black yin-and-yang print on the chest, along with spray-on blue denim bootleg jeans and a blue sparkly choker. I created a look with blue and white eyeshadow; blue mascara for my lashes and my frost-tipped hair; and glitter and crystals glued on my cheeks.

When I got to my friends' place to meet everyone before heading to the party together, they were all in the standard gay uniform of jeans and a singlet. I felt like Elle Woods walking into that frat mixer dressed as a bunny. Residual high school hypervigilance resurfaced at the speed of light: it felt like my friends had set me up and then laughed at me. My immediate thought was to run home and change but I let myself be talked out of it. Everyone said there'd be people at the party wearing makeup.

When we got to the party and I didn't see a speck of glitter, I was triggered. At school, once I'd realised fitting in wasn't an option, I'd mastered standing out: offence was my best defence. Now that I'd found my tribe, all I wanted to do was fit in. In this new world where it was fine to like boys, it seemed imperative to look and act like a boy. Upholding masculinity was even more important now that I was subverting heterosexuality. But try as I might, it was consistently proving to be a challenge for me.

So there I was at Frisky, covered in glitter and blue mascara, feeling betrayed and wrong. I wanted the walls to curl down around me and suck me into a void. In lieu of that my legs carried me to the bathroom so I could burst out crying in private. I peeled the plastic crystals from my cheeks and scrubbed my face with cold tap water to get rid of the glitter and glue. Someone came into the bathroom so I ran into a cubicle, locked the door and sat there sobbing into my hands. I was humiliated.

Before long, the tears stopped flowing and I became conscious of the music. Well, I wasn't going to sit on a toilet all night. Red-eyed, but my face now clean of makeup, I went back to the party determined to have a good time. I found a different group to spend the night with and started to dance it off.

'Do you want a White Dove?' asked someone I'd just met, handing me a white tablet with the peace dove pressed into it.

'Sure.' My first whole ecstasy. *gulp*

Within an hour I was incapacitated, lying on the stage wedged against a speaker blasting a trance remix of 'Silence' by Delirium. Disconnected from the pain of the physical world, writhing in ecstasy.

Feeling overwhelmed by the drugs, I left the party with Princess, a friend who had also been at Frisky, and headed back to the Broom Closet. Princess identified as a lesbian and I identified as gay, but when we got back to my place we jumped the homosexual ship and committed a heterosexual act of treason on my disintegrating foam couch-bed (which was actually a couch on this particular occasion). In high school my attraction to women had allowed me to sexually explore, despite the attraction to boys bubbling just below the surface. I sought it out, in part, I am sure, because that's 'what boys did', but I genuinely enjoyed it as well.

Since my discovery that being attracted to boys was possible I had dived in headfirst (figuratively speaking… mostly). It seemed that where before I'd been given only one option, now

I had two: gay or straight. But what about bisexual? It was more of a theoretical concept than a label that was practically available to me. Most men on the gay scene insisted that any attraction to girls was a hangover from a heteronormative upbringing, and any suggestion of being attracted to both men and women was dismissed. I was gay… tbc.

One night a few years later, I was at Arq with some friends, still ringing in the evening before. For your visualising context, I was dressed as a boy.

'Blake and I are taking Valentin home with us – do you want to come?' Cameron said, staring right into my eyes with a sexually direct gaze. There was something about Cameron's giant green eyes that hypnotised me whenever I looked into them.

Valentin was a hot, straight German model who'd been helicoptering around the gay scene all summer. Blake and Cameron were a couple. I kinda had a thing for Cameron. Which was confusing, not because Cameron and Blake were a couple, but because they were both women.

For some reason, I hadn't been able to stop staring at Cameron ever since we'd met. When we talked she would stare straight into my soul. I'd stare straight back until I'd start to feel intimidated, always darting my eyes away coyly, no matter how hard I tried not to. I think we were both intrigued by each other, in a way I certainly wasn't sure how to explain.

We got back to my place as the sun came up over Darlinghurst. Our posse had grown – Valentin came with a plus-one: his girlfriend (those Berliners are so progressive). I was well and truly outnumbered. Three beautiful women, one straight man and one twink (me). Valentin was more interested in the girls and he fucked his girlfriend on my couch while watching Cameron, Blake and me perform a live sex show on the day bed. I was really turned on, if not a little intimidated, to be there with two beautiful women having sex and, yes, even going down on them. It's not something I would normally have actively sought, but when presented with the opportunity I was more than happy to enjoy the pleasures of the human body.

The irony is that I am trying to justify a heterosexual sex act, like I have to explain why it is perfectly normal – there's nothing untoward about it. A completely natural form of human expression. Just know plenty of gay men reading this have their faces scrunched up right now like they're sucking on a slice of lemon. I guess this is where my sexuality deviates a little from the garden-variety homosexual. I won't lie, I get a kick out of telling the story, but I also genuinely enjoyed myself. I am a faggot; I am most aware and proud of that. (I should add the caveat that if you are not a faggot you shouldn't use that word. At all.) Most of my attraction is for men, but every now and then I'm drawn to a person in a way that transcends lines of gender and sex. I understand it might sound queer, me having sex with women, because that's something 'real men' do. It is farcical – me and a woman – but it happens… and it has, quite a few times.

Being a good friend, and sensing that I was missing out on the man-on-twink action that was the initial provocation for the soiree, Cameron started going down on Valentin.

'Shane, I want to know how to suck cock like a gay boy. Is it like this?' She was flicking the tip with her tongue as if it were a clitoris.

'Nah, it's like this.' I grabbed Valentin's penis and engulfed it in the back of my throat.

'Oh, like this,' Cameron said, taking back the penis.

'NO! Like this!' And we continued to pass his cock back and forth and back and forth until he climaxed.

COURTNEY FACT

The term 'gold-star gay' is sometimes used in the gay community to describe a gay man who has never had sexual relations with a woman; taking the idea one step further is 'platinum-star gay', describing a gold-star gay born by C-section. (Just to spell it out, that would mean he has never touched a vagina.) While I understand these terms are perhaps used as jovial affirmations of one's early, unwavering knowledge of their sexuality, I can't help but find them to be misogynistic. These phrases often seem to be deployed with a tone of repulsion at the idea of sex with women and vaginas. You can have a positive attraction to one gender or physicality without being disgusted by the alternatives; that disgust is neither healthy nor an inevitable consequence of any orientation or identity. To me, active repulsion points towards something unresolved… and it stops you from being open to the many wonderful ways of being queer.

Queer is an umbrella term used to describe people who are not exclusively cisgender and heterosexual. Trans, non-binary, bisexual, lesbian and gay people can all identify as queer, but the word 'queer' can allude to more than just those discrete labels. Queerness is a framework that seeks to challenge society's expectations of sexuality, gender performance, beauty and body standards, and politics. (Bear with me: I'll explain these concepts in more depth soon.) It should be noted that 'queer' is a historical slur, and some older members of the community don't have fond memories of it. While the slur has been reclaimed, I appreciate that it's not for everyone, though I personally feel the label 'queer' describes my experience best.

Bisexual people make up the majority of the LGBTQ+ community but are the least visible. Simply put, bisexual people are attracted to people of more than one gender. Many people think that being bisexual means a person is attracted to men and women 50/50 but it doesn't, not necessarily. Activist Robyn Ochs says it best: 'I call myself bisexual because I acknowledge that I have in myself the potential to be attracted – romantically and/or sexually – to people of more than one gender, not necessarily at the same time, in the same way, or to the same degree.' Another common misconception is that if a bisexual person is in a same-gender relationship they're gay, or if they are in a different-gender relationship they're straight. Bisexual people remain bi regardless of who they're dating, having sex with or married to.

Pansexual describes someone who has physical, emotional and/or romantic attraction to people regardless of their gender. This term started being used because some people thought 'bisexual' wasn't inclusive of trans and non-binary people, but as our understanding has evolved, so has language. Now the 'bi', meaning two, in bisexual represents attraction to people of the same gender and to people of different genders. Pansexuality falls under the bisexual umbrella.

Asexual people experience an absence of, or very low, sexual attraction, sexual desire or sexual interest. Some describe this as their sexuality, while others describe it as an absence of sexuality.

Gay – At this stage in the book, do I need to define this?

Straight – You almost certainly don't need a definition for this one either.

This is by no means an exhaustive list of sexual identities; it gets real nuanced the further down the rabbit hole you go.

As the year 2000 ended, I'd become a completely different person from who I'd been at the start. In the six months since my first trip to Sydney, I'd come out (to myself and my new friends), found a broom closet to call my own, and I was now working as a barman in the cocktail bar upstairs at the Midnight Shift. Oxford Street really felt like a home, and it was: it was the beating heart of Sydney's LGBTQ+ community. This wasn't a convenient gathering: it was a necessary part of our survival.

Many of us had either been disowned by family or were in the closet in fear of rejection. In the queer community we have a 'chosen family'. If love from biological families becomes conditional when our true identities are revealed, our chosen family becomes that unconditional love support system everyone needs. The scene was a safe haven that had been built over decades, where we could gather to socialise, work and live. Where we could walk down the street being visually different without feeling the very real threat of violence that was all too familiar in the default world. Within a hostile world that was never built for us, we created a bubble where we could thrive, with gay cafés, a gay bookshop, a gay music shop, gay newspapers, a gay radio station, bars and clubs, sex-on-premises venues, a gay gym, a gay accountant, a gay internet café, drag shops, gay clothing stores with very gay clothes – a whole world where we were the majority. Though I should clarify that the 'we' here mostly applied to white gay men. I know that the inclusion I felt in this scene was due largely to the privileges of my skin colour and sex; as in the world at large, prejudiced attitudes and behaviour can easily be found on the gay scene.

Despite all its ups and downs, if I had to pick a place in the world that feels like home, it would be standing on Taylor Square looking up at the big rainbow flag blowing in the wind. From the minute I set foot on Sydney's Golden Gay Mile I was welcomed, supported, challenged, entertained, employed, educated and loved. The community was made up of the locals and tourists who patronised the bars, shops and restaurants and the people who worked there, the bartenders, drag queens, DJs, security staff, Rosie from Olympic Yeeros, Chelsea at House of Priscilla, Ricca at Stonewall, Mazz Image the scene photographer who was always dressed in head-to-toe purple – even her hair was purple – and Beryl, one of the loud and colourful people experiencing homelessness (anyone from that era will have a soft spot for or at least a good story about Beryl). Our queer community was vibrant in its defiance; everyone who lived in the 2010 postcode knew everyone else – one big extended chosen family.

My friend circle grew every time I went out as I settled into the scene. I was becoming familiar with all of the regular faces and they were becoming familiar with mine. I earned the nickname 'Baby Shane' on account of how young I looked: I had to carry ID everywhere. I'd blossomed into a 'twink' – a young, slim queer boy. I am still yet to retire the twink label, although these days I add in the qualifying prefix 'oldest living'.

8

Another new label I was about to assume was *drag queen.* For New Year's Eve a couple of my non-drag-queen friends, Princess and Mona, and I were off to Melbourne for a dance party called Magnitude. It was a special occasion, and Princess suggested that I do drag for the first time. She could see it brewing inside me and knew I needed an excuse. I needed no persuasion: it seemed to be the logical path.

Now that I had a goal, my strategic brain kicked in. For years I'd been reading business books like *Rich Dad, Poor Dad* and Richard Branson's autobiography *Losing My Virginity* and I was determined to be a millionaire at 21 and a billionaire before I was 30. Unfortunately neither happened, but one of those books had a good suggestion: if you want to get ahead, invite someone you admire from your industry out for a nice meal and pick their brains. Everyone loves a free lunch. Vanity and I were acquaintances who chatted once in a while, and she was the gold standard for what I wanted to be in drag. So I invited her to an Italian restaurant called Stilla on Crown Street to discuss my drag debut. Vanity didn't come to the lunch in drag of course; we were just a couple of boys discussing being beautiful women over a bowl of pasta. He told me what essentials I needed to buy and where to get them and then we moved onto the subject of drag names and character. I wanted to be a redheaded shag-cut nightclub singer called Ginger LeBon. I was obsessed with the soundtrack from a musical called *Smokey Joe's Café* and in particular the track 'Pearl's a Singer'. I wanted to be the smoky-voiced woman who sang that song.

Vanity thought a cuter, girlier name like Courtney would be better. At first I was indifferent: the name seemed a bit basic. A drag name needs to have wit and a certain sensibility. It needs to be striking and have a twist. I said the name 'Courtney' slowly and broke down the syllables trying to find a hidden meaning. Court-an-ey. Caught in the. Caught in the Act! And there it was. My name. Courtney Act. Poor old Ginger LeBon never got to see the light of day. Probably for the best.

On Vanity's advice, before I left Sydney I went to House of Priscilla, a specialty drag and costume shop on Oxford Street, to get specific items like foam boobs and a tucking G-string. In Melbourne, Princess and I went shopping for the rest. I got two aqua-blue stretch sequin boob tubes from a shop called Ice. I wore one as intended and the other as a skirt, breaking fashion and gender convention in one fell swoop. The strappy gold heels I bought would become a staple in my wardrobe for the next few years. Then we made the pilgrimage to the wig store. This was the year 2000: Amazon didn't exist and there weren't wig shops in every shopping centre (at least not in Australia). There was one wig shop in Melbourne I'd heard of, and it mainly serviced older Orthodox Jewish women. Walking in there was nerve-racking, and I was glad I had Princess with me because I was too on edge to even try on a wig. I pointed at an ash-blonde shoulder-length layered bob on a mannequin head on the wall, and the woman who worked in the shop reluctantly got it down.

'Is this for you?' she said, looking at Princess.

'No, it's for him,' she said, pointing at me but still looking straight at the woman, giving her a moment to register what was going on.

'Oh. *Oh!* Ah, yes, here, sit down and pop this stocking cap on.' She fumbled, not quite sure how to react to a boy trying on a wig. I sat down in the chair and slipped it on my head. The style was called 'Gillian': she was very natural, realistic and elegant. Nothing draggy about her – in Sydney the girls, even Vanity, wore big hair piled on their heads, but no such resources existed in this wig shop. I also kinda loved how natural Gillian was – she seemed to suit my face.

'I'll take her!'

At the markets I picked out some jewellery: a necklace and an armband. In the ladies' department of Myer I found aqua-blue feature knickers and a blue denim handbag. I also bought a pair of sunglasses because, as a Boy Scout, I'd learnt to always be prepared (for stumbling out of the club when it's daylight). The sunglasses were two tone, like something pop star Anastacia might have worn in the 90s. They faded from dark violet at the top to hot pink at the bottom and had a cute little love heart out of crystals in the top right-hand corner.

Now for one final stop: the Napoleon store on Chapel Street, to get my makeup done. When I called and booked the appointment I made sure they knew it was drag makeup and that the artist knew what they were doing. Even though I wanted a more girl-like aesthetic, like Vanity, drag makeup was very different to girls' makeup. These were pre-Kardashian days, before the influence of drag on mainstream makeup became noticeable. Nowadays, there isn't much difference between how I do my face and how a makeup artist would do Kim Kardashian's face.

People joke that all I wear is chapstick and mascara, but in reality the magic of makeup is what you don't see. With drag makeup you're restructuring the bones of the face with a brush and some paint to feminise and create an illusion. Obviously my drag makeup isn't as intense as many of my sisters', but there's still a lot going on behind the curtain. I cover up my 'boy' eyebrows to make room for a larger eyelid, deeper sockets, and a higher, more arched eyebrow. When the eye is bigger and the eyebrow is higher everything else appears relatively smaller – it's all about 'proportionising'. Women's faces (generally) differ from men's faces as they have narrower and lower foreheads, larger and more angular eyes and eyebrows, smaller noses, fuller lips and cheeks and finer jawlines: these are the secondary sex characteristics we assign to a 'feminine' aesthetic. Manipulating perspective just a little bit on each of those features creates an illusion one way or another that's greater than the sum of its parts. It's nuanced and detailed and it has taken me years to get the balance, and even so I learn new things every time I put on my makeup. It's a process – an evolution.

Back at the makeup counter, my 18-year-old androgynous bones didn't pose too much of a hurdle for the ill-fated makeup artist, but my eyebrows did.

COURTNEY FACT

The first and most structure-altering step in drag makeup is the repositioning of the eyebrows. This can be done by shaving them off and drawing them on in a new position: the easiest solve for the moment but the most consequential in the near future, and not just due to the obvious repercussion of having to walk around in general society without brows. Eyebrows assist in human communication, as well as stopping sweat from running into your eyes. It's well documented that eyebrows do not grow back as they once were, as many an over-plucked drag queen or woman can attest. You can, of course, draw brows on as a boy, which is a fix of two of the three issues above, but then you are left with the constant worry of smudging your eyebrows, sweating them off and even the stress of getting eyebrow-shaped tan lines when you cleanse off your pencilled-in brows during the summer months.

In Sydney in the noughties it was also frowned upon to shave off your brows: drag is an artform and this was one of its guidelines at the time. The guidelines mattered – they ensured you were going to do it properly and be a part of the club. A higher brow required a flawless application of special-effects putty to smooth and cover up the boy brow. We would block our eyebrows using Grimas Eyebrow Plastic, which was imported from Germany and cost about $40 for a 25-millilitre tub. You would scrape a bit out of the tub with the end of a makeup brush and press the gummy, sticky putty into your brows, trying to cover as much as possible. Using a cheap barber's comb you brushed against the direction of the hair to coat every last one in product, then brushed back the other way so that all the hairs sat at a 45-degree angle up and outwards on the face. Next you smoothed them down with your finger, the warmth of which helped to melt the product, smoothing away the edges and wiping off the excess. Then, to complete the job, you added a layer of translucent powder, a layer of thick Kryolan Paint Stick, more powder, foundation and another layer of powder. Even if you got it looking smooth and concealed, the texture of the wax would create a sticky surface that was problematic when trying to blend pigmented eyeshadows from eyelid to artificial eyebrow, so we would use Kryolan Supracolors as an eyeshadow base – this created a creamy wet layer to blend the powdered eyeshadow pigments into. You still weren't guaranteed the wax wouldn't grab the product, creating a line on the outside bottom edge of your pesky boy brow, which made achieving flawless eyeshadow application a real artform (one I never quite managed to get right). Eyebrow wax is temperamental too. Even if it's applied well, you would constantly have to press it down with a powder puff throughout the night to keep it from lifting up. And on big nights, which they all were back then, a sunrise stumble out of a club would reveal more than just your five o'clock shadow. The world would be blessed with bloodshot eyes framed by defiant, Kryolan-caked brow hairs poking through the Madame Tussauds wax façade that had once been your face.

Eyebrows were hierarchical in the Sydney scene; a well-maintained and smooth wax job was a badge of honour and skill. It took me ten years and moving to LA to learn that the same effect could be achieved with none of the downsides by using an Elmer's Glue Stick for $0.59 from Target. I like to credit myself as the drag explorer responsible for bringing this superior foreign process back to my mother country and revolutionising the way drag queens in Oz do their eyebrows (I don't know if anybody else does though).

To prepare for my first drag look, I shaved the nine hairs that grew from my chin. I'd never attempted my own makeup and I didn't know how to wax down a brow, but it quickly became clear that the girl doing my face knew even less. She had a stick of Kryolan wax that looked like a candle, and I guess because of that she thought she'd try to melt it with a lighter as if it were one. She scraped and melted the wax to cover up my brows and it seemed to work OK. Maybe. Sort of. She worked on my face for what seemed like forever, with all manner of brushes and products, painting away on the new face with which I would ring in the New Year. To complete the look I pulled 'Gillian' out of my bag, gave her a shake and plonked her on my noggin. Oddly I have no visceral memory of seeing myself in hair and makeup for the first time. You'd think it must have been some sort of transformative moment where the world stopped turning – but it wasn't. Maybe because I got to watch the process unfold and there was no big reveal. Maybe because the end result didn't live up to the expectation and I felt a little underwhelmed. Or maybe because I still saw Shane looking back from the mirror. I'd expected to see someone else staring back, but it was still me, except with makeup on.

The photos show that I looked pretty gorgeous when they hurried us out the shop door at closing time and onto the Toorak sidewalk. Now I was in drag from the neck up, but still wearing a 'boy' outfit: my four-inch-high Buffalo Boots, skin-tight dark blue denim jeans, and my boomerang-print Peter Morrissey button-up shirt.

With my shopping bags slung over my arm I strolled up the street – but before long my eyebrow wax started to crack. Imagine you drip candle wax on the back of your hand. You let it cool solid, and when you start to move your hand the wax buckles, cracks and falls off. I held out my hand and one of my eyebrows dropped straight into it, followed by the next. *Shit.* It was 6 pm, Sunday 31 December 2000. What was I going to do? When no good solution presented itself, I decided to pop on my Anastacia shades and wear them all night.

A few hours and half an ecstasy later, I strutted into that party like I owned the motherfucker. A friend told me someone had come up to them thinking I was Kylie Minogue – which, thinking about it now, was either a lie or the person was an idiot, but it doesn't matter 'cause it filled me with the delusional confidence I needed. From photos I appreciate belatedly how banging I was. My smooth, tight and tanned 18-year-old body, the flattest stomach, longest legs, and skin glossed and glowing in the light of the green lasers that broadcast wave-like patterns through the smoky nightclub air. In that dim-lit party I read as a woman: I 'passed'. I was in control of the narrative and, it turned out, I loved the feeling of being a girl. It came very easily to me, much easier than being a man. As Courtney I had the opportunity to perform femininity in a socially acceptable way.

Melbourne nightlife was known for attracting more mixed crowds than Sydney. Even though it was a gay event there was a contingent of straight partygoers there: the gays had the good music back then. A muscly, shirtless straight man dominating the go-go podium sat down next to me and started flirting. When he leant in to kiss me, I stopped him.

'I'm not… I'm a… I'm not a girl.'

'I know.'

We spent most of the night dancing and making out. I had no lip liner, lipstick or powder to touch up with and left the party with very little makeup on the lower half of my face. But I did have a unique new sense of ownership over my identity: I'd discovered something. In drag I felt powerful around straight men in a way I never had before. I'd also got to be something different for the night: it was still me, but in a parallel universe. It all came with an intoxicating sense of freedom. Night turned into morning, and Mona, Princess and I jumped on a flight back to Sydney.

The next night in Sydney I had a ticket to a Frisky party. Wanting to keep the dream alive, I called Vanity and begged her to put me in drag. Reluctantly, she agreed. Vanity was my friend, my inspiration, the co-creator of my name, and now I was having my mug beat by her too. Her studio apartment on Crown Street was like a drag cave. Mannequin heads with wigs on them, a dress form, sewing machine, stacks of CDs, costumes strewn everywhere and a futon bed in the corner.

'I'll do your face once, and once only. You can accept it's the best you'll ever look and quit while you're ahead, or forever live in the shadow of how good you once looked.' Vanity's golden rule was partly because she didn't want to paint people's faces all the time, but the other reasons were more complex. She was conscious that she was potentially about to induct me into a cutthroat world. Being a queen is a tough life, with social ramifications unperceived by the civilian eye. Drag takes over your life: it's a job and a social life; it often costs more than it makes; the work hours are akin to a particularly punishing non-union shift worker roster; it usually involves (or involved) being around booze and drugs; and often friends with 'real' jobs don't quite understand. On top of all the challenges that still exist, back then it wasn't socially acceptable to do drag like it is now: it was the arse-end of the entertainment industry. So becoming a drag queen any time prior to the last decade (aka a pre-*Drag Race* world) had to be an act of completely free will. But I knew this was just a one-off, since I had serious entertainment career aspirations.

With Vanity doing my glam, my second hit of drag promised to be even better than the first. I watched as she skilfully waxed down my brows and contoured my foundation. When she put my wig on she took sections from the front, twisted them back and pinned them in to keep them off my face. She made me look beautiful; the contrast with the makeup counter girl's paint job was stark. There's a difference between doing generic girl makeup on Shane's face and doing Courtney's makeup on Shane's face. When I looked in the mirror, I was Courtney. I saw for the first time the reflection I've come to recognise as being 'her'.

After going to Frisky in drag, I knew I'd been bitten by the bug. The contrast with the last Frisky, three months previously, was dramatic thanks to the social power of drag. My next opportunity to do drag was the Harbour Party, in the run-up to Mardi Gras. Vanity, Destiny and I all got dolled up to attend: our first of many outings together as three drag sisters. I had a feeling that for the three of us drag extended beyond just costume, and it was exciting to have these two to share our unspoken enjoyment of the feminine.

The following weekend was my first Mardi Gras – the highlight of the Australian queer calendar. Of course I was going in drag: any excuse to get dressed up. Weirdly, I still needed an excuse. My goal was to be a respected entertainer in a very straight industry, and doing drag wasn't going to bring me closer to achieving that. Another factor – though I wasn't yet aware of it – was misogyny: we've all grown up in a society that teaches us women and femininity are 'less than'. Regardless of how much those around me celebrated it, dressing up like a girl was degrading somehow. But Mardi Gras! That other stuff could wait…

My outfit began its life on Mardi Gras morning. Lincraft, purveyors of sewing and craft supplies, had a store in the city and I scoured it for something I could turn into a costume. Equipped with plastic leaves and vines, a nude G-string and a nude boob tube, I headed to Vanity's place. She sewed the leaves onto the boob tube and tied a vine around my waist. Breaking her golden rule, she did my face a second time and pinned a mass of blonde curls on my head. I had the night of my life.

Even though I'd been going to the Oxford Street bars and clubs for about eight months, they were nothing like Mardi Gras.

When straight people and the media refer to 'Mardi Gras' they're talking about the largest night-time outdoor parade in the world, but when queers say Mardi Gras we mean a multi-week festival packed with arts, cultural, sporting, social events and more, with thousands of visitors from interstate and around the world. The crown jewel of the festival is a giant circuit party that happens after the parade for 17,000 of your closest friends. It rages from 10 pm to 10 am at Fox Studios, and all sections of the community come out for a huge night of celebration. In the bars and clubs I frequented, the main demographic was white gay men aged 18 to 35. At Mardi Gras, there were people of all ages, genders, colours and subcultures. Mardi Gras used to be a members-only party and every member could only buy four tickets so, despite the enormity of the crowd, it was highly curated. 78ers, bears, leather daddies, butch dykes, lipstick lesbians, drag queens, trans people, Asian marching boys, Indigenous groups, people in wheelchairs, straight allies, and fresh-faced twinks like me. I danced all night in a sea of strangers and met countless new people. It was the first time I'd been in such an inclusive and diverse crowd, and my perception of my community was once again expanded beyond what I imagined was possible. The thread of our queer sexuality and gender bound us all together despite our physical differences.

I clip-clopped out of the party when it ended at 10 am, still in my six-inch Fredericks of Hollywood white patent-leather stripper heels, content from a magical night of conversation, exploration and even a few make-out sessions, and hurried along to the Midnight Shift, where I was working as a barman… that morning, though, I was a barwoman.

Cymone Rose, Osher's girlfriend, was a kids TV host at Nickelodeon; she told me they were casting for a new host and wondered if I might be interested. She put me in contact, I went in to meet the producers and I got the job. (Thanks, Cymone!) What a coup: I was the host of *Snick Flicks*, Saturday night on Nickelodeon. I was careful not to mention my sexuality because I was sure being a kids TV host and being gay were mutually exclusive back then. We'd film four episodes – a month's worth – in one day, and I had the other days off.

Now that my finances were healthier, I moved out of my $200/week broom closet into a $220/week studio apartment. Everyone who'd ever visited the Broom Closet was shocked at what a hovel it was, and at last I understood what they'd meant. It was like going from black-and-white to colour, and only for an extra $20 a week. My new place was on the fifth floor of a modern building with a lift, and although it was still only one room, the new place was at least five times bigger in floor space.

I was a 19-year-old needing to work only one day a month: my idle hands were drag's playground. Without the means to buy professional stage makeup like the working showgirls used, I improvised. At the pharmacy I could afford a Maybelline pan stick, an Innoxa blush and an Australis lipstick. Eyebrow wax and eyelash glue could only be found at House of Priscilla, so I asked the drag queen who worked there (to this day I'm not sure if it was Chelsea Bun or Tess Tickle; both say it was the other) what was best for gluing on eyelashes. She recommended spirit gum. What a stitch-up. Spirit gum – the dressing-room staple of my werewolf days – was made mostly of alcohol and tree resin, and shouldn't be used near your eyes.

Even without running eyes from spirit-gum lashes, my makeup was dodgy. But it didn't stop straight men hitting on me or gay men asking if I was Vanity Faire: the latter was the biggest compliment of all. Vanity was a work of art, and to be compared to her was an amazing confidence boost. Maybe a reality check would have been more helpful, because all photographic evidence from that time unequivocally shows I was a busted novice. The lighting must have been dim in those bars and clubs.

A friend was throwing a private birthday party at the Manor House, a boutique gay hotel on Flinders Street, and invited me to do a number in drag. When I mentioned that gig to another friend, Hillary Eternity – who hosted a show in the back bar of the Albury – she asked me to do a number there too! For this double booking of my first drag performance I did 'Dance: Ten, Looks: Three' from *A Chorus Line.* I wore a black fluffy knitted dress, some black undies, black fingerless gloves and Gillian, my blonde wig. It was exhilarating to be on stage again and I realised how much I missed performing. For someone with my ambitions, drag might not have been a noble path but it was a path to being on stage and performing live. This is what I craved; this was my passion. As Shane I wasn't getting any offers that came close.

I started getting dressed as Courtney whenever I went out, making a name for myself as a new queen. There weren't any other new queens on Oxford Street back then, so I had the market cornered. Despite intellectually knowing that drag wasn't the right career move, there was just something about it I loved so much that doubts – and shame – took a back seat.

It was August, which meant the 2001 DIVAs were approaching. In 2000 I'd gone as a boy, but this year I was definitely going in drag. From Grace Bros, a department store, I bought an aqua-blue bias-cut dress with big translucent paillettes. I borrowed a wig off Vanity called Robyn and asked Hillary if she'd do my makeup.

'Those flashbulbs are like a weird narcotic for you, queen, so keep away from those photographers! It's bad enough you're even going in drag. But photographic proof is a sure-fire way to lose your job as a kids TV host,' she said as I sat in the makeup chair. I rolled my eyes.

This year the DIVAs were at the Metro Theatre, where Frisky was held, but by any comparison this was a classy affair. As I walked up the stairs with my date, Jake, someone called out 'Vanity' and waved at me. I was chuffed. Then one of the photographers from the *SSO* asked to take a photo and I decided not to heed Hillary's warning. I'd forgotten to pack a camera, and she'd done such a good paint job, and the likelihood of me ending up in the social pages was slim, especially on a night packed with Sydney's drag elite. Our seats were pretty far up the back, while all the working showgirls were seated down the front. Vanity won Entertainer of the Year, which is the big gong of the night. She was wearing a dress made of hessian, proving that Marilyn wasn't the only one who could look good in a potato sack.

A few days later, Hillary called me to inform me I'd made the paper. And not only that – I was on the front page of the *SSO*, which sat in the doorway of every gay-friendly business in Sydney.

'As if they're going to be reading the fag rags, Hillary. And even if they were, I'm unrecognisable.'

'Hi Shane!'

It was a producer from Nickelodeon.

'Look… we have some bad news. We are not going to be needing you as a host for *Snick Flicks* any more.'

'Oh. OK.' I just assumed this was all a coincidence. Nothing to do with my pic at the DIVAs.

'You should have already been paid for August, so I think that's all there is. It's been a pleasure working with you!'

'Yeah. Thanks. Is it possible to get a VHS of some of the episodes?'

'I'm sure we can arrange that for you. By the way, loved your blue dress at the DIVAs on Monday night.'

'What? Sorry? Not sure what you're talking about… I've got another call coming through – got to go. Chat soon.'

Time to look for a new job I guess, which meant a day job in the default world, where being gay also couldn't be acknowledged. Though I'm sure I didn't fool anyone by changing the way I dressed, spoke or acted, it was simply what had to be done. Lots of my friends worked in call centres so I figured I'd give that a crack. After lining up appointments with a few recruitment agencies, I knocked up a CV. As I headed off to an interview in the city I felt stifled tiptoeing back into the closet.

There'd been an ad in the gay papers for a recruitment agency called Staff-It, run by two lesbians, so I gave them a call next. There's a whole level of ease when 'keeping it in the family', a common understanding that doesn't require explaining or coming out. At Staff-It I could be myself and allow them to place me in a job where I fit. They offered me a temp role as receptionist at their agency, and I embraced the normalcy of going to work each day and being mentored by the folks there. My social life was growing increasingly wild, so having a day job with lovely office-working queers was a nice contrast to the drag queens, door bitches and DJs of my night life.

9

My identity was expanding fast in Sydney: I was becoming all of these new things and having so many fresh experiences. But as far as everyone from my Brisbane life knew, I was the same old Shane. When Lisa and Jessica were down in Sydney and we caught up for a meal, I wondered if they could tell I was gay. Unfortunately that was the week I tried plucking my eyebrows into an extreme lady arch because waxing them down with putty was proving such a chore. It worried me how ridiculous and obvious I looked. What would they think about me if they knew? What might they tell Colleen? And would she tell my parents?

I'd always had such an honest relationship with Mum and Dad, but now I was struggling to have regular conversations with them because everything I said felt like a lie. There were so many negative messages about coming out: boys I met in Sydney told me about being disowned by their parents; some were grateful their parents were at least talking to them again. No one had a positive story to tell. Coming out was tied to rejection, and I didn't want this wonderful new discovery of who I was to ruin my relationship with my parents.

Mum and Dad announced plans to come to Sydney, and I started building myself up to tell them my secret. I met my friend Sarah for a drink at Gilligan's to discuss my impending coming-out. She'd been sharing her experiences of being trans and we had a trust in each other. After listening to all of my fears, she told me that no matter what happened, my chosen family in Sydney would always love me.

My parents were staying in Kings Cross, and when we met for dinner at the Holiday Inn it was wonderful to see them, but there was a disconnect. I'd evolved in the year since I'd seen them last and didn't know how to be the same Shane they expected me to be. I felt like a marshmallow being pushed through the slot of a piggy bank. We'd talked on the phone – calling long distance charged by the minute, which was hideously expensive from a mobile, so our conversations, while regular, were always brief.

Attempting to ease into the inevitable, I regaled them with stories of my new life and new friends – Mogadonna, Vanity, Nic and Ben, Mona, Princess, Destiny and Girl Craig – careful to never talk about *my* sexuality. But clearly Mum was picking up what I was putting down.

'Is Girl Craig your… special friend?' she asked.

'I have to pee,' I blurted out.

'I'm gunna top up my drink,' said Dad.

We both stood up from the table. I rushed to the bathroom, worried I might throw up. Clutching at Sarah's earlier support, I phoned her from the toilet cubicle to get her thoughts.

'It sounds like they *want* to know if they're asking questions like that,' she said soothingly. Despite her reassurance I just couldn't do it. On my way back to the table I detoured via the marble-countered wine buffet for a refill. No one mentioned the topic again for the rest of the meal.

After dinner I walked out of the Holiday Inn and stood at the intersection of Darlinghurst Road and William Street, unsure what to do. The neon Coca-Cola sign buzzed overhead. Kings Cross was alive with people out for a big weekend. I only had one more chance to tell Mum and Dad before they went back to Brisbane. I called Sarah as I walked down the hill towards Hyde Park and asked if I could stay at her place that night because I didn't want to be alone.

Nothing Mum and Dad had ever said or done had given me the impression that they'd have an issue if I was gay, but still I was crippled by fear. I cried most of the walk to Sarah's as the cool night air evaporated my tears. I felt so confused, so afraid. I didn't understand what was going on in my brain. Nothing inside me seemed to match the world outside. Everything my childhood had taught me to be wasn't how I'd turned out. It wasn't only that I liked boys; it was everything. I didn't fit. I wasn't what a boy was supposed to be.

Up in Sarah's high-rise apartment, we sat on her bed with the sliding doors open, looking out at the city. I wondered about all the things I should be but wasn't. All the ways I'd fallen short where the other boys from Sandgate High had succeeded. I shouldn't like boys, I should be at university, it was wrong to do drugs, it wasn't right that I liked dressing as a girl. I'd failed at being a man. The last one stung the most. I wasn't a man like Ezra or Ritchie, or the boys at A block. I wasn't a man at all.

One of the first assumptions we're able to make about someone is their gender: whether someone is a man or a woman. As Courtney I felt so much freer: none of the socialised expectations imposed on women applied to me – or if they did, I wasn't aware of them. Dressing up in different clothes allowed me to express myself without consequence. I could just be me. As Shane I was always going to come up short, but as Courtney it seemed I had something extra. *Maybe that was it,* I thought. *If I'm not a man, I guess I must be a woman.*

It might be good to pause the narrative here and dive into some biology, sociology and psychology. Then we'll return to the dramatic cliffhanger!

COURTNEY FACT

If I'm preaching to the choir here, why not see how many times you disagree with me because: a) how I see it is different from how you see it; b) you're reading this in the future and everything has changed and what I've written below is now deeply problematic and offensive and I've been cancelled on Twitter; c) you're one of a handful of people left on the planet, you're busy trying not to get eaten by a lion, but you found this book in an abandoned discount bin and though you really don't give a fuck about gender theory you're hoping that reading might distract you from impending doom or; d) we now live in a utopian future where everyone has an equitable chance regardless of their sex, gender, race, sexuality, disability or other defining characteristic.

Put really, really simply, sex is what's between your legs and gender is what's between your ears. Gender is who you go to bed as; sexuality is who you go to bed with.

The slightly less simple but altogether more useful version goes like this:

Sex (the noun) – male or female – is made up of a bunch of factors but is usually determined at birth by a doctor based on whether you have a penis or not. Except it's not quite that simple. Your sex isn't determined purely by your donger (or lack thereof – and that's not me being sexist: the medical system is phallocentric, i.e. obsessed with dick; same). Sex is also determined by your internal genitals, hormones and chromosomes.

Intersex people are born with a combination of sex characteristics not typical of male or female bodies. Sometimes these characteristics are visible at birth, sometimes they appear at puberty, and sometimes they are not physically apparent at all. In many countries around the world, intersex infants, children and adolescents are subjected to medically unnecessary surgeries, hormonal treatments and other procedures in an attempt to forcibly change their appearance to be in line with societal expectations about female and male bodies. When, as is often the case, these procedures are performed without the full, free and informed consent of the person concerned, they amount to violations of fundamental human rights. Some intersex people identify as men or women with intersex characteristics.

Gender – man or woman, traditionally – refers to each culture's social roles for how the sexes should act. Judith Butler writes, *We are assigned a sex, treated in various ways that communicate expectations for living as one gender or another, and we are formed within institutions that reproduce our lives through gender norms. So, we are always 'constructed' in ways that we do not choose.* If you're male you act/look/think/feel like a man; if you're female you act/look/think/feel like a woman. Unfortunately these widely accepted and imposed definitions aren't accurate for a lot of people and are therefore the cause of much oppression. And I'm not only talking about trans and non-binary people – gender expectations have huge ramifications for cisgender (i.e. people who aren't transgender) people too. I would argue that the rigid and imposed system of rules defining how to be a man is responsible for a vast portion of the fucked-up shit in the world today.

Gender comes in different parts: **gender identity**, which is how we feel on the inside, and **gender expression**, which is how we present our gender to the world. The two don't always match. Some people experience a mismatch but don't express their gender as would feel natural to them because their personal safety would be compromised if they did. Some people are unaware of having a mismatch because (like me most of my life) they don't have the language, tools or support to understand.

Like money, language, religion and time, gender is also a social construct – a set of parameters our society made up and agreed upon to help with the functioning of our world. Just because it's made up doesn't make its impact any less real. And because we made up the rules, when they no longer serve us we have the ability to update them. We know gender is a construct because people have historically shown a wide range of gender expression in different cultures around the world.

Rather than thinking of gender as binary – man/woman – it can be seen as a spectrum with feminine on one side, androgynous in the middle and masculine on the other. Sam Killermann, in his book *A Guide to Gender*, points out that to be more of one thing you don't have to be less of another, and suggests visualising identity as two (or more) parallel continuums.

One continuum goes from 'null' to feminine and the other goes from 'null' to masculine.

While 'feminine' and 'masculine' are still socially constructed categories, and the rigid definitions of them can be a source of shame and internal conflict for everyone, including cis and straight people, I find them helpful for describing how I feel in the least confusing way – provided we can challenge the idea that feminine is only for women and masculine is only for men.

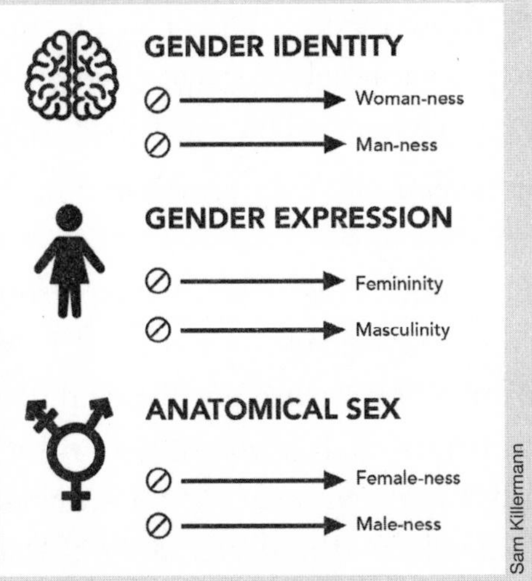

'**Masculine**' descriptions include: strong, authoritative, self-assured, courageous, ambitious, direct, logical, physical, active, compulsive, aggressive.

'**Feminine**' descriptions include: caring, attentive, submissive, sensitive, thoughtful, empathetic, emotional, compassionate, delicate.

Throughout my journey – and it has become more apparent in writing this book – I've discovered identity labels that better described how I felt on the inside. They gave me an intellectual framework with which to understand myself relative to the world we live in. Essentially all of these labels and language are signposts to help us deprogram the gender indoctrination we've all experienced growing up in this world. We were born inside a jail, unaware of the freedom that lies beyond the bars of prescribed identity.

Back to the plot: I'm at Sarah's place having a full gender crisis. All of the above information would have been mighty helpful, but sadly I was only aware of two options: man or woman. If I wasn't one then I must be the other; it wasn't possible to be both. I'd tried so hard to be a man, but I also loved being a woman. The choice I had to make about my fundamental nature left me tortured. Was I a transgender woman like Sarah? I was lying on her bed uncontrollably kicking and screaming, like someone having a demon exorcised from their body.

What was it about drag? I loved the performance aspect, but it wasn't *just* performance, as much as I tried to tell myself it was. The truth is the clothes, the makeup, the identity, and the way I was perceived and treated gave me a fully justified and celebrated way to embody my own integral femininity. But I had no intellectual understanding of that at the time. All I knew was that I enjoyed dressing up like a girl, but also I really loved being a boy – although I *did* notice there was a specific type of girl and specific type of boy that I longed to be. Both versions were extreme: on one side was... not Barbie; more like a Bratz doll come to life. A 90s supermodel? Maybe more like a swimsuit model. Long hair, big eyes, full lips, breasts, curves, long legs. Hyper-feminine. Sexual. And on the other side was the desire to be like one of the boys on the cover of *DNA Magazine* or the Calvin Klein underwear box. Perfectly chiselled jawline, piercing eyes, a body of bulging muscles and an engorged, throbbing member. Also sexualised.

I was so stuck trying to be these diametrically opposed options that even I noticed the contradiction. Did it make sense that the two things I desired were the most aesthetically exceptional version prescribed by society? Passive, plastic, receptive, fertile. Was there something in that? Was this a clue that external forces had shaped my desire? There was me on the inside, and this man and this woman I aspired to be on the outside were merely the superficial casings of consumerism.

This was a brief, profound moment of observation. What I wanted was what all of us had been sold, and because most people either wanted to be one or the other, the fact that I wanted to be both of these extreme things seemed absurd. It was this binary construct that was competing with the true nature of my being, and seemingly winning. I couldn't be a man, so that must make me a woman? *No. Way. I am not a tr*nny!* A wall of denial shot up, trapping this idea behind a sign proclaiming *GENDER IDENTITY – DO NOT OPEN.* These were the kinds of thoughts and conversations my friends and I were having at the time because of the rigid binaries we believed we needed to fit into.

'I want to be a woman, not a tr*nny.' These words from Destiny's mouth made me hurt, for her most of all, but also for myself. Those words summed up our internalised transphobia: what were we? Vanity, Destiny and I had become sisters who loved to share a party and also shared queries surrounding our gender identity. Yes, we were drag queens, but it was more than just performance for us – it was tangled in our gender identity. We took it off the stage and would spend all weekend in drag at the recovery party. It was fun, but it also allowed us the opportunity to express ourselves in a feminine form.

One such Sunday afternoon, still awake and still in drag from the night before, we were at a recovery at Desto's place on Albion Street in Surry Hills. Sitting on her bed, she reached into her bedside table and pulled out a pill and placed it in my hand.

'What is it?' I asked.

'Ask me no questions, I'll tell you no lies.' Who was I to look free drugs in the mouth? It was a pharmaceutical-looking pill as opposed to the hand-pressed ecstasy we usually took. It was white with the letter 'U' on it with a circle around it.

'U for… upper?' I said out loud as I swallowed the pill back with a chug of blue Gatorade. I wondered what effect this pill would have on me: would it be trippy? Or speedy? Or smacky perhaps? I waited for it to kick in.

After a couple of hours of feeling nothing, I asked Destiny if she was feeling her pill yet. 'Oh that? That was a hormone, darl.'

'WHAT?'

I went into a state of internal panic. I should have known better than to trust that Destiny was giving me free drugs – she would have kept them for herself! These were hormones she'd got from a friend because she was experimenting with the idea of transitioning. Now she'd given one to me, but I didn't want to be a woman. Well… I didn't know that, but I hadn't taken any action either way and had had my hand forced. Clearly lacking an understanding of chemistry and biology, I thought that when I woke up in the morning I would be a woman. That overnight I would grow a mane of long hair, breasts and a vagina. I was anxious when I fell asleep that night and in the haze of waking the next morning, I remembered having swallowed the oestrogen tablet and quickly and nervously grasped for my chest and crotch to see what had transpired, but everything was still as it had been when I went to bed. I breathed a sigh of relief.

When the sun came up the next day at Sarah's place, the storm inside me had abated somewhat. All I knew for sure was that I had to come out as gay to Mum and Dad before they went back to Brisbane the next morning. From Sarah's house I headed straight to work – at an internet café on Oxford Street where I checked in customers who wanted to use one of about 40 PCs. It was pretty simple customer service, but I couldn't focus. When my lunch break came I headed home; I needed to be somewhere private to try to gather myself. Instead, I fell apart. Someone had left a bottle of white wine in my fridge so I cracked it open and began to drink. This was out of character: I wasn't one to drink unless in a bar, and certainly not in the day by myself.

Still looking for distraction, I turned on my TV and the highly emotive *Touched by an Angel* was on. There was no couch so I sat on the floor watching and drinking and crying. The full-body cry. The ugly cry. The fear of rejection by my parents was unbearable, to the point of making me feel physically ill. Suddenly, I had to pull the trigger. I couldn't keep my secret any more… it couldn't wait another second. I took out my Nokia 3210 with its black-and-green screen and wrote a text message to my mum: I am gay.

The world was a different place back then. Texting was barely a thing; I think of myself as quite the pioneer! Writing 'I am gay' on a numeric keypad involved pressing 4 4 4, 0, 2, 6, 0, 4, 2, 9 9 9 *send*

Mum replied. That's nice dear, see you at dinner.

I was in shock. *That's it?!* I'd wrapped myself into an emotional knot. This was the hardest thing I'd ever done and *That's nice dear, see you at dinner* was it? How anticlimactic! A crushing weight lifted off my shoulders and I wept a whole new wave of tears. Tears of relief. I'd done it. I could be honest with my parents again: that was the most important thing to me.

Now, I know what you're thinking – they must have known already, right? But it turns out they didn't… Mum said the idea hadn't crossed her mind. Most of the boys she knew, who were my friends, were just like me. I guess it hadn't occurred to her that perhaps Fame attracted a fair few boys with inclinations towards the less fair sex. She hadn't tried to filter me through a set of labels society had laid out to try and discover who I was. Kim liked jiu-jitsu, and I liked singing and dancing. I was her son, who was scared of the dark, loved the Spice Girls, and once got his tongue stuck to the fridge. I was her Shaney.

Over dinner, I discovered I wasn't Mum and Dad's first brush with a queer person.

'Remember Jim and Rudi?' Mum said. I vaguely recalled meeting two guys who were a couple when I was younger.

'Or The Lesbians?' referring to some other friends who were, as their appellation suggested, lesbians.

'I think so…'

'Do you know Carlotta?' Mum asked. Apart from when I used to watch her on *Beauty and the Beast* in high school, I had met the Aussie icon a couple of times.

'I waxed Carlotta's legs once,' she continued. 'All the Les Girls used to come to the Persian Room, where I worked, for a knock-off drink after they finished up the road.'

'Gosh! I used to love going to see the Les Girls show. They were wonderful!' added Dad. 'Hey, Shaneo, did I ever tell you I lived with six drag queens back in the 70s?'

Mum and Dad were unintentionally one-upping each other with their proximity to queerness, but Dad's revelation floored me. Why hadn't I known any of this 24 hours earlier?

I spent most of my childhood in Brisbane trying on different costumes and identities. Some suited me more than others did!

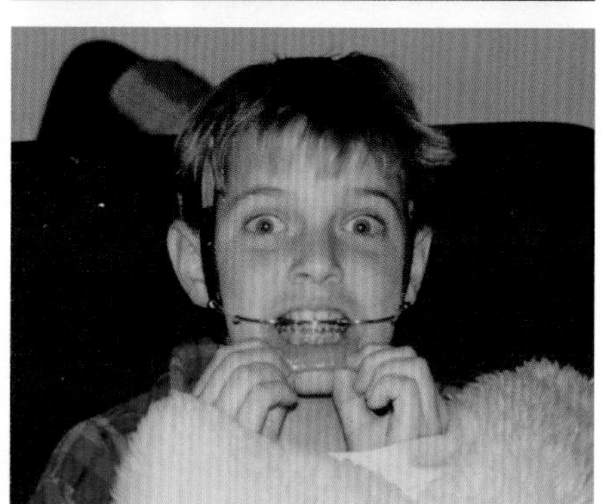

Top left and right: My early forays into performance at Fame.

Middle left: Baby's first beard! My infamous kiss with Miss Tiny Tot 1987.

Middle right: I will forever be grateful for modern orthodontics.

Right: Has there ever been a more 80s family portrait?

Above: With Mum after a Fame performance in my late teens.

I made so many important friendships at Fame. Stephanie and I clicked from a young age, and years later we went to a reunion with Mr Kennett, the director of Fame, pictured with us below.

Top: You're supposed to wear braces *or* a belt – but I was a rebel. Jessica, Beccy, Lisa and me in our Spice Girls covers group, Mixed Spice.

Above: We were the hit of the Queen Street Mall with our Christmas show.

Left: The Veronicas and Courtney Act – or, as we were known then, The Yabba Dabba Doo Young Entertainers.

Darren Tieste

Above: Catalogue model! Just in case it's not clear, I am on the far right.

Left: I had my nose photoshopped smaller here because I thought it was too big and wanted a nose job. I'm glad I barely had money to pay rent, let alone for a rhinoplasty, 'cause I like my nose now. This comp card also featured my fax number!

Below: Before I was the 'oldest living twink', I was just a twink.

Mazz Image

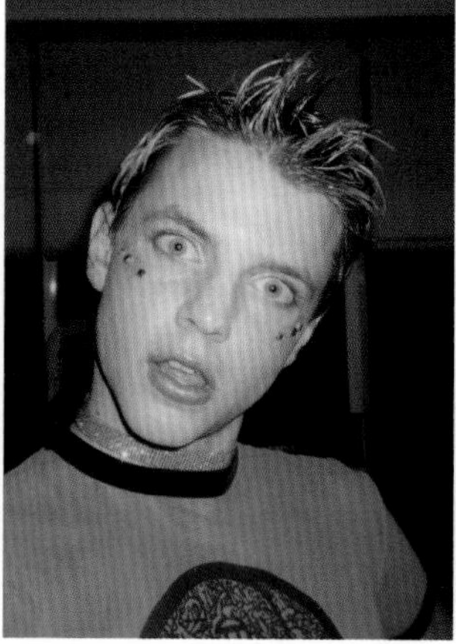

First time in drags at a mall! Strutting the footpath in Melbourne, New Year's Eve 2000.

The first time Vanity painted my face, and my second night in drag: New Year's Day 2001.

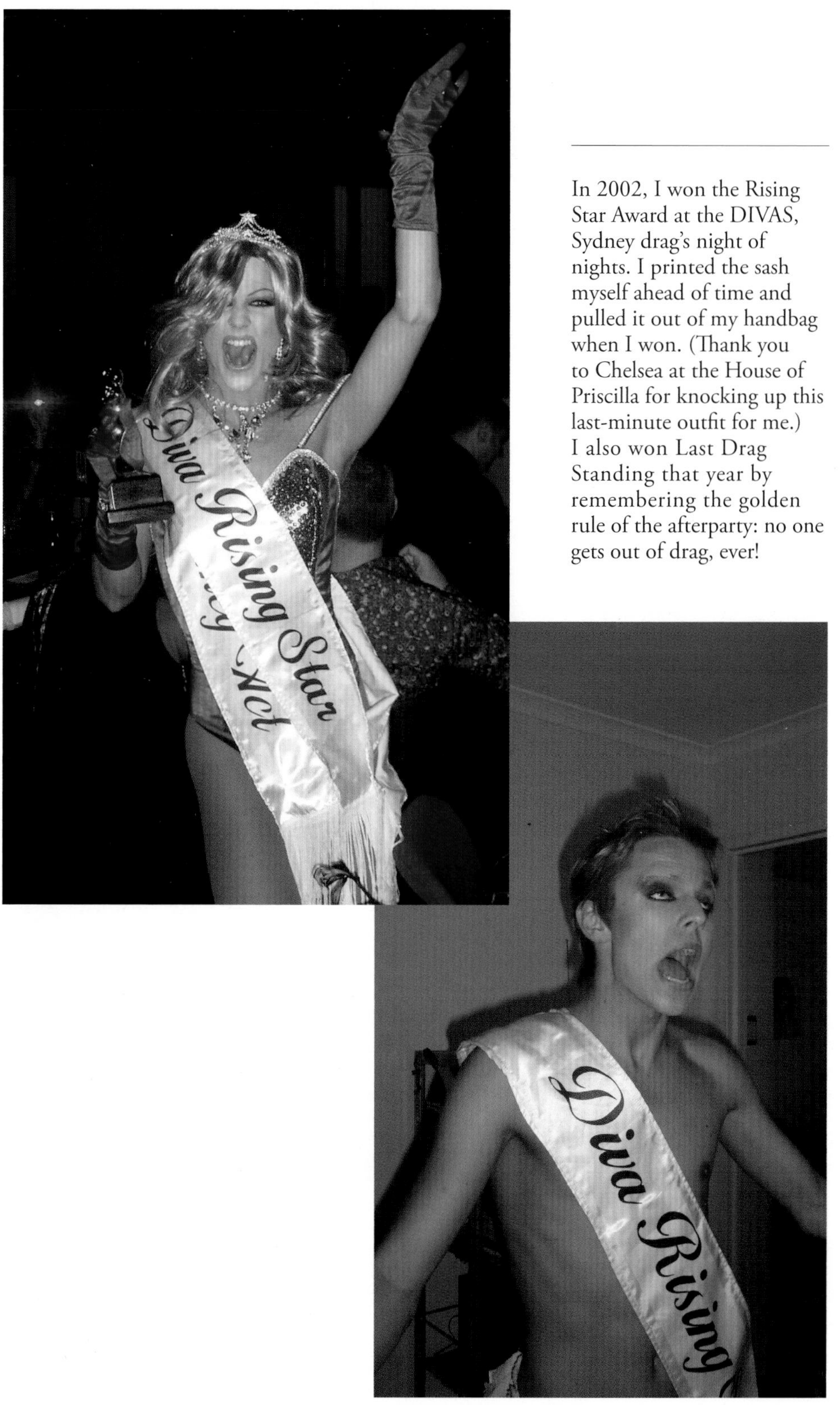

In 2002, I won the Rising Star Award at the DIVAS, Sydney drag's night of nights. I printed the sash myself ahead of time and pulled it out of my handbag when I won. (Thank you to Chelsea at the House of Priscilla for knocking up this last-minute outfit for me.) I also won Last Drag Standing that year by remembering the golden rule of the afterparty: no one gets out of drag, ever!

My drag family: Vanity and Ashley Swift taught me so much about the art of drag. Together we were Divastated!

Kamp Quality

DIVASTATED

ASHLEY SWIFT • VANITY FAIRE • COURTENY ACT • MATT • SIMON

FRIDAYS FROM 10PM • FREE ENTRY

DJ'S BRETT HANNATH • RONNIE JAMES • SEAN MANLEY

themidnightshift club

GAY GAMES VI 2002

BACARDI BREEZER

85 Oxford Street, Darlinghurst • www.themidnightshift.com

Photograph: Eric Manukov

Before I worked at the Midnight Shift as a performer, I was a barman – or on this occasion a barwoman, as I stumbled in as Courtney after my first Mardi Gras.

'You'd look pretty good dressed as a sheila,' Dad said. Sheila is Australian slang for woman.

'Well, since you mention it…'

May as well hold the bag open so a few more cats could run out.

'… I also do drag.' It was a pity our phones didn't take or store photos back then: I had no pictures to show them. I told Mum and Dad my name was Courtney Act, that I'd started doing drag socially for fun and had even performed a couple of times. We drank more wine and I was surprised by how well Dad was taking the news. He was really leaning in (more than I was), interested to know about my love life, drag, my new world, relishing this fresh level of honesty as an opportunity for connection with a part of my life previously kept at arm's length. This was the opposite of the rejection I'd anticipated. Mum was being supportive too, but I suspected that below the surface she was hashing over all the frightening scenarios that had made it so hard for me to come out. If I'd picked up negative messages from the world around me about being gay, then my parents must have too, albeit in a less personal way. And mums build fairytales for their sons – there'd be no falling in love with Beccy and us having babies and living happily ever after.

'We'll have to come and see you perform next time we're in Sydney,' Mum said.

'Oh yeah. That would be great.'

'I went to Sleaze Ball in Brisbane once in drag.'

'WHAT?! Dad! This is *my* coming out!' Dad telling me this made me weirdly uneasy; I didn't know where it was going and the possibilities made me uncomfortable. I was too filled with shame about my own identity to reconcile the story Dad was telling me with the images sons build of their dads.

'Yeah. The girls dressed me up one night. Got rid of all my body hair!'

'Even your moustache?'

'Especially my moustache! Had a great time. Don't know how you can wear heels all night. Bloody killed.'

That left me speechless, mouth agape, eyes bulging.

'Was working on a construction site at the time. At work on Monday I had a hell of a time explaining to the boys why I had no body hair.'

It was tempting to put my fingers in my ears and start singing loudly. I wasn't quite ready for Dad's level of solidarity. 'I need to go to the toilet.'

When I returned to the table I was looking forward to starting a new topic of conversation.

'Hey, Shaneo. You tried any drugs?'

Wow.

Sheepishly I replied, 'I have dabbled in a few things,' then proceeded to rattle off a list of illicit chemicals: 'Ecstasy, GHB, ketamine, speed—'

'What about coke? You ever tried that?'

Mum interrupted. 'All right! There are some things a mother doesn't need to hear.'

Despite having momentarily breached the limit of Mum's comfort zone, it felt so good to share these things with my parents. I didn't care what other people thought, only Mum and Dad. Now I could walk around in the world with that confidence. That primary bond is fundamental to self-acceptance. Not the *only* thing fundamental to self-acceptance – I still had to resolve society's impositions, which would take years to do – but knowing my parents thought that who I was was worthy of love affected me in ways I doubt I'll ever be able to appreciate. I love you, Mum and Dad! Thank you.

10

One Thursday a month I'd work the door, as a boy, at Fruits in Suits at the W Hotel. It was a mixer for the Gay and Lesbian Business Association. I stood at the front greeting everyone with a smile and writing each person's name on a sticky name-tag as they came in. One week, someone I considered a mentor pulled me aside and told me that if I wanted to be taken seriously in the business world I should stop drag. That really hurt. I mean… I knew it was true and they meant it to be helpful – I wanted to be an entrepreneur or an entertainer; drag was never going to lead to any success. Had I already ruined any hope I had of a mainstream entertainment career because people knew I was gay? Because there were too many photos of me in drag? There were few out gay people on TV, few gay actors or characters: it was just the way it was. But it was growing obvious to me that while there was no chance I'd be able to keep being gay a secret, maybe if I stopped drag now, nipped it in the bud, it wasn't too late. This sounds so absurd now, but these were very real and legitimate fears at the time, reinforced constantly by the entertainment industry and world at large.

Concluding that the drag had to stop, when I got home I grabbed Gillian (my one wig) and hacked into her with a pair of scissors. I couldn't do drag without a wig and I couldn't afford the $400 to buy another one. This seemed like the perfect intervention, a sort of suicide of Courtney. *Snip.* The damage was done. I started to sob and cut and sob and cut. I hacked away at those synthetic fibres like I was Joan Crawford in the rose garden, henny. I was free from the monster. Or so I thought.

The folks at Staff-It found me a placement as an office manager with a company whose product was called the Pocket Sock. It was a sock… with a zipper pocket in it. The company was a mother-and-son team in a home office doing big business around the world. I was responsible for answering the phones, liaising with the factory in China to chase up orders, and doing the bookkeeping and general office admin.

Even though Courtney was out of my life, it's not like my social life ended. One night at Arq on the dance floor, craving chewing gum to satiate my grinding jaw, a business idea passed through my entrepreneurial mind. What if there was a person with a tray of all of those dance-floor essentials like gum, lighters, mints, lollipops and fans wandering the club? Those things everyone wanted at some point during the night but never seemed to have.

Over the next couple of weeks I registered the business name, got a Costco membership card and caught the train to an industrial suburb on the outer limits of Sydney, where I had a plastics fabrication company manufacture a tray with adjustable dividers, a clear perspex hinged lid and a neck strap. I started doing an online TAFE course, Certificate III in Financial Services, and purchased Quicken so I could invoice and run the back end of my business venture. When I approached Ricca Paris at the Stonewall Hotel about starting Disco Medic there each Friday and Saturday night, she loved the idea and loved my entrepreneurial spunk even more. But

Ricca said that for it to work for Stonewall, she'd need a drag queen working the tray. I couldn't afford to pay one, so I decided I would have to be the drag queen. This was different to social drag; this was a business idea. The drag was a means to an end now. I had a career trajectory and I could use it to justify the shame of doing drag… and boy was I glad Courtney was back!

I went to House of Priscilla and bought a white PVC nurse's outfit and a red bobbed wig. I needed a functional yet fashionable shoe, so I got a pair of white knee-high boots from Raben Footwear with a platform and a solid heel, and Hillary agreed to do my makeup again. The first night, I pounded the pavement of Oxford Street, up and down all three levels of Stonewall and upstairs at the Shift for five hours. I made about $100 and was pretty happy with myself. The next night I went around to Hillary's place for a makeup lesson. She worked on one eye and then stopped. 'OK,' she said. 'I've done one half of your face. If you want to leave the house in drag, you have to copy what I've done on the other side.' Now I kinda had a basic idea, I could do my own face. The man had been taught to fish.

People noticed Disco Medic and they were impressed. I started getting known in drag. I would do laps of the strip selling gum and glowsticks; it was hard work, but it was satisfying and I could usually add an extra 50 per cent on top of my weekly wage at Pocket Sock. At about 1 am business seemed to die down, so I would cloak-check my box at Arq and party all night; this always involved drugs, usually ecstasy, GHB and ketamine. I was the new queen on the block, making a name for myself as a businesswoman and party girl.

Noticing my initiative, Mogadonna asked me to be in her new show at Stonewall with Tess Tickle. Disco Medic showed Mogi (and others) that I wasn't *just* some drug-addled twink. She knew I had a background in performance and most importantly, being in a show would help refine my otherwise limited drag skills. It was hardly the Sydney Opera House, but being back on stage was exhilarating. I was 19 and earning money from my passion of performing, which is kind of the dream.

I asked Mum and Dad if they wanted to come down to Sydney to see the show, and a few weeks into the run they were in the audience. Dad's moustache was a hit and everyone commented how much I look like my mum. It's a big deal when someone's parents come to see a drag show: everyone's on their best behaviour, as if it were their own parents. Unfortunately for a lot of people in that bar, having their parents support them in such a way wasn't a reality. I think my parents being there gave them hope, just as seeing Amelia's mum at the Albury had done for me. I was so proud and knew I was lucky, but I don't think I realised at the time just how lucky I was.

Other queens started asking me to be in their shows and little by little I absorbed the culture, getting to know the regulars at the shows and the quirks of the different venues. I was the bright-eyed new girl and I was prepared to pay my dues.

Chelsea Bun, who owned House of Priscilla, created some wonderful and wacky costumes for me. A drag wonderland full of costumes, wigs, shoes, makeup and everything that sparkles, House of Priscilla is a must on any queer tourism guide to Sydney, especially if you need a Mardi Gras costume.

I loved looking like a girl and I loved socialising in drag after the shows. The vibrant colours of the costumes overwhelmed my sloppily applied earth-toned makeup. I shaved my legs because I wasn't that hairy. And when I finally did start wearing lashes it was only ever one pair of whispies, not multiple pairs of giant 301 lashes like most drag queens wore. I loved performing and being in these shows, but my physicality, my skill level and my desire for femininity meant I wasn't all that good at doing traditional drag. Vanity was feminine and glamorous, but she was also skilled and her look was heightened: it worked with the style of drag we were doing. I was like her little sister playing dress-ups.

The work built up. On Saturdays I was at Stonewall then had a second gig at the Flinders. This required a little back and forth. After we finished the second show at Stonewall I'd clip-clop through the kitchen, out past the beer kegs, into the back lane, down Little Bourke Street and past the kitchen window of my old Broom Closet to be on stage for a 12.30 am spot number, then turn straight back around to make it to Stonewall in time for the 1 am show. I can still hear the sound of the exposed metal pin in my worn-down black knee-high boot scraping on the bitumen as I walked. Why I never thought to pack a pair of flats I'll never know. Walking the streets alone at 19, dressed like a trollop, hoofing it through the backstreets of Darlinghurst: personal safety was never a thought, and not just because I was young and naïve. The streets were considered safe. Although I wish I had considered the safety of my knees. Be kind to your knees, kids – you'll thank me when you're older.

I saw that drag could earn me enough to pay my bills, so I quit my job at Pocket Sock. It was for the best: I wasn't being the most responsible employee, my sick days were becoming more frequent and having a day job just wasn't working with my nocturnal lifestyle. I knew working in an office wasn't for me. My home was definitely on the stage, I just loved it too much. I outsourced Disco Medic to fledgling queens and started doing drag full time. An apartment next door to Nic and Ben's became available, number 16 (or 'suite 16' as we called it) in the Taylor Grand. Nic and Ben were my friends who kept me grounded, so I was glad to be moving closer to them.

After only a few months of me doing drag shows, the DIVA judges approached me at Stonewall. They asked if I could stop doing one of my favourite spot numbers – 'Cherry Lips' by Garbage – as they wanted me to perform it as the lead in a show at the 2002 DIVA Awards! This was a huge honour. I was gobsmacked – a full production at Sydney Town Hall, which made it feel all the more prestigious, and I was nominated for an award too. When the presenters of DIVA Rising Star, Vida and Atlanta, called out my name as the winner I leapt to my feet and ran to the stage. 'I really had no idea I had a hope of winning this award…' I said, as I pulled a white sash out of my handbag that had *DIVA Rising Star* printed on it. It was smug, but in a very 'Sydney drag sense of humour' way.

The DIVAs were always on a Monday night; as with hairdressers, it was drag queens' unofficial day off, so it was likely that most working showgirls could attend. The afterparty went on for days. We had a golden rule: 'no one gets out of drag, ever'. Once Town Hall kicked us out we headed to the official Bitch or Boast afterparty before retreating to my place. In the morning we stumbled to Stonewall for Breakfast with the Stars, where everyone was mostly out of drag, before gaining some more tag-alongs and heading back to mine. The party devolved into debauchery as we took more drugs and one by one we would concede and get out of drag. But I was DIVA Rising

Star and I wanted to make the night last. I think I won Last Drag Standing that year, and no one was ever sure if that was something to be proud of. It wasn't about keeping the look well presented. It was about not conceding to the consensual reality of 'normal' life. People see drag as an illusion, a costume, but it's actually the hand pointing at the moon. Its flaw is being so captivating that most people end up staring at the hand instead of what it's pointing at. Drag is intended to break the illusion of our everyday lives – the illusion that clothing and fashion are 'real', that gender is real, that any of these social constructs we accept so readily and without question are real. On those magical DIVA nights there was a critical mass of drag queens. We could suspend our own disbelief. As long as we didn't take the drag off, as long as we didn't go to sleep, we could keep the dream alive.

Sydney was dominated by a certain style of drag in the late 90s and early 2000s. Its proponents were called the Beige Brigade on account of everyone having the same beige high heels, the same elbow-length gloves and the same earrings. You had to have black liquid liner eyebrows, sockets and lip liner. Drag was a business and there were rules if you wanted to be in a show; ironically, being a drag queen meant you had to conform.

Ashley Swift was an outlier to the old guard. He didn't follow their rules and his performances were always spectacular. He asked Vanity and me to join him in a new Friday night show called Divastated, upstairs at the Midnight Shift. It was going to be like nothing else Sydney had seen: Ashley, Vanity, me; two male dancers, Simon and Matt; and occasional cameos from dance mum and costume sewer Mamma Shirl. All of us invested countless hours into every detail. For weeks we met up to have costume-sewing bees and dance rehearsals.

These performances were next level – like an MTV music video come to life on stage. On opening night, the club was packed and we took ages getting ready. As the hours ticked on the crowd got agitated. Ashley told us, 'People will forget you were late, but they won't forget if you're shit.' Divastated became the hit show on the strip, breathing life back into the Midnight Shift and making us the stars of the Sydney scene.

Around this time I was only working three nights. From Thursday to Sunday I'd be flying high but would come crashing down in a deep, dark depression during the week. I'd fall asleep on Sunday night or in the wee hours of Monday morning and awake on Tuesday to find texts on my phone from the dealer asking for money to pay for the drugs I'd got 'on tick' – always money I didn't have. I'd ask if I could pay it back when one of my jobs paid and I always had a way of robbing Peter to pay Paul – paying rent late or setting up a payment plan. But on Tuesday afternoons at around 2 pm my brain, void of feel-good neurotransmitters, would begin consuming itself with thoughts. Every fear and doubt was magnified and my brain would spiral into darkness. How would I pay rent? How would I buy food? Why did I hate myself? Why hadn't any of this stuff been covered in my first 18 years of life? What was I doing with my life? What would my mum think? The wounds of growing up queer in a straight-as-default world were cured when I was high on the weekends, but became paralysing and insurmountable midweek when coming down. I'd lie in bed crying in hopeless pain.

Party drug use was the norm. Overdoses weren't uncommon. If someone started dropping on the dance floor we'd get them out and back to someone's place. If someone overdosed on the dance floor they could be taken to hospital in an ambulance then be back at the club or the recovery party a few hours later, still with the heart monitor stickers on their chest. Many of us had no respect for ourselves or our lives. We were chasing the extremes. Sometimes I think the point was to get as close to death as possible without actually dying. Not because I wanted to die, just because I'd been presented with such a limited reality for so long I wanted to see how far the edge actually extended. The nature of GHB meant that it made you feel happy, horny and full of energy, but there was a very short distance between an optimum high and unconsciousness. It's often described as a date-rape drug in the media for good reason.

One Wednesday evening, having just emerged from my darkened bedroom, recovering from a long weekend at the disco, my nose started to bleed – which often happened as a result of snorting all sorts of different drugs to maintain all sorts of different highs. I had a particular love for ketamine, the horse tranquilliser-cum-party-drug known as Special K. I went to the bathroom, sat down on the toilet, leant forwards and waited for the bleeding to stop. I sat there for ages but the blood kept gushing: it wouldn't clot. I tried the old-school method of tilting my head back and pinching the top of my nose. Still bleeding. There was blood everywhere, all over the white marble tiles, the toilet, the basin, my face and my body. The bathroom looked like a crime scene. My nose just wouldn't stop bleeding and I didn't know what to do.

Luckily, my friend Linus popped in for an unannounced visit (the front door was always unlocked in those days).

'Shane Shims! Are you home?'

'I'm in the bathroom, Linus Lims. Don't get a fright.'

'Why? What did you… SHANE! NO! BABY NO! PLEASE NO!'

Linus grabbed my arms and looked at my wrists. He thought he'd caught me mid–suicide attempt and he was trying to find where I'd cut myself. Linus was screaming hysterically, panicking and unsure of what to do. I tried to explain that the blood was coming from my nose, but he was in such a state he couldn't hear me.

'WHY?!' He sobbed, shaking my shoulders and staring me in the eyes. We were both covered in my blood. Overwhelmed with his emotion, I started crying too.

'LINUS! IT'S MY NOSE. IT WON'T STOP BLEEDING!'

He was confused, but when he finally understood what was going on he was so relieved that our tears turned to laughter. With the blood still refusing to coagulate we agreed it was best to go to the emergency department. We cleaned the blood off me and headed to St Vincent's, where they had to cauterise both nostrils. A chemical swab singed and sealed all of the blood vessels inside my nose closed so they would stop bleeding. Time to give snorting drugs a break.

Sydney hosted the 2000 Olympics, and in 2002 the city hosted the Gay Games. The Gay Games, in part, was an attempt to reconcile that all-too-often negative experience many queers have with sport by creating a safe space where they can come together and have an opportunity to enjoy ball sports and water sports of a different variety to usual. The opening ceremony was in Aussie Stadium and I got to lead a group show where all the drag queens were cheerleaders; we performed a rewrite of the cheer from *Bring It On*. I was also in the finale featuring 24 drag queens in gorgeous red sequin gowns performing 'Le Freak' by Chic. There was something monumental and legitimising about being on stage at a queer event in front of 45,000 people.

After the opening number I ran up to the grandstand to watch the show. I sat there sobbing, listening to k.d. lang sing 'Hallelujah', and then the Honourable Michael Kirby's speech. Michael Kirby was an openly gay judge who'd sat on the Australian High Court, the highest court in the land and final court of appeal. This man was one of the most important and powerful people in the country *and he was gay*. I'd never heard of such a thing. A gay public figure who was a respected intellect, interpreter of the constitution, and who held one of the highest and most respected seats in the country: this was a groundbreaking concept. Justice Kirby's words moved me to tears that night. I'd never heard someone talk about being gay in such a dignified way. As his words echoed around that stadium I felt the importance of what he said:

'Under different skies, at the beginning of a new millennium, in an old land, and a young nation, we join together in the hope and conviction that the future will be more kind and just than the past… Acceptance, diversity, inclusiveness, participation, tolerance and joy. Ours is a world of love questing to find the common link that binds all people. We are here because whatever our sexuality, we know that the days of exclusion are numbered.'

Watching this speech on YouTube still brings me to tears. I cry for the beauty of Justice Kirby's words and message, I cry for all of the suffering my community has endured, I cry because I'm reminded of my own struggle to understand myself and my place in the world, and I cry because I know

I'm still one of the lucky few who have the freedom to express their gender and sexuality freely on this planet today.

No longer was I just some kid from Brisbane alone on a personal journey of self-discovery; I was part of a community, a bigger picture. I benefitted from the work of all those who had gone before me, who had fought, been persecuted – and prosecuted – and died for my right to exist. Justice Kirby acknowledged the First Nations peoples of Australia, he included all members of our community, and spoke to marginalised groups around the world – the courage of those of the past and hopes for those in the future. His words were illuminating. They were like balm on wounds I hadn't known existed.

The Gay Games brought visitors from all around the world and the proliferation of an exciting new drug too. We didn't know anything about it except it had a similar effect to cocaine but was one sixth of the price at only $50 a bag. And where a bag of coke would last a couple of hours between a small group of friends, this new drug would last you and your friends all night and well into the next day. Crystal meth (or 'ice' as the media now calls it) would become a scourge that would ravage queer communities the world over, but initially we knew nothing of its reputation or ramifications. We smoked it out of a little glass pipe and the effect was instant. It wasn't mind-altering like the other drugs; in fact it was sobering but moreish.

The week of the Gay Games I had a gig every day and night. I would go to sleep with a prescription benzo and then four hours later I'd snap back awake and light up a pipe to get me going and ready for the next gig. It seemed totally normal at the time, but looking back those were dark and hectic times.

Crystal meth, or Tina, as she was also known, changed the vibe of Sydney. Partying went from being fun, lovely times on ecstasy to a more solemn and focused energy. We'd still pile into the toilet cubicle at the club, but the fun wasn't there any more. We'd pull a glass pipe from a pouch in a handbag and mindlessly pass it around the cubicle. The focus became the drug and waiting for the pipe to circle back around so we could have more. We still did E, K and G, but T became the star. It wasn't that its effects were better, we just seemed to do it more.

At the recoveries the same thing happened. The focus shifted to the pipe, or pipes, circling around the room. The community connection I'd been so drawn to on ecstasy was no longer there on crystal. It was a very insular drug, making each person focused on one thing. We cut off our connection with humanity and developed a new one with the drug. I remember the rush of holding a jet lighter just below the glass bulb and watching the white smoke swill around as I gently sucked it deep into my lungs. I'd inhale deeply and then hold the smoke inside me for as long as I could, pinching my nose and covering my mouth with my hand, ensuring none of it escaped. I wanted every ounce of its effect. It was insidious, but no one seemed to notice what it was doing to us.

The following Mardi Gras, I remember friends kept asking me if I was all right. I didn't know what they meant, but people not in my immediate circle kept pulling me aside for a moment and saying, 'Shane, are you OK?' Despite being able to see the life being sucked out of my face when I looked in the mirror, I was in denial about the effects of my crystal use: my usually flawless skin had welts and scabs popping up, and the bags under my eyes got harder to conceal with makeup. Even though it was only on weekends – well... Thursday to Sunday... well... Monday morning, I guess – it was still just social use. I didn't wake up every day and have a pipe: I only wanted to do it when I was with friends so we could keep the party going. We were all doing it. It went with our nocturnal lifestyle. I still turned up to work to do the shows and paid my rent. It wasn't behind closed doors or secretive, at least not a secret from each other, but I knew these were all justifications for something that was wrong for me, and I decided it was best to give it a break, at least for a weekend.

I made it all the way through Thursday night without a drug, but then Friday night after the shows I found myself sucking on the 'glass cigarette' again. *Oh well, I'll try again next weekend*, I'd tell myself. Thursday rolled around and I made a stronger resolve.

Hey, Shane, remember how you said you weren't going to do meth this weekend? And you said the same last weekend too? And the one before that? I think this might be turning into a problem. What would Mum think of this? A moment of conversation with myself. It seemed like the simple method of 'just stopping' biting my nails Mum had suggested wasn't as effective when it came to a narcotic more addictive than heroin. It was hard to avoid, especially because my work life revolved around drug culture. I felt like I was wasting away.

I'd moved to Sydney a few years earlier with big dreams for my future and now I struggled to understand what that meant in real-world terms. There was no obvious path for me to follow. I wasn't sure where I was going, but I knew what the next step was. I needed to stop all of the drugs.

I knew the drugs clouded every aspect of my being, and perhaps with a drug-free mind and body I would find the clarity to recognise or devise the next step. My goal was to make it through one single weekend, which might sound like a pretty piss-weak goal, but from where I stood that was an achievement.

I made it through Thursday night working at Arq, Friday night at Divastated, Saturday night at Stonewall and I stayed in on Sunday night. I'd done it. A whole weekend clean. I didn't feel like I'd missed out on anything – in fact, it felt like an accomplishment. I've learnt over the years that setting small goals and achieving them is really helpful given how my brain is wired. I've tricked myself into writing this whole book by setting a 20-minute timer and then sitting down to write. The idea of writing a book was too massive for my mind to comprehend, too scary, too much of a commitment, but by negotiating with my brain I could at least commit to writing for 20 minutes. It was the same with drugs. There was no way I could imagine never taking drugs again, but I could imagine not doing them for 24 hours and so I did that, and then I did it again.

Instead of being cooped up in the apartment all Saturday I spent the day with some non-drug-den friends. I was fortunate to have Nic and Ben and a circle of mates who weren't wrapped up in the same world but who I didn't have to hide that world from. Those friendships filled the gaps of drug-taking with something far more real and important, and for once on Comedown Tuesday I wasn't sitting in front of the TV watching Oprah, crying my eyes out. I wasn't cured, but my brain chemistry wasn't swinging from left to right for a change. I know now that there are so many free and effective support services out there if you're struggling with addiction or need help. Most LGBTQ+ organisations can point you in the right direction, or a quick google of a 12-step program might be the way through. Asking for help can be hard, but struggling with addiction alone is harder.

The next weekend I committed to not taking drugs again. And then the next. And then the next. It had been a month: I'd broken the cycle. Maybe taking six months off was an achievable goal. I had an unusual sense of discipline; people would offer me stuff and I'd politely say no. I'd still go to the kikis (afterparties, in layfolk terms), where everyone was high, and I'd be completely sober with no desire to do drugs. I don't know where this determination came from – it isn't a common experience when it comes to habitual drug use, especially with something as addictive as crystal meth.

I think there are probably degrees of addiction and, despite what I've described, I don't think my drug use crossed over into the depth of full addiction. This distinction is important, because suggesting that an addict can just stop would be unfair and irresponsible. Based on his research into addiction, Johann Hari writes that *the opposite to addiction is not sobriety – it's connection*. I was very lucky to have the foundational love of my parents, the support system of close friends and community, and a dream that was bigger than myself. Together these provided me with a sense of connection that was greater than the grip of meth.

After my six months of sobriety, I'd occasionally do drugs again if it was a long weekend party, but the frequency was down from every weekend to a couple of times a year. Of the people I used to party with 20 years ago, some made it out but many lives are still impacted: some still use 'casually', others are in a constant struggle, many went to jail and several are dead.

I can't categorise my drug-taking years as good or bad: they were nuanced and filled with all sorts of experiences. For all the dark times there was a lot of fun too, though the fun was part of the problem, part of the addictive nature of drugs. But I can honestly say that nothing was added to my life when I did meth. Take it from your Uncle Courtney and don't even bother trying it. I did, so you don't have to. I don't condone drug use or suggest it, but shutting down the conversation with a hard no is not healthy or realistic. People, especially young people, are going to try drugs, and we need to be able to talk about that. If there was more information about drugs when I was younger I might have not had to do all the learning in secrecy, using trial and error as my metric.

11

I'd cleaned up my act and as the months trucked along I got offered my own headlining show on Saturday nights at the Shift. I was going to make it my first live singing show. Up until that point I'd only lip-synced when performing, as was customary for Sydney queens, until Vanity convinced me to try singing live.

'But drag queens lip-sync,' I said.

'But you can sing.'

It had never occurred to me I was allowed to sing live in drag. The showcast included four male dancers and a cameo by a quirky Sydney queen called Joyce Mange. The night was called *Queen* and the show went from Kylie's version of 'Dancing Queen' to a glam-rock finale with Queen's 'We Will Rock You'. We were a hit.

Something I've always loved about the drag community is how intergenerational it is. In a dressing room the ages can range from 18 to 70 and beyond. There's a whole creative underworld that works at putting on the shows too. We sat with sound engineers in studio for hours, crafting and editing the soundtracks; we had expert choreographers and genius costumiers. And because the budgets for these shows weren't big, the cast of the show would all pitch in at sewing bees to put our various skills to work.

Before the Gay Games I had a costume fitting with Abbey Rhode, a drag queen and renowned costume designer; his outfits were always stunning and beautifully finished. When I'd gone to his place in Surry Hills for a fitting, he swathed me in plastic wrap and brown packing tape and started drawing all over my body – an unexpected method for making patterns. I asked him to make the costumes for *Queen* and would go over and hang out and help cut things, or glue things and use my skills where I could. He'd regale me with stories of the 80s and 90s in Sydney and tell me all about the drag legends who'd paved the way: the crowds they attracted, the visibility they commanded and the glamour they brought to the world. The stories of legendary shows and unbridled creativity that left audiences stunned. Abbey also told me of the trauma of the AIDS crisis and how he himself was HIV positive. He told me of the way the community rallied together in support of those who were suffering, how they mourned the loss of a generation of young men, and how those who lived suffered the guilt of surviving. I'd had no idea. This stuff wasn't recorded anywhere: it wasn't in history books or in TV dramas, you couldn't google it. It only existed as memories in the hearts and minds of those who'd survived. It was so special to sit with Abbey absorbing the oral history of my people and my city. Like when Justice Michael Kirby spoke at the Gay Games, I felt fortified by these stories. I belonged to a lineage of queer people: those before me had fought for my right to exist. This understanding of intergenerational connection is pivotal to how I see myself now: what before seemed surface and ephemeral turned out to be deep roots of history.

The week after my *Queen* show opened I heard about auditions for a TV show called *Australian Idol.* I didn't really know what it was, but I'd heard about the American version in *TV Hits* magazine and decided to go along. I figured I may as well double my chances by going one day as Shane and the next as Courtney. There were two rounds of auditions: one in front of the show's producers and the other, if you were successful, that would make it to TV. The first-round cattle-call was at the University of Sydney campus, and thousands of people turned up. The first day I went by myself and don't recall talking to anyone – just waiting in line until I was shuffled into a little room with three producers seated behind a trestle table. I sang 'Your Song' by Elton John and they told me to come back for the TV auditions a few weeks later. *Well, that was easy... maybe this was my big break, my chance at being a straight male pop star. I don't think I should go back tomorrow, I can just play it straight, pretend that Courtney doesn't exist.* I really genuinely thought that... for about an hour until I snapped out of it and realised that what Portia Turbo had told me one night in the dressing room at Stonewall was true: drag was my strength, not my weakness. Courtney is what made me unique.

That night Ashley, Vanity and I created a look that felt TV friendly, and by 'Ashley, Vanity and I', I mean... Ashley created the outfit, Vanity did the hair and I tried to operate the hot glue gun. I marched along the next day as Courtney, feeling uncomfortably conspicuous. It's *awkward* when you're in drag in an everyday situation. Part of the way I made drag socially acceptable was being 'in on the joke' – I was on stage or in a club with an audience who knew I was a boy dressed as a woman – but being in drag in daylight, by myself with no context, was confronting. I felt the need to make a public announcement that I knew I was in drag and everyone could therefore relax. If there is a hypervigilance that comes with being queer in straight spaces, being gender diverse in daylight in a heteronormative space puts it under the microscope.

So after standing in line for hours, waiting for my *Australian Idol* audition as Courtney, I finally got into the audition room. I sang 'Woman' by Peggy Lee and the people behind the panel asked me to come back for the TV auditions. Maybe it was the right decision to come back as Courtney. As I was exiting, one of the producers on the panel stopped me and asked if I'd auditioned yesterday out of drag. He remembered me. This took me by surprise because there were several rooms churning through thousands of people a day. I could tell this idea excited him; he, like me, saw the potential that Courtney offered for good TV.

The footage of the second round of auditions tells the next part of the story better than I can. Basically, I went along to the audition as Shane, got knocked back then returned the next day as Courtney and made it through. The judges weren't told about my double act until after they'd said yes to Courtney. People still come up and tell me they remember that moment. Young children around the country watching TV with the family, sitting in their suburban living rooms as a drag queen struts onto their cathode ray tube. There was no outrage – no vituperative letters were written to the network – only appreciation for the charisma, uniqueness, nerve and talent on display.

I went on to the top 100, then the top-40 live rounds, but was beaten out of a spot in the top 12 by Paulini, a diva with Whitney Houston range, and Rob Mills, a cheeky singer with a penchant for soft rock. However, a second chance awaited me when I was put through to the wildcard round.

'I think wildcard is more my style,' I declared, and I did the Angus Young duckwalk across the *Idol* stage, belting out the Aussie rock classic 'You Shook Me All Night Long'. As if I hadn't already overturned the proverbial apple cart merely by being there, now a drag queen was singing AC/DC. Alas, Cosima De Vito deservingly got put through to the top 12. There I was, unlucky 13, but I wasn't about to be overcome by triskaidekaphobia: I was going to hustle my way into the mainstream by hook or by crook.

Ian 'Dicko' Dickson was a beloved *Idol* judge and a record executive at Sony BMG, and he became a big champion of mine. Dicko came from the UK, with its long tradition of drag, queer and camp in the mainstream, and he saw the entertainment value in what I was doing. Where a regular Aussie bloke might feel too threatened to flirt with a glamorous woman who happened to have a penis, Dicko leant in, making quips about leaving his wife for me and how I was his daughter's favourite because I was a real-life Bratz doll. What might have just seemed like a good time and good TV was actually groundbreaking leadership on Dicko's part. For many years afterwards I'd smile politely as a male TV host would 'wink wink, nudge nudge' at the fact I was a bloke in a dress, but while Dicko was in on the joke, he never made *me* the joke. And through his acceptance of me, he led Australia to accept me too. He also put his money where his mouth was – as the credits rolled on the wildcard episode, Dicko and I shook hands on a gentleman's agreement and he signed me for a record deal. Over those weeks from *Idol* audition to wildcard round, life as I knew it started changing. People would recognise me basically any time I stood still. At the check-out buying groceries, waiting to cross the lights, and definitely at gay bars.

Something that I had seen and thought about from the non-fame side many times was suddenly happening to me. Once, in high school, I was with Mum doing the weekly shop. I wandered off to sneak in a bag of these little German gingery/spiced cookies Dad and I liked called Pfeffernüsse. As I rounded the aisle with the cookies, chocolate and chips in it (an aisle our family usually skipped straight past) I was stopped dead in my tracks. *Oh. My. Gosh.* My little heart started racing; my face got flushed. I couldn't believe it. *What are the odds of spotting a celebrity at Woolworths in Sandgate!? It's that woman from* Neighbours*! No. It's the woman from that travel show Mum and Dad like.* Getaway. *No. No that's not it. I know! It's the woman from the Brand Power TV commercial. Yes! And she's walking right towards me with her shopping trolley.*

My natural instinct was to about-face and go back from whence I came. I ducked round the corner and stood in front of a Vegemite display, trying to compose myself. I heard Mum's wise words in my head: 'Deep breaths, Shaney.' I could hear the wobbly red wheel of the woman's cart getting closer, and as the steel cage emerged around the corner I put a big grin on my face and… froze. I couldn't move. I just smiled, waiting for her. I stopped breathing. As she came around the corner her head of shiny brunette hair bounced in slow motion, her eyes meeting mine. I tried to speak, but all I managed was a wince. Still smiling. She slowed her stride, then smiled and gave a polite nod. I couldn't move. She raised her eyebrows and cocked her head to one side as if to say, 'Can I help you?' but it was as if someone had hit the pause button on me. With a bemused look she picked up her pace, diverted her path around me, and headed down the next aisle.

I was in shock. A real-life celebrity. I stood there staring off into the distance for a few more seconds in awe before heading down the aisle to grab a bag of Pfeffernüsse to hide in Mum's trolley when she wasn't looking.

Obviously my scale of fame was relative to my life experience when I was 12, but what is it about 'fame'? Seeing famous people doesn't always have that same impact; I'm glad to say it didn't happen again for another 18 years. The next time I was rendered mute and frozen was in 2012 when I met Oprah, which I feel is reasonable. When we notice famous people we often think, *Oh! Wait till I tell *insert best friend's name* about this.* My mate Maxi Shield says she'd root any celebrity for the story, just so she could sit around with her sister girlfriends and say, 'Guess who I had sex with? The woman from the Brand Power commercial!'

Fame has a mystical power, but it also has a way of hijacking reality. While I was gaining a lot on *Idol*, I was losing something too: something I didn't know was a thing. My anonymity. When strangers started greeting me, telling me how proud they were, it was such a thrill but also a peculiar experience. (Describing this is hard because I sound ungrateful, and I think that was the problem: I wasn't grateful. Gratitude came later.) People started giving me their opinion on what I could have done better or what I should have done instead. It was said with the best of intentions, but I was inundated and overwhelmed by it all. Everyone usually wanted to know what I was doing next, and I always felt compelled to announce something worthy. I didn't want to let them down. Conversations stopped being two-way and became solely focused on me. Every conversation, even with a stranger, was like I was being interviewed. People seemed to subjugate their own existence just because I'd been on TV.

Loss of anonymity wasn't something I could understand without experiencing it, but the best way I can put it is – it felt like there were no strangers left in the world. Everyone knew something about me, before I knew anything about them.

Obviously the whole world didn't know something about me, but it felt like everyone in my world did. It might not sound like a big deal, but it was incredibly hard to comprehend and process. It was like everything had changed overnight and I hadn't caught up yet.

For the first time I went to see a psychologist about the mental anguish I was going through. I felt like I was getting my dream, but the struggle inside my head was much greater than the reward. I'd started blaming Courtney for all of the things I was finding challenging. The therapist swiftly and simply pointed out that in fact Courtney acted as a buffer between Shane and fame, and that if anything I should thank 'her' for that. The therapist acknowledged that the shift in my life was a big challenge for me to cope with, but that it was a by-product of having a successful entertainment career. She explained that it was OK and healthy for me to have boundaries about what was public and what was private, and she helped me prepare some polite responses to people when I was out trying to socialise and they wanted to talk to me about *Idol*. She was a cognitive behavioural psychologist, and I liked her advice. It seemed practical. Those sessions helped give me some perspective on and appreciation for what was going on.

Despite me not making the cut on *Idol*, the producers brought me back for different moments throughout the season. One such assignment was hosting the red carpet for the 2003 ARIAs (Australia's answer to the Grammys). But before I interviewed people on the red carpet I got to walk it. My first red carpet. I wore a purple backless gown and fresh irises in my hair. Australian pop sweetheart Delta Goodrem had recently been diagnosed with cancer, and as a symbol of support I had her name and some flowers body-painted down my back. As my car pulled up, she'd just hopped out of the vehicle in front of me and was greeting the crowd. I stepped onto the carpet to the roar of thousands of people cheering and the line of paparazzi yelling my name. It was the first time I'd experienced anything like that. Momentarily I stood frozen like a deer in headlights, not knowing what to do. I'd watched red carpets on TV before but experiencing the real thing was terrifying. In front of me, Delta was waving and taking photos with fans in the crowd. She was so effortless and natural, I decided to copy what she was doing – and it worked. I just pretended it was totally normal to have thousands of people screaming my name and hundreds of people taking my photo. Whenever I find myself on a big red carpet I think about Delta at the ARIAs and I know exactly what to do.

Doing my best at holding my foot in the door of fame, I went along to sit in the audience of the 60s-themed episode of *Australian Idol.* Loving any opportunity to dress for the occasion, I wore a Wayne Cooper baby-doll dress with Brigitte Bardot-esque hair and makeup. The producers asked if I wanted to be a go-go dancer in someone's number, and of course I jumped at the chance to be on camera. Dress for the job you want, kids, not the job you've got.

That live show was the same night as *The Matrix Reloaded* premiere at the Sydney Opera House, as in the Wachowski film, with Keanu Reeves, Jada Pinkett-Smith and Hugo Weaving all in attendance. *Idol* larrikin Rob 'Millsy' Mills and I got invited along, but when we got to the door our names weren't on the guest list and we had to wait out the front while the publicist came and got us. We didn't care: we were amazed we'd been invited to a big Hollywood movie premiere in the first place. Apologetic, the publicist asked if there was anything she could do to make it up to us. 'A photo with the Hilton sisters will suffice,' I said, half joking and half hopeful. Australia is such an isolated place that when an international celebrity comes to town they're big news, and Nicky and Paris were all the media could talk about. We were whisked off to meet them and snapped some photos, and I chatted to Nicky, wingmanning 'cause Millsy thought Paris was hot.

It seemed Paris thought Millsy was cute too, as we ended up hanging out all night and into the next morning. Many Australians will remember the infamous covers of newspapers featuring papped photos of Millsy and Paris lip-locked on the balcony of the Park Hyatt. I was inside the room, still in drag, too afraid to step into the daylight.

A few days later was the Melbourne Cup, the nation's largest horse-racing event, aka 'the race that stops the nation' (I don't support cruelty to animals these days, but back in 2003 I was none the wiser). Paris asked Millsy and me if we wanted to come along, which of course we did. We spent the week in Melbourne going to different events, and I started to get to know Paris away from public life, hanging out in her suite at the Lyall Hotel in Melbourne. Privately she was really kind, sweet and smart. It just felt like we were a couple of girls talking about boys and stuff. To me, she had an 'in drag' persona for the public and an 'out of drag' persona for private. Her voice, which was higher pitched like a young girl's voice in public, became deeper in private settings. This dual persona reminded me of what I'd learnt in therapy about boundaries.

Later that week we were in the back of the car on our way to the Wayne Cooper fashion show Paris was walking in. I was wearing an aqua-blue mini-sequin halter neck, a white rosary

(I have no idea why), white acrylic bangles and a short blonde wig with the front of my own hair pulled back and pinned in for a 'natural' look. Paris was touching up her lip gloss.

'You should wear lip gloss. Here, try this.' She leant over and applied a coat to my lips. It was actually life changing.

'What is that?'

'Mac Lip Lacquer in Tongue-in-Chic.'

'That's hot!' I said, mimicking her now immortal phrase.

Ever since that day (in drag), unless wearing a red lip, I have worn Mac lip gloss. Tongue-in-Chic was discontinued so then I switched to Pogo Pink, which was also discontinued, so now I use Oyster Girl. I'm obsessed with it: the perfect frosted glossy lip finish.

It was so eye-opening, getting a tiny glimpse into the life of one of the most famous people on the planet. I enjoyed getting to know Paris and she sent me a beautiful email (trapped in an old Hotmail account that has probably since been deleted in some digital housekeeping) about how much she enjoyed our time together, which was really sweet. I was glad to realise she enjoyed my company too.

Idol rang for other cameos throughout the ratings-smashing season, which culminated when I opened the grand finale with a live performance on the steps of the Sydney Opera House. It was such an honour and the biggest live crowd I'd performed to. I borrowed a dress off Kitty Glitter that Abbey had made; I borrowed some diamonds off jeweller Adrian Lewis – so Hollywood; and I got my mate Michael Boyd (one of my many unrequited crushes) to dance with me. The grand finale of *Australian Idol* Season 1 was the ninth highest rated TV show in Australian history. The nation loved us – probably more specifically Guy Sebastian, Shannon Noll, Cosima, Paulini, Millsy and then me… but I was one of the 'unforgettable' stories referred to on the giant McDonald's banner draped across the back of the Opera House forecourt stage.

These days, watching that performance on YouTube, I'm ready to cringe, but also proud. As a 21-year-old baby, I totally owned that stage. It wasn't the strongest vocal delivery, but it was a great performance. I knew I couldn't compete with the 'real' singers on the show, so I put on a show of my own. I wish I could go give myself a hug as I came off stage and say, 'Good job. I'm proud of you.'

12

Hot on the high heels of the TV show came the arena tour in January 2004. Fourteen thousand screaming fans a night in sold-out venues nationwide. I sang 'I Should Be So Lucky' by Kylie and then Rob Mills and I did a duet of 'Kids' by Kylie and Robbie Williams. The *Idol* tour was epic. We were rock stars. We thought we were the most famous people in the country at that time, and we possibly were. It was exactly what I imagined being famous would feel like. I didn't fully register that the fame wasn't mine alone, that I was a part of a much bigger machine. We were whisked around the country with security guards and fans screaming everywhere we went. We got drunk each night after the show and lived our best 90s rock-and-roll touring fantasy. After the show in Perth, I caught the last flight back to Sydney to shoot the music video for my debut single, squeezing it into our day off. Then we were off to Adelaide for the next day of tour. I was living on the thrill of it all. This was it! I'd made it. All the hard work was over. Lol!

The record label gave me a bunch of songs to listen to, including a demo Kylie had recorded but never released (squeal), and a track called 'Caught in the Act' that had been written for me by one of the lads who'd written 'Don't Call Me

Baby' by Madison Avenue. I thought it was the right vibe – the verses were all about hiding who you are in the shadows, the bridge was about being tired of that and how it was time to make some noise, and the chorus featured the literal sounding out of my name in an affirmative declaration: 'I've been caught in the act' and no one was going to stop me now! There was another track, 'Rub Me Wrong', which was a better pop song and the production was more slick, but the energy of the song wasn't right for me. It was too sexualised in its sound and lyrics (even Mum said so).

The vibe from management and the record company peeps was that 'Rub Me Wrong' was the way to go, although Vanity and Ashley were very vocal that 'Caught in the Act' was the better choice: it would appeal to the young female audience who loved me on *Idol.* But I was so young myself, and was being handed my dream. And who was I to question a record company's judgement: these folks *had* worked on the biggest pop acts in Australia. I was lucky to even be there. So I did what they suggested and chose 'Rub Me Wrong'.

The storyline for the music video, as best I could tell, was that I was a glamorous mistress or possibly an escort booked by a Hugh Hefner type for a home-invasion sex fantasy – which, although I could get away with today, at the time felt inappropriate to me. I was the country's sweetheart, a national trinket, not a Playboy bunny. I was being produced to match the fantasies of the straight white men in boardrooms rather than the girls, gays and grannies who loved me on *Idol.* I was the first drag queen in the world to debut on a major label, which was a huge coup. But something didn't sit right. I tried to explain what I wanted, what my vision was, but they told me, 'You don't know who you are' – and I think they were right. I didn't. But despite my lack of self-knowledge, I'd managed to intuitively tell a pretty strong and unique storyline on *Idol* just by being myself.

I was told by my label that in all press interviews I was to assume the identity of a female. I wasn't a drag queen and I shouldn't refer to myself as such. I wasn't Shane in drag. I was a female pop star. This made no sense to me, since the cornerstone of my story on *Idol* was that I went along as a boy, got knocked back then bent the rules and my gender when I returned as Courtney. It was the defiance and the larrikin nature of the scheme that Australians found endearing, along with the fact that I wasn't trying to put one over on them. We were all in on 'the joke'.

Press would be briefed that they weren't allowed to ask me questions about being a boy or being a drag queen, so my *Idol* plot twist was therefore off the record, even though it was really what everyone wanted to talk about – there was a pink glittery elephant in the room. The message I got from this was that I was to be seen but not heard; my story wasn't important. It made for such uncomfortable interviews, but more than that was the shame it reinforced about my own identity. I couldn't be myself: my job was to pretend I was a blonde bombshell pop singer. They overlooked the fact that the country already had a Sophie Monk, and she was much better at it than I was.

Be cordial, Courtney, don't do anything to make the nice straight people uncomfortable, and pull up the ladder behind you, would you? We don't want any more undesirables following you up.

One such interview was on *Good Morning Australia*, a highlight of my TV landscape growing up. Bert Newton was the host of the show and the most revered person on Australian TV as far as I was concerned, and I was in Melbourne as a guest on his show.

'How long have you been Courtney Act?' Bert asked.

'Ummmm...' *nervous giggle* '... all my life. I popped out a glamorous diva, I think.' I was trying desperately to answer the questions without lying but without telling the truth. It was so awkward and when I watch it now I squirm (it's on YouTube). All I wanted to do was answer the king of Australian TV honestly, but I understood I wasn't allowed to. I had to pretend to be a woman. I feel so stupid now for not asserting myself in the first place and saying, 'No you bunch of nongs, I'm a bloody drag queen! That's how I got here and that's how everyone knows me.' I'd been accepted as a drag TV performer and that had relieved my shame, but this validation was quickly quashed by the ideals of the corporate entertainment industry. It's one thing to try and manoeuvre your way out of social boxes, but it's another to be placed back into one by the powers that be.

Even so, I don't blame the record and management companies I worked with: none of us knew what to do with me and we lived in a very different world from the one we live in now. I don't want to paint the experience and the people involved as a blanket negative – everyone was doing what they thought was right. There were a lot of wonderful people working hard to make my career happen, and I'm very grateful for the opportunities I was given, the chances that were taken and the lessons that were learnt. Do I think they could have done better? Sure, but when considering history you have to understand it through the paradigm of the day. Back then in the entertainment industry, actors and singers were encouraged by agents to stay in the closet (I'm sure plenty of them still are), and most out celebrities didn't come out until after they'd 'made it'. In the late 90s Ellen had come out and seemingly ended her career. Any gatekeepers who were queer were often reluctant to be pro-queer for fear of seeming self-serving.

We started doing publicity and promotion for 'Rub Me Wrong' around Mardi Gras 2004. I'd always fantasised about having this success growing up and how it would feel, but now it was happening I felt a bit like an impostor. I was pretending I knew what to do, how to be a pop star, but I was just a drag queen still trying to work out how to do her hair and makeup properly.

On 23 March 'Rub Me Wrong' debuted at #29 on the ARIA charts before dropping out of the Top 40 the following week. After that, the label wasn't going to take me up with an album option and… that was it. The ride was over. The *Idol* juggernaut had moved on.

While this is an 'all good in retrospect' statement, I'm glad success didn't come to me in the way I hoped for back then. If the record company's Courtney had given me commercial success, I'd never have had the opportunity to fail like I did and then to work it out on my own terms. The success would have been built on a false narrative, and the closet Courtney was being pushed into would have grown locks. Closets (self-imposed or externally generated) can feel like a form of protection, but ultimately they negatively reinforce a secret that pushes us deeper and deeper into shame.

From that episode I learnt that there are many ways to do things and no one can predict what will succeed. It's all trial and error. But whatever speaks to the truth of who I am is always going to deliver the best result for me. Commercial success is worthless without authenticity and dignity. I truly believe that. I don't want to be 'rich and famous' for no purpose: the loss of anonymity that comes with fame isn't worth the price tag without a purpose greater than yourself.

With nothing else on offer and eager to 'keep my brand alive', I accepted every red-carpet invite I got. Anything with a step and repeat and a chance to get my face in the gossip column or the social pages of the newspaper and I was there. A premiere, a brand launch... the opening of an envelope. Life inside the red-velvet rope wasn't as thrilling as it seemed from the outside, I discovered. The events became a circuit of familiar faces. There were certainly nights that stood out and people I loved seeing, but by and large it'd be a bunch of people sitting in a room drinking free booze.

I always felt socially anxious arriving at these events, always by myself, never quite sure who I'd run into. In essence, I was some kid off reality TV in drag, in an off-the-rack dress a fashion PR company had lent me, a light lady face and my own fringe pulled through the front of a wig. I'd do my best to blend in, to look like a 'real woman' and to draw no more attention to myself than was necessary. Yet my identity was malleable – I was still in my early 20s – and once I got used to people wanting to talk about me all the time... that's what I started to do. It permeated my whole life: everything was about me and my career, and I became a bit of a brat. Paris was back in Australia; after we went to a party, the media called me 'the third Hilton sister'.

The truth of my existence was anything but glamorous: I was running out of money, my music was a flop and I hardly had any work. High-paid corporate gigs and club gigs were piecemeal, and there wasn't anything major on the horizon. Management suggested I move into a swankier apartment befitting my new life, and I did. It was all white, grey and sleek with big glass doors on a high floor of a brand-new building that was a block away from the Broom Closet and the Taylor Grand. But the money was going out faster than it was coming in, and my bank account was getting lower and lower until finally it was like my eyebrows – overdrawn! My management said they'd pay me a monthly retainer recoupable off money I earnt, but month by month I was getting further in debt.

I had high expectations that were built up by the people working on my career, and while encouragement is important, expectation management is important too. I'd been promised the world and been given an atlas. But my friends and drag community expected more from me, so I had to keep up appearances and I couldn't let them know I was a failure. Once again I was trying to be something I wasn't. *What's wrong with me?* I put on all of these airs and graces to try to bolster my image and my self-worth by pretending I was better than I was, and better than everyone else.

At the 2004 DIVAs I won Entertainer of the Year and gave what is hopefully the most cringey speech I will ever make. I thanked 'my team', my manager, publicist, record label, and a slew of people I was only mentioning to make myself sound more important. I looked like a real dickhead. I should have been thanking the people in that room who helped turn me into the drag queen I was: Vanity, Ashley, Chelsea, Mogi, Hillary, Ricca, Abbey – the people of my community who'd given me a place to belong – and the venues that employed me like the Shift, Stonewall and Arq. Instead I'd snubbed them. If people didn't think I was a tosser from my thank-you speech they certainly did by the last line:

'I'd like to thank Paris Hilton because she's my friend and not yours.'

Reliving that moment, I want to be swallowed up by space and time. This isn't me hating on myself: it's me being objectively aware that I was a douche. I just wanted to be liked, and somehow I thought being pretentious was an effective method. If everyone liked Paris and we were friends then everyone would like me too.

I hope I'm not sounding like some out-of-touch wanker with these stories: 'Oh poor Courtney. Everybody knows her name. How horrible.' I'm aware of my privilege and how lucky I am. But this particular brand of good fortune isn't without strange and unexpected challenges. My love of performing had always been about the fun of it. As a kid, Fame was a place I could express myself fully, away from a world telling me I had to be a certain way that I wasn't. I'd always dreamt of being someone on TV, but from our living room in Kennedy Street I couldn't understand what that meant. Now I'd arrived, all I wanted to do was fit in. I wouldn't change anything about the experience, but it was bloody challenging to deal with at 21 years old with no instruction manual. I was struggling to find purpose in it all.

Then one day in the wake of *Idol* I opened a fan letter written on a page torn from a school exercise book.

Dear Courtney,
I've been having a hard time at school and I don't know if I am gay or straight but I know I am different. I couldn't take it any longer and I tried to kill myself. It didn't work and I am glad 'cause when I watched you on Australian Idol you were so happy and proud and different and I realised that if it was OK for you to be different, then it was OK for me to be different too.

I've decided to keep on living.

Thank you.

Felix

As I read those words, tears rolled down my cheeks and onto the paper. Its fine blue horizontal lines held a brief but powerful message that shifted my entire world. This wasn't about I, me, mine any more – it was about us. That letter was one of the greatest gifts I've ever received.

All I'd been focusing on lately was the question of what was in it for me, but that letter instantly connected me with that boy and through that boy myself, and all the other young people made to feel less than because they didn't fit into some box that society, their family, their friends or their church said they should. When I was growing up, I'd longed to see someone like me on TV. Now I was that person for someone, and I felt imbued not with the burden of responsibility but with the privilege and power of authenticity. Simply by being myself I could be of service to someone else; I could save a life. What an honour – the greatest, perhaps?

From being on *Australian Idol* – in a narrow bandwidth of storytelling – I learnt the power and beauty of reality TV and how its ability to tell diverse stories could profoundly impact the lives of people watching. I'll be forever grateful that I got to share who I was and be accepted by the Australian public.

13

When I got the call that my management was letting me go and the fiscal reality hit, it was time to finally drop the act. I moved out of my 'lifestyles of the rich and famous' pad and into a shared apartment in Edgecliff. I got a job working at the House of Priscilla store in Stanmore and caught the morning train to work each day. It was time to get real again.

The bubble had burst. It wasn't the end of the world by any means, but it was the humbling I needed. And unexpectedly, out on my own without management I felt empowered, calling all the shots myself. It was exciting to be back in control of my hustle without the restrictions of the identity that had been crafted for me. Bring on a new season of shows at the Shift, *Courtney Act's Search for a DNA Coverboy* in Brisbane, Melbourne and Sydney, followed by a cabaret show called *Boys Like Me* that toured the country. The cabaret venues were only small and it wasn't always an easy sell, but it was so good to be on stage doing what I loved.

I was invited to be the special guest act on *Carlotta's Priscilla Show*: hosted by the legendary Carlotta, it featured seven trans women and a comedy queen in a classic showgirl revue that toured the RSL and leagues club showrooms. In Australia we have working-class members clubs that are entertainment hubs in their suburban and regional communities. They offer a well-priced buffet, affordable drinks, poker machines and a decent showroom that plays host to touring acts. The audiences were very straight and a good chunk of them were older, but they all knew Carlotta: a variety performer and Australia's most famous transgender woman. She started out her career in 1963 at Les Girls, the 'all-male revue' in Sydney's Kings Cross that even Mum and Dad had gone to see in the 70s. In 1972 she became one of the first Australians to have gender-affirming surgery (formerly known as a 'sex change'). Headlines like *Balmain Boy Becomes Beauty* were splashed across the newspapers, and Carlotta was launched into the nation's vernacular. In 1973 she became the first openly trans actress in the world to play a trans character on TV on the hugely popular drama *Number 96*. I grew up watching Carlotta, as a guest on *Good Morning Australia* and a panellist on *Beauty and the Beast* in the 90s. These days, after a 58-year career, and approaching 80, Carlotta is retiring from showbiz as beloved and adored as ever.

I loved standing beside the stage watching Carlotta weave her magic. I'd take notes, steal jokes and observe how she worked the crowd: it was a real masterclass. Show in, show out she made every night feel fresh: she'd draw from her pool of jokes and stories, but she assembled them in a way that was unique for the room, so everyone felt they were getting a show created just for them. Every night someone would try to heckle, but they were no match for Carlotta, with her quick wit and brilliant one-liners.

Drunken yobbo: Where do ya put it?

Carlotta: Open ya mouth and I'll show ya! You know, it's blokes like you that make women appreciate blokes like me.

Knowing the audience were there, in part, to see 'the sheilas who used to be blokes', Carlotta would get them on side by making herself the joke before they had the chance. Anyone who'd come to gawk or mock was disarmed by the humour and undeniable glamour. Is self-deprecation the healthiest form of comedy for the artist or the movement? No. But I'd argue that it was the only, and therefore most effective, option available to her in those days. Activists have long battled heroically in public and private for our rights, and I don't want to discount their amazing, often unsung work. But I saw Carlotta carve a place for herself and her trans identity in the Australian psyche during a time when trans people weren't at all a part of the cultural conversation. For many years the greatest public outreach was Carlotta on the TV and in the RSLs making dick jokes and using glamour to shift people's perceptions.

Being on tour was a unique demographic and gender experience too. I was a boy in his mid-20s, on a minibus full of performers in their 50s and beyond. Such a contrast to the default world, even that of the Oxford Street drag dressing rooms. Despite the show being called *Carlotta's Priscilla Show* and its billing as an 'all-male revue', the cast were actually trans women. The term wasn't widely known and was too high a concept for the general public of the day anyway: the GP are only starting to grapple with these concepts now.

It might be time for another Courtney Fact.

COURTNEY FACT

Trans, transgender and **gender diverse** are words used to describe people whose gender differs from what was presumed for them at birth (sometimes referred to as 'assigned at birth'). This concept may sound complex at first, but really it's that simple.

Because the words 'transgender' and 'trans' are adjectives, they should always come before a noun; for example, trans person, transgender folk. For clarity, although I've been talking about drag (the artform) and trans (the gender identity) alongside each other, it's important not to conflate the two. While there is a visible subset of the trans community who do drag, most trans people don't. They're bank tellers, real estate agents, CEOs, doctors, hairdressers. You name it.

Folk is often used as a non-gendered collective suffix. Trans folk, queer folk, etc.

A **trans man** is a man who was presumed to be female at birth.

A **trans woman** is a woman who was presumed to be male at birth.

Sistergirl and **Brotherboy** are terms used by First Nations transgender people; they sometimes use these terms alongside or instead of transgender. Off the coast of Darwin, the Tiwi Islands are home to what is believed to be the highest concentration of First Nations trans people in the country.

Cisgender/cis describes someone whose gender identity matches their assigned sex at birth. A cisgender person is someone who is not transgender. 'Cis' is Latin for 'on this side of'.

Transgendered is a not even a term. Imagine if I was to describe myself as an Australianed person… it just doesn't make sense. It's a past-tense verb, like something was done to a person, as opposed to an adjective describing their identity.

Transition is the process a trans person goes through to affirm their gender. (Note that the act of transitioning doesn't make someone trans; they are trans regardless of how they present.) This process can include social, medical and legal steps – including, but not necessarily: how they present their gender to the world (gender expression), changing their name and/or pronouns, hormone therapy, gender-affirming surgery, and changing legal documents and identification to reflect their gender. Each transition is a different journey, and the destination is whatever the individual feels is right for them. Sometimes gender reassignment surgery (GRS), where genitals are changed, is incorrectly seen as a 'complete' stage of transition. Many trans people have no desire to undergo GRS. It's all a matter of personal preference. For many people this concept is a bit tricky to wrap their heads around, but some women have penises and some men have vaginas. Quite often in society, trans people are reduced to conversations about the very personal subject of genitals and surgery, which, as you can imagine, is dehumanising – and we miss out on learning about their lived experience.

Passing is a verb that describes a trans person's ability to appear cisgender (as their essential, not assigned, sex). It used to be seen as the gold standard because if you could pass, you could blend in and get a 'normal' job; you didn't have to suffer the stares and aggression, and were less at risk of ending up in jail for 'cross-dressing'. Now the idea of passing is understood as conforming to society's ideas about gender, and puts an unrealistic expectation on many trans people. The objective of being trans is about how one feels and shouldn't be about meeting other people's expectations of what a man or a woman should look like. Trans beauty is unique and should be celebrated as such, rather than shamed for not conforming to cis beauty standards.

Tranny, much like faggot or the n-word, must only be used by the people who identify as such. I use it as sparingly as possible in this book as it's now seen as a pejorative when used by people who don't self-identify as trans; where it's necessary for the story I use 'tr*nny'. When I was emerging on the Sydney drag scene it was the most common word used to describe trans people, even in a friendly way. To me, the word always felt vaguely aggressive. Back then, we simply didn't have the language, which is probably indicative of how marginalised trans folk were. Thankfully, the evolution to more inclusive and affirming language was a simple one. Swapping out a noun and slipping in an adjective here and there was so easy.

Transsexual and **sex change** were the other words we had when I was in my 20s. These terms describe trans people who've undergone gender-affirming surgeries. The terms aren't used as much today because they centre the concept of genitals and surgery.

Drag is an artform that subverts the status quo of identity and uses the heightened costume of gender to entertain. It can take many forms and be performed by anyone. The origins of the word 'drag' are widely contested. One story links it to Polari, an anti-language spoken by gay men in the UK when being gay was illegal. It was like a secret code – a way to talk in public without being understood. The story goes that the word came into Polari from the German word 'drauf', meaning 'to put on'. Another story (though largely debunked) is that 'drag' is short for *DRessed As Girl* – a stage direction scribbled in the margins of scripts in Shakespearean times, when women weren't allowed to perform so their roles were played by men dressed as women.

Drag is also a term for one's social costume. It can be the costume a drag queen puts on, or the clothes you put on to leave the house. To quote RuPaul: 'We're all born naked and the rest is drag.'

Drag kings are often lesbians, trans men or non-binary folk dressed up in masculine costume for performance.

Showgirl can refer to a trans woman who does drag (obviously there are also Vegas showgirls and Moulin Rouge showgirls, and 'showgirl' can refer to other performers too). Some identify as drag performers, some as drag queens; there's a lot of nuance. It's important to note that not every trans woman who performs on stage is a showgirl or a drag performer; many trans women on stage are artists, singers or cabaret performers and have nothing to do with the artform of drag.

Drag queens are often gay men, trans women or non-binary people dressed up in feminine costume for performance. Cis women are increasingly enjoying the performative femininity of drag these days too, and after different labels like bio-queen and hyper-queen were floated to describe them, it's now usually agreed that cis women in feminine drag can also identify as drag queens.

A **cross-dresser** is someone who dresses up in clothing not usually associated with their sex, often for personal or sexual enjoyment, not as a public performance. 'Transvestite' is the dated word for cross-dresser.

Those are the most basic and inclusive descriptions of these terms I could come up with. In truth, the meanings vary culturally and geographically and, as with all language, they constantly evolve and overlap. Don't worry if you're finding it confusing: we're on an ever-evolving journey of identity. It all changes, so learn it, love it and don't hold on to it too tightly.

In the specific context of the tour I was on, I was working with seven trans women who were performing in drag. But it was different from the drag you might see today on TV: they were tall, leggy women with full breasts, in towering headdresses and feather backpacks. In their everyday lives they all lived as women because… they were women… but they dressed up in a showgirl style of drag, a costume, for the stage.

It was wonderful to hang out with these women when it was just us. Getting to hear unguarded conversations and girly gossip was a privilege. It was also fortifying to find out about those who'd come before, to get the legendary anecdotes and queer history. As with my oral history lessons with Abbey, these stories weren't being told in books or on the internet; they were only passed down through conversation.

Although I didn't have the language, I was still struggling to understand my own gender identity. The thought that I might be trans would re-emerge every now and then and I'd push it down just as fast. But spending quality time with a big group of trans women helped me to understand this identity that I was so afraid to investigate inside myself.

I'd heard that in the 60s and 70s, if you did drag you also lived as a woman: 'It's just what you did.' This always struck me as peculiar logic: doing drag and being trans are two markedly different things. There was certainly an overlap in these identities for some, and drag can be a pathway for *some* trans women to explore femininity before they transition, but trans is who someone *is* and drag is something you *do*. To me, living in drag 24/7 would have been like a police officer never taking their uniform off. Taking hormones, modifying your entire endocrine system – all because of your job – seemed extreme. What I hadn't perceived before was the context of earlier eras, like Carlotta's: there was no theory, there was only intuitive and reactive exploration of pre-existing gender constructs. The shows were high-glamour female illusion in a rigid world of gender expression, where men were men, and women were women. People drawn to this occupation probably *were* on the gender spectrum. Some radically conforming to the male/female binary, going 'all the way' to 'the other side', while others were possibly closer to the middle. Except 'the middle' didn't exist yet – not as an endpoint anyway; it was more a 'passing through' point. This was the only justifiable way to express femininity for someone assigned male at birth.

These trans showgirls I was touring with, and now counted as friends, were gender revolutionaries simply by being trans. I saw how people treated them; I heard how people talked about them; and if I'm honest, I thought of them as being 'other' too. I saw how they developed their armour and what they had to go through just to be themselves from the moment they stepped out the front door. For some of them, experiencing constant micro- and macro-aggressions created hypervigilance. Coupled with the emotional highs and lows of hormone therapy, this could understandably manifest as manic and depressive states. In certain ways, the more time I spent with this group of women, the more my own internalised transphobia grew. Their strength was inspiring, but it wasn't aspirational: I knew the way society treated them was wrong, and I didn't want that for myself.

Even at that stage of my career, my drag harked back to the Les Girls era of glamour with realness. Rather than today's over-the-top theatricality, my drag is more about amplified yet nuanced femininity, like that of the Hollywood movie stars of old. Consequently, the women in this show saw me as one of their own: a trans woman, albeit one who wasn't quite aware of herself yet. More than my style of drag, they noticed my femininity and the questions I was asking. To them there was urgency: if I was to undergo medical transition to maintain my female-passing bone structure, the clock was ticking. The longer I left medical transition, the harder it would be to 'pass' and the harder my life would be. They also loved the idea of fostering a new generation of showgirl to carry on their legacy. Despite their best of intentions, I didn't feel that their experience quite reflected mine.

For now, I was comfortable with my body and OK getting by the way I was. As Shane, I continued trying to be a man as best I could. Provided I could justify drag as a job, I didn't have to worry about revealing to myself or others that I secretly enjoyed being a girl. Only two options appeared to be available: trans or cis (another binary!). Although I knew I wasn't a man, I didn't want to *be* a trans woman – this was distinct from feeling that I *wasn't* a trans woman. Best not to look too closely for fear of the truth.

Meanwhile, I loved touring with Carlotta's show, where my femininity was celebrated. Being in control of my career and identity again felt so good. On top of all that, I was earning money. Then came a little reminder from outside the bubble: at the opening of a musical in Melbourne a respected woman in the entertainment industry, whose opinion I valued, walked up to me and said, 'Carlotta's show. Bad career move. You've damaged your reputation doing that.'

And she walked off. Like, wtf? Talk about hit and run. She was saying that 'Courtney' needed to be separated from the world I came from if I wanted a real career. The prevailing queerphobia had just gone out of its way to reassert itself. That hurt. Especially as when I'd tried it their way I ended up with no work and in debt. Now I was back with my community, getting to do what I loved, *and* I could pay my rent.

Another step on the road to financial stability came from a business and creative partnership that still holds today.

In 2003, Vanity opened a bricks-and-mortar shop on Oxford Street called Wigs by Vanity to sell and style wigs catering to the drag industry. Vanity is a wig master! A wig witch! The wig whisperer! But, by her own admission, business skills eluded her. Knowing my entrepreneurial streak, she invited me to join forces as an equal partner and tackle the business side while she handled the creative. What we didn't realise at the time was that we were about to change the face, or rather the hairline, of drag wigs around the globe.

Different wigs serve different purposes. The wigs most drag queens wear these days are lace-front wigs. A fine tulle-like lace is sewn onto the front of a regular wig then hair is hand-tied to the lace in the shape of a natural (or unnatural) hairline. Depending on the thickness, colour, quality and cleanliness of the lace, at best it's undetectable to the eye. The hair looks like it's growing out of the scalp. In the early noughties, Vanity and I would marvel at how flawless RuPaul was in his lace-front wigs. Apparently they cost thousands of dollars and were custom made.

What if we could create an 'off the rack' one-size-fits-most lace-front wig suitable for drag and bring it to the masses? It took us over a year in product development, flying to China and working with wig makers, but that's what we did. Drag queens all around Sydney were wearing our 'Uber Riahs' ('riah' is Polari for hair, and is also hair spelt backwards) – then drag queens all around the country, and pretty soon drag queens all around the world.

For a few years we held the market exclusively, then knock-off brands started popping up: factories began copying our wigs and offering a cheaper generic version to different wig sellers around the globe. But none ever compared to the quality, craftsmanship and design of our often imitated but never replicated Uber Riah.

Another professional relationship that gave me much-needed stability fell into place around this time. I landed the role of Angel in the musical *Rent* over in Perth and I realised that the deal was too big to negotiate myself, so I asked Rob Mills to connect me with his manager, Wendy Richards. Her background was touring big acts like U2, Destiny's Child and Tina Turner around Australia. She was a woman who'd forged a successful career in what was very much a man's world. I'd met Wendy on the Australian Idol Arena Tour, and then again in Melbourne when she came to see my cabaret, *Boys Like Me*, at the Chapel off Chapel. She mentioned that if I ever needed help I was welcome to give her a call. When I did, Wendy really took the time to listen and explain. She was direct but also compassionate and seemed genuinely interested in what I was about. It didn't seem she was there just to earn a buck, but that she wanted to ensure I was treated fairly. We decided to see how we gelled through the process of *Rent,* and from the start our professional manager–artist relationship went smoothly. After doing everything myself for the previous few years, it was lovely to have someone standing by my side.

14

'I'm a girly top who one day dreams of being a butch bottom,' I would proudly proclaim with a smirk when defining my preference of sexual position. For uninitiated straight readers, a top is the person who inserts their penis into another's butthole, while a bottom takes it up the arse. Someone who is vers (versatile) likes it both ways. Despite my exterior and disposition, which often leads people to assume I am a bottom, back then I was very reluctant to put anything up my butt on account of how much the prior attempts (banana, Destiny and occasional other men) had hurt.

My friend Linus was a proud bottom and temporary house guest for a week while his place was being repainted. He always talked about anal sex with such gusto and glee that I was inspired. A few months before he came to stay, I'd found myself acting on this inspiration as I nervously asked the man behind the counter at a sex shop, 'Could you please put something from that wall of d-d-dildos into my bag that might assist me with becoming a bottom? I don't want to see it; I would like you to just put it in my bag please.' When I got home I put the black plastic sex-shop bag straight under my bed, too nervous to examine its contents.

Not long after Linus arrived, he told me about how he'd had a full-body orgasm that didn't involve him, or anyone, touching his junk. I couldn't imagine such a fantastical reality, so I decided to duck off to the privacy of my bedroom to make use of the pink sparkly monster under my bed. *I'll call you Pinky,* I thought as I cut open the package then tried to put it in my butt.

'OUCH!' *Fuck! That really hurt.*

I tried with some lube. 'AHHH!' Nope: still hurt.

'Linus!' I called out.

'Yes, Shane Shims?' he called back.

'Can you teach me how to be a bottom?' I grabbed a towel and wandered out to the living room with Pinky in hand. 'I tried putting this in me 'cause I want to learn how to be a bottom like you, but it hurt too much. What am I doing wrong?'

'Well, did you use lube?'

'A bit.'

'You have to use lots. Especially if you're new.' He started explaining what angle I had to put it in and lots of other things that seemed far more complex than I was expecting. I sat there with a perplexed look on my face and, sensing my bewilderment, he huffed, 'Here, let me show you,' then stood up and marched to my bedroom.

'Lie down, take off your pants and hold up the sheet. No funny business!' Linus and I had fooled around when we'd first met, but now our friendship was strictly platonic. He simply knew that a practical lesson was going to be much more beneficial than a theoretical one.

Lying on my back, I held the bedsheet up so we couldn't make eye contact and he proceeded to insert the dildo. We were giggling like schoolgirls, which isn't the usual mood you want during penetration, but these were extenuating circumstances.

'So you want to put lots of lube on the dick and your butt, and you put it in really gently. Take your time and push out as if you are trying to take a shit. Don't worry: you won't.'

Though I was kind of mortified by my friend inserting a pink glittery dildo into my butt, I was also glad we shared the kind of bond where we both felt so comfortable with each other. Once the 'Bottoming 101' presentation was over, Linus turned off my bedroom light, shut the door and left me to explore my inner sanctum. A true friend.

When it came to a phallus that was attached to a human, the situation was a little less straightforward. That first night at Stonewall, aged 18, I'd ripped off the lid and tried to make sense of the contents. I loved what I found and knew it was for me. A box full of candy, and I was trying to shove as much in my mouth as possible – so to speak. But without any framework, this exploration could be confusing. Nothing had prepared me for dating boys, and all that sugar started giving me a toothache.

Away from the eyes of anyone I grew up with, the newness of my identity mixed with the carnal thrill of sex and attraction became a second puberty, where I could finally unleash those pent-up teenage hormones – a little later than scheduled, and with even more vigour to overcompensate for what I'd missed. The subconscious aim was to pick up every time I went out. Actually, that was the function of going out: to have sex; the socialising and fun with friends was secondary.

Physical intimacy was easy, but adding in emotional intimacy was tricky: same-gender love required a skillset that young queer people were never prepared for. We'd grown up with no examples of two men, two women or gender-nonconforming people in love – not on TV, not in movies, not in real life. Mimicking heterosexual models didn't seem to work because the dynamic was so different. That left us poking around in the dark, both figuratively and literally. In the early days of the internet the only queer content to be found was porn. While I've never really got into porn, it certainly provided some of my first examples of two men being intimate, and for a lot of gays it's a pastime that heavily informs their sex lives.

For me, sex was a lot about validation. It seemed the best and most fun way to prove others liked me, and that therefore I could like myself, was one man at a time. Admittedly it's a flawed approach, but it was the only approach I knew. The fringe benefits often born out of those one-night stands were friends. Back then nearly everyone I was friends with I'd met by having sex with first – the gay handshake. Once we'd got the physical part out of the way we could be friends, though I always wanted more, and they never seemed to. This narrative is common for many queer men.

Well… it wasn't *just* one-night stands: I also had deep, ongoing infatuations with boys who never seemed to love me back. I'd fall in love with boy after boy, only for it to be unrequited. If I ever got around to telling George, then Sam, Paul, Cameron, Michael, Daniel… that I was wildly in love with them, they would laugh off my advances, bringing on a flood of shame. I'd laugh too and pretend I was joking; we'd stay friends after that, but all the while I'd be pining for them. I always had a boyfriend; he just never knew it. These unrequited relationships felt like my formative crushes on Ezra and Ritchie at school. My sexuality had been forged in the secrecy of the closet, so being in love with boys and never telling them felt familiar. All I ever wanted was one of these friends to love me back, to break the cycle, to prove me wrong. Unrequited love is destructive, and constantly feeling desire that is never reciprocated perpetuates the narrative that who I am is unlovable.

But every encounter is a chance for a do-over. Maybe not to rewrite the script, but at least to edit a few lines. At 25 there was Jack.

Nic, Ben and our group of friends were at Harbour Party, the outdoor party the week before the Mardi Gras parade that I'd attended in drag all those years earlier. This year I was there as a boy and the party got rained out. Unable to get a taxi, our group walked from Mrs Macquarie's Chair with our step in sync, trying to share body heat all the way back to Oxford Street. Shivering and drenched, we took refuge in Slide, the first gay bar on the strip, where we danced our bodies back to warmth. There was a stripper pole on the light-up dance floor and 'Love Shack' was playing. I was spinning around the pole living my best life as the song built to its crescendo – 'TIIIIIINNNN ROOF! RUSTED' – when I spotted a cute boy approaching. Quickly I stopped queening out and butched it up. I hoped he hadn't seen me acting femme.

'I know you!' he said. *Oh damn. My cover is blown, he knows I'm Courtney Act.* 'You're the boy from yoga class?'

'Oh… yes.' I was pleasantly mistaken.

Jack and I were the same age; he'd recently moved from Toronto, Canada. This was good news. If he was from Canada maybe he wouldn't know about me, about *Idol*, about the fact that I was a drag queen. Since starting drag professionally, I'd found that gay boys were less interested in me. It was known as the 'drag curse' among my Sydney sisters: the idea that if you did drag, gay men wouldn't want to have sex with you, and certainly wouldn't date you. For clarity, gay men aren't sexually interested in guys when they're in drag, but even when the drag came off there was a carry-over effect on a queen's sexual desirability.

Jack and I got chatting, and he knew nothing about me.

'What do you do?'

'Errr, I'm a singer.'

I'd found a loophole in the drag curse! As long as he didn't know I did drag, I was safe. We started kissing and then went back to my place to work on our downward dogs (that's a euphemism). He stayed the night, and the next morning I felt comfortable enough to mention I did drag.

By our second date I was already in my second longest relationship with a guy. Jack arrived at my door carrying vegan apricot balls. Jack's mum is a nutritionist – like my dad – so we bonded over our love of health foods.

We hung out most days that week, but Saturday was Mardi Gras and I didn't want to commit to anything, not even to spending the party with Jack. Mardi Gras was gay Christmas and I wasn't ready to have my style cramped by a boy I'd just met. The excitement of reciprocated lust and infatuation *was* fortifying, but thus far I'd lived a life free of commitment, and despite my yearning for intimacy with my unrequited boyfriends, that suited me. I loved spontaneity, and now I was finally confronted with dating someone, I worried I would lose my freedom. Despite my initial reluctance, though, we did leave the party together.

Six weeks in I was still on the fence when I went off to a gig in Broome, Western Australia. Talking on the phone with this most lovely and most perfect candidate for a boyfriend, I said that I was scared to commit because I'd always imagined myself in an open relationship. Freedom, no restriction, a bond that transcended convention and ownership. That wasn't what Jack wanted, but he was willing to give it a crack. I didn't know it then, but my tentativeness ran deeper than that. Jack had stuck around despite seeing parts of myself I felt deep shame about, so my subconscious concluded that there must have been something wrong with him. *How can he like me if I don't like myself?* Even so, something about him tempered these fears.

That August we went on a trip to Europe with Nic and Ben, my first time there. We spent a week in London and a week in Ibiza, then Jack and I went our own way and spent a romantic weekend in Paris for our six-month anniversary. Exploring Europe with Jack strengthened our union.

Back in Australia, Jack and I moved in together. He met Mum and Dad, and then his family came over from Canada to meet me and my parents. Things were getting serious. But then, all of a sudden, my sexual attraction to Jack disappeared. I was falling in love with him, but I no longer wanted to have sex with him. Affection was fine, but the idea of sexual contact made me feel uneasy. After two weeks of struggle and internal inquiry, it emerged that my feelings of love for Jack reminded me of the love I felt for my family. Because I'd only ever experienced unconditional love with family members, I got confused as I developed those same feelings for Jack. Once I was able to apply a little critical thinking I could see that this kind of love with Jack was different – it *was* unconditional love, but it was also sexual. After our break in the bedroom we were back on track, and the honeymoon period prevailed.

As the months rolled on, Jack and I had a wonderful time loving each other, supporting each other and growing together. Insecurities inherited from adolescence faded as I accepted Jack's love as more worthy than society's shame. A relationship can't make you whole, but beyond doubt the act of requited love heals and soothes. I always thought I had to answer the big life questions by myself, but getting to love Jack and being loved in return was one of the greatest things I ever learnt: Bowie was right.

Our trip to Europe made a big impression, and after another year went by we decided to move there. Jack wanted to move to Barcelona for work, and I knew the next step for my career was London. If I was ever going to have a meaningful career in Australia I had to get out, find success overseas, and then Australia would accept me – that's just how it worked. No one took an Aussie act seriously unless they were famous overseas first. Living in different countries would be a challenge but it would be a thrill. Moving to Europe with the man I loved felt like a dream.

But before we made it there, along came a boy called Harry Little.

To me, an open relationship meant sex with people outside the relationship with no strings attached. I'd become familiar with the often emotionless, transactional sex on the gay scene, as the lack of healthy relationship-building in our formative years had left so many of us joining the dots between sex, intimacy and love as adults. But for Jack, an open relationship involved a more human connection with the people he was seeing. He liked to go on dates with boys, getting to know them and forming a connection first before having sex. It seemed absurd to me: that wasn't how 'it' worked – he was doing it all wrong!

I met Harry Little at Nic and Ben's place one night; he had a fun and dangerous energy about him. By chance we left at the same time, and in the elevator on the way down it got really flirty. I was heading out of town for a gig but we swapped numbers.

While I was away, Harry and Jack went on a date. Neither of us realised at first that we were flirting with the same boy; it wasn't until we swapped stories that we made the connection.

When I returned to Sydney, I bumped into Harry when I was out with some friends at a bar. The sexual tension had built up over text messages, so I asked him home. By coincidence, Jack was out with some of his friends that night and turned up at the same bar not long afterwards. My friends told him that I'd left with Harry.

Meanwhile, Harry and I could barely keep our clothes on in the elevator up to our apartment, and as soon as I shut the front door it was on. In the front hallway of the apartment. Why not? After a while we progressed into the bathroom and fucked in the shower.

Suddenly there was a knock on the door.

'SHANE?!' Jack spoke with a tone that signalled I was in trouble. I wasn't aware I was doing anything wrong, so I excused myself from the steamy shower scene with Harry and opened the bathroom door.

'Hi, Jack! Can't say that on a plane any more.' I used one of my favourite dad jokes to try to make Jack smile. He didn't.

'Is Harry in there?' His voice was stern.

'Yeah. Wanna join?' I asked with a cheeky grin, hoping to break the mood.

'No, Shane!' He slammed the door and stormed off. I was a bit confused; I didn't know why Jack was angry.

We talked about it the next day, but there was still confusion between Jack and me. I can see now that we didn't quite have the tools we needed to navigate an open relationship, which was still a relatively new concept to us. We had a full-disclosure rule when we hooked up with someone else, but this had recently created a competitive tit-for-tat dynamic: if I slept with someone, Jack would feel the need to as well, or vice versa. When we both realised that we'd been courting the same guy, things got messy.

Even when Jack articulated his feelings to me, it didn't help. My intention hadn't been to hurt him, and I thought my intention was what counted, not the impact. But when you step on someone's foot you're still sorry for hurting them, even if you didn't mean it. I didn't understand that and was unable to hold space for Jack's feelings. Growing up queer, I got really good at hiding my own feelings, and was more inclined to bottle things up than actually feel them. On the surface we patched over it, but there was a crack deep in our foundation now.

The next weekend, plans to go to the cinema and see *Sex and the City: The Movie* collided (a gay conundrum as old as time itself). I wanted to go see it with Jack, but he'd made plans with Harry, so I imposed and we all went together. Harry wedged himself between us during the movie, and I became fixated on all of the non-verbal communication that might be going on between him and Jack. Were their legs touching? Did he brush his hand against Jack's thigh? Did their hands touch as they both reached for the popcorn? I couldn't control my jealousy and I didn't like it. I wanted to sit next to Jack – he was my boyfriend. I felt physically and emotionally separated from him by Harry.

When Carrie got out of the limo and started beating Mr Big with that bunch of flowers, I lost my shit. Thankfully it was an emotional part of the movie worthy of tears, but that's not why I was crying. I was crying because while I felt that it was fine to have sex with someone outside of the relationship as a one-off, I now found myself competing for my boyfriend's affection and that felt like a betrayal.

Over the coming months Jack and I talked about our different interpretations of sex and relationships, but even though Harry was out of the picture, the cycle repeated. It was a struggle for me to understand Jack's perspective without my own healthy understanding of sex and relationships. And more than that, in challenging situations I lacked empathy; in fact, I lacked empathy in general. I'm not saying Jack's way or my way was the right one, but I didn't have the emotional intelligence to listen and feel. Instead of acknowledging my feelings, I would apply logic to my emotions and deny they existed. Emotions felt messy to me, unnecessary, avoidable. I was wrong. Repressing them made me feel powerless, and that feeling built up and manifested as anger.

This situation culminated in a fight in our living room on New Year's Day. I became overwhelmed, yelling angry words that tried to convey love: the louder I yelled the better he might hear me. But our efforts to communicate were futile. Embittered at the situation, I grabbed a vase full of lilies and threw it across the room. Not at Jack, but next to him. I didn't want to hurt him – it was simply all I could do in that moment to express myself where words had failed. The vase shattered against a floor-to-ceiling window. Glass and water and flowers went everywhere. I was crying and screaming, and so was Jack. He picked up the flowers from the couch and threw them back across the room at me, and water splashed across my already tear-soaked face. We couldn't communicate our way out of this. We tried talking. We tried not talking. We tried couples counselling. We tried everything.

A few weeks later Jack sat me down in the bedroom and told me it was over. He had to tell me a few times because I couldn't comprehend what was going on. I had a deep trust that we were meant to be together forever, a fantasy of relationships that had been instilled in me by Hollywood, and here he was telling me that we weren't. I felt like a failure. I didn't really know how to process my emotions, and this time I couldn't rationalise away the enormity of what I felt about Jack and me ending.

I decided I was still going to move to London as planned. So I began packing my life into storage boxes and organised to sublet my apartment.

Jack had left the house for a few hours while I packed, and in my melancholic state I tried to find songs to help emote what I was feeling. This was one of the only tools I had for transferring and releasing my emotions. Starting with my old favourite, *Smokey Joe's Café*, I skipped through songs of love and heartbreak, searching for meaning, and cried and cried as I sang along.

Then I went to the soundtrack from *Grace of My Heart* and cried my way through all the tracks – 'Born to Love That Boy' and other knife-twisters. Then I cried through another favourite soundtrack, *The Boy from Oz (Australian Cast Recording)* with songs like 'I Honestly Love You' and 'Don't Cry Out Loud'.

When Jack arrived back home, I asked him if we could have one last dance together, and put 'I'd Rather Leave While I'm in Love' on the stereo. I put my arms around his shoulders and stood on his feet, and we slow-danced around the living room crying in each other's arms as the song played.

While I wanted to pretend I was the singer of this song, that I was strong and insightful enough to be able to leave while I was still in love, Jack was the one metaphorically singing those lyrics. This was the first time I'd been in love. Previously I assumed that only the absence of love meant the end of the relationship, but now I realise that while relationships end, love never does. When you love someone a part of you will always love them, and waiting around for the feeling of love to switch off in order to end a relationship is futile. That's how I feel about Jack. After two beautiful years together, leaving while we were still in love, before our beautiful union got too damaged, was actually the perfect ending.

There was no time to cry over spilt vase water, though: I had a gig at Gay Ski Week in Whistler, Canada, performing at the Mr Gay World final!

I spent the first day in my hotel room with the curtains drawn. Sleeping and crying. Using music, once again, to emote where I was otherwise incapable of connecting with my feelings. I put 'And I Am Telling You I'm Not Going' from *Dreamgirls* on at full volume (the Jennifer Holliday version, obviously). I sobbed and sobbed, still in denial that the relationship had ended – a very emotional moment personally, but I get that the optics are too gay to take seriously.

When I was finally all cried out, I pulled myself together and headed up the mountain to ski. I met some lovely Canadians on the ascent and they invited me to join them for the ski back down. They were slightly faster than I was. Spotting one of them whiz down a trail, I hurried after, not realising it was a double-black-diamond run. It was basically a 45-degree slope of moguls intended for only the most skilled athlete. I was not capable. I ended up with two broken bones – tibia and fibula – and needed surgery to patch up my leg with a titanium rod and a whole bunch of screws. Five days later I was released from hospital on the day I was meant to do my show. As I'd learnt at Fame, the show must go on! I asked the promoter to drive me back up the mountain. I parked my wheelchair in front of the bathroom sink of my hotel room and painted my face – years of party drugs and drag had prepared me for doing this on morphine. I don't know how I got into my gown, or my tucking G-string for that matter. Someone must have helped me, but I honestly don't remember. I sang 'You Shook Me All Night Long' and reprised Angus Young's duckwalk; this time it was my only choice of independent transport.

Leaving hospital and getting straight into drag probably wasn't the smartest idea, though it seemed right at the time. I'd been flown to the other side of the world to perform and felt responsible to deliver. I was so jacked up on painkillers I was unaware of my body or the seven-inch surgical wound that now ran up the inside of my leg.

Those final days in Canada are a haze. I'd been prescribed 80 morphine tablets – way too many. Despite my dedicated foray into illicit drugs at age 18, I was loath to take unnecessary pain medication. The pain was gone after three days, but I still had 72 morphine tablets to go. It's quite apparent to me now how the opioid crisis cycle begins on an individual level.

I flew back to Australia. One broken heart and two broken bones. My plans to move to London were foiled. I couldn't even walk, let alone move across the world. But Jack could, and off to Barcelona he went.

My first love, the one I thought I'd live happily ever after with, was gone.

Performing best friend duty perfectly, and showing me the value in expressing emotions without a musical soundtrack, Vanity was there to grieve with me, listen, and hate Harry Little. I hadn't realised how much Vanity hated Harry. There must have been some pre-existing issue I wasn't aware of: whenever Harry's name was mentioned Vanity would fly off the handle.

'OH GOD I HATE HARRY LITTLE!' It was said with such vitriol too. It was kinda soothing having someone who seemed to hate Harry more than I did. Over the next few months, any time his name came up Vanity would seethe. Her fists would clench and she'd get viscerally angry. Eventually I became curious.

'Why do you hate Harry Little so much?'

'For you.' She stared at me as if it should have been obvious.

'But I don't even hate him that much.'

'I know. I hate him so you don't have to.'

'What? That's the most ridiculous thing I've heard!'

'No, it isn't. That's what friends do for each other.'

'Where did you even meet him?'

'I didn't. I've never met him.'

15

Now that I was able to walk again, I needed to think about work. My friend Tim Duggan was starting a new club night at Nevermind, a venue on Oxford Street near Stonewall, and asked if I'd go in with him. At a meeting with the stakeholders, we agreed to take over this failed straight club and turn it into a pumping queer discotheque. Welcome to Disgraceland!

Back in a time when Facebook was fresh and the digital meeting place of young people, we rode the crest of social media marketing using Facebook Events to tell everyone about our parties, which had a new theme every week. Our night quickly became the place to be in queer Sydney, attracting a fresh, fun crowd of kids who normally weren't seen on Oxford Street.

Everyone who worked for us became a part of our Disgraceland family. Our DJs were key to our success too. Where previously in gay bars the DJ was off to the side, ours was on the stage surrounded by a state-of-the-art floor-to-ceiling LED video wall, and we positioned the music they played differently too, introducing a novel electro-pop sound to the strip.

For me the crowning glory, and I might be biased, was our shows. We had a great team of dancers – Wil, Daniel G, Jess and Carly. Each week we'd do a brand-new fully choreographed and costumed number tied to a theme that also dictated the decorations and the video content on the LED wall. We used that as the backdrop for the shows.

Fun little sideshow moments also featured. One night, as the crowd started arriving, the show cast – all dressed to the nines – were sat on stage playing a game of strip poker. Dressed in 1940s glam we drank and gambled our clothes away until we were naked – as was legally allowed with our entertainment licence. Another night, a group of guys and girls and I played Spin the Bottle on stage. Under a dull wash of pink lighting, pretending we weren't in a packed nightclub, we drank, spun the bottle and never broke the fourth wall. One time, dressed in a nude bra and undies, I lay covered in delicious sweet treats beside a sign saying *Eat me*.

Disgraceland was so successful that it became my only job – and it only happened one night a week. I was able to dedicate all my energy to it, and we could afford to pay a wonderful creative team of people to make it all happen. The weekly show would start around 11 pm, and then the big production show began at 1 am. These shows, which ran for about three months, were massive. Big budgets, amazing costumes and sets, and extremely well-produced soundtracks. We were living in a post-Gaga world and her over-the-top fashion, persona and music really influenced us creatively. I channelled what I'd learnt from the Divastated shows and Ashley Swift all those years prior. Then we expanded to Saturdays – 'Saturday Fucking Night', we called it – which had slightly harder music sounds and chicly dressed go-go dancers on podiums high above the audience, like the go-gos I'd ogled at in Ibiza. Disgraceland was my Oxford Street renaissance.

Around the time of Mardi Gras 2010 I got the first of many bookings on Atlantis Events gay cruises. The first was from Auckland to Sydney, and the crowd of mostly Americans loved my show. I was booked for four more cruises that year: three in August and September around the Baltic and Mediterranean Sea, and one in October around the Caribbean. There was a big chunk of time off between the last date in Barcelona and the first date in Florida, and the cost of schlepping from Europe back to Australia and then to the US was prohibitive, so Wendy set about rustling up some gigs for me in America.

Initially I wasn't crazy about the idea of going to the US: the idea didn't interest me. Aside from the country's new Democrat President, Obama, it seemed like a backward place. I wanted to live in Europe, where the people and culture seemed much more liberated and progressive.

Wendy contacted booking agent Michael Benedetti, who we'd met when we flew New York nightlife legend Amanda Lepore out to Australia for the opening of 'Saturday Fucking Night'. In July 2010 Disgraceland was going from strength to strength, and I released an original song with a schmick music video called 'Welcome to Disgraceland'. Using the video as a promo tool, Michael booked me a tour around the US. I was gobsmacked at the number of gigs and the money: nine cities! In Australia there are only eight capital cities, so when touring I'd perform in Brisbane, Sydney, Melbourne and possibly Perth, the gigs splattered out over a year.

Wendy and I flew from Europe to Chicago. I knew Oprah had a gift store at Harpo Studios, so I had to visit the promised land. I didn't see *The Oprah Show* or Oprah, just the gift store, which was honestly so exciting! There is a section called

Oprah's Closet, where she sells used items of clothing, like an Oprah Car Boot Sale, and all the money goes to her School for Girls. I purchased a pair of pre-loved purple and gold Louboutin sandals. At $175 they were significantly cheaper than if they'd been new, *and* Oprah had worn them! When I skyped with Vanity to show her she dared me to lick them. At first I refused, but then to amuse my friend I leant in and licked Oprah Winfrey's pre-worn shoe. That's when I heard the screenshot sound and realised Vanity had captured this beautiful moment for posterity. For the last ten years those shoes have sat on a mantle, credenza or bookshelf wherever I have lived.

We had lots of time for gigs and LA life before the cruise. The first gig weekend was Cleveland and Columbus, Ohio, then to LA before heading to Vegas and NYC. I was getting a smaller fee in these three cities, but I decided it was important to make a splash in these hubs, so we booked dancers and choreographed a Disgraceland-style spectacle. James St James, legendary NYC Club Kid who now worked with the production company World of Wonder, came to my gig at Cherry Pop, a weekly party held at the West Hollywood club Ultra Suede, and filmed an episode for his YouTube show called *Freak Show*. I was so excited he was coming; he was such an icon and was interested in making a video about little ole me.

At that time World of Wonder had just started a new show called *RuPaul's Drag Race* on the small cable network Logo. A bunch of drag queens participated in *Project Runway* meets *Top Model* challenges with the chance of winning $20,000. It was a pretty low-budget show, but I loved seeing drag on TV and had watched every episode. Most importantly, the host of the show was none other than RuPaul, of legendary 90s *Supermodel of the World* fame. He and I had exchanged a few emails after I sent him a YouTube video of myself, and I had vague hopes of working with him in the future.

During my 2010 tour, Vanity was in Toronto setting up the hair and makeup department on *Priscilla the Musical* before it opened on Broadway, so she flew to Vegas to join in some fun. And boy, did we have fun: I remember a pool party at the Hard Rock Hotel in Vegas – it was 38 degrees Celsius and I was in full drag in a nude Swarovski-encrusted one-piece swimsuit. One of my photography idols, David LaChapelle, was there and it blew me away to meet him – his photos had inspired me and just about every drag queen in the world, I think. His books are on the shelf next to Oprah's shoes. After the gig we ended up at someone's Vegas penthouse doing cocaine as the sun came up. I'd taken off my fabulous, but very uncomfortable, look in exchange for the luxury of a white bathrobe, and when it came time for our walk of shame I couldn't bear to lace myself back into my black studded J'Aton corset. Fortunately our gracious host allowed me to mop the robe. On the long walk back to our room Vanity made us search the casino floor for an hour to find a Wizard of Oz poker machine. I was still in high drag, looking slightly dishevelled and in a bathrobe. Nevertheless, I looked way more put together than any of the punters left at the blackjack tables at that time of morning. It was the perfect trashy Vegas experience, and felt so chic and glamorous compared to the humdrum life of Sydney.

We crisscrossed the country doing shows – DC, LA, Florida. Some stand out more than others, like the night I did Patrón shots and gave a gobby to a go-go dancer in the dressing room at Honey Pot in Tampa, Florida.

Then it was Mobile, Alabama, to a club called B-Bobs. The regular showgirls working the night, Miss Cie, Venus and

Regine, made me feel very welcome, and Jerry the owner was a delight. In the dressing room I watched as one of the girls tore three strips of silver gaff tape, stuck them into a triangle, sprayed them with Elmer's spray adhesive and then proceeded to tuck with them. That's how serious they are about tucking in the South.

Back to LA for another week to wash my wigs, and Wendy and I went to a few meetings, including one with World of Wonder. We met with Randy, Fenton and Tom, the heads of the company, who were a super-lovely bunch, and they said that while they loved meeting me they already had RuPaul as their priority with this new show *Drag Race.*

Wendy headed back to Australia, and Michael (now my US agent) and I were off to McAllen, Texas, to wrap up the tour. How was it possible to do so many gigs in a couple of months and still have plenty of other cities left to perform in? And look… Cleveland, Ohio; McAllen, Texas; Mobile, Alabama… they weren't exactly tourist destinations, but they were the ones that paid the most, and more than anything there was something thrilling about being a travelling showgirl in a foreign country. I felt like a star – this was success! I started to grasp the magnitude of the USA. Australia had a population of 22 million and the USA had a population of 309 million, with 50 states and several cities in each state with potential to perform in.

The *Drag Race* girls weren't yet ubiquitous in gay bars across the world. Drag icons like Jackie Beat, Coco Peru, Lady Bunny, Sherry Vine, Varla Jean Merman and Joey Arias still ruled the school and were touring the gay bars of the

USA; the only new girl on the scene was Derrick Barry, who'd been on *America's Got Talent* a couple of years earlier impersonating Britney Spears. And aside from drag queens, club divas like Kristine W, Ultra Nate and even Jennifer Holliday were on the circuit too. Mike said the reason I had such a solid uptake with all the gigs is because the last new music act who had done a gay bar tour of the US was Lady Gaga right before 'Just Dance' came out; a bunch of the bars had said no and regret it to this day. So when they saw my Gaga-esque music video for 'Welcome to Disgraceland' they jumped straight on it. After not even wanting to come to the US to do the gigs, suddenly I wanted to move there in a matter of weeks: I was sold!

Even though I could scarcely afford it, when I returned to Australia in November 2010 I set about making that dream a reality. Wendy could tell I was serious too. We began the application for an O1 Visa so I could be an *alien of extraordinary ability* (that's the actual title of the visa) and live in the USA. On this visa you need an agent and a work offer. Michael Benedetti was my agent and Luke Nero, the cocktail waiter who had given me the safer sex talk my first week in Sydney, would end up as my work sponsor. Luke had gone from mixing the Oxford Smash at Gilligan's to serving the Mr Black Smash in NYC's hottest club. He was infamously known as The Ass because he wore a black waiter's apron with nothing underneath. The Scissor Sisters song 'Let's Have a Kiki' is about the final night of Mr Black in NYC, when the police shut it down. Luke had moved to LA and brought the party with him.

Luke and I hadn't spoken in ten years, but when a friend introduced us I asked him, 'Do you remember in the year 2000 you pulled a twink out of the toilets at Gilligan's and sat him down on a pylon on Taylor Square and gave him a safer sex talk? That was me, and I have to thank you; it really changed the course of my life! I was wearing Buffalo Boots with—'

'A big yellow puffer jacket! Yes. I remember!'

Luke was starting up a new night in WeHo and offered me a regular job as one of his hosts, which fulfilled the requirements of the visa. Interestingly, Luke had intervened in the outcome of my life twice: on arrival in both Sydney *and* LA.

While I didn't move straightaway, I made a couple of trips. The first time was to host the red carpet for the opening of *Priscilla the Musical* on Broadway for Logo TV. It was an exciting night to be an Australian drag queen, and even more exciting was standing on the red carpet interviewing Bette Midler, Joan Rivers and Christie Brinkley. I got to see New York icon Sherry Vine again, and meet some of the local queens, including Flotilla Debarge and a quick-talking lady with big lashes, far too much makeup and a cold-shoulder baby-doll silver sequin dress: Bianca Del Rio.

Vanity was there too – working as the makeup designer and wig supervisor. I was such a proud friend seeing her go from Darlinghurst to Broadway. We were sisters in drag in NYC. The next morning, after the day had broken, still in drag we stumbled out of the hotel-room party of Stephan Elliott (the writer and director of the 1994 film and writer of the musical) in SoHo House. It was snowing and we were in swimsuits and open-toed shoes. Vanity and I chuckled and shivered as we hailed a taxi home.

For the next few months my body might have been in Sydney but my head was in LA. I was plotting and planning my move. And when it came, the timing was auspicious.

Right before I flew back to LA, Lady Gaga performed at our club in Sydney. And I don't mean this as a platitude – it was legendary. I was standing in the dressing room waiting for her to arrive and heard the crash doors of the fire escape fly open. I could hear screaming fans calling her name on the street below, and while I couldn't see her yet there was no mistaking the silhouette cast onto the wall by the hundreds of flashing cameras. A few moments later a tiny woman dressed in vintage Versace, with an aqua side pony, heavy bangs, red lips and a strong winged eyeliner appeared before me, looked me right in the eye and with a warm smile said, 'Hi, Courtney!'

The year before, I'd sung at Gaga's birthday party in – wait for it – the Canberra Botanic Gardens. Not a bucket list birthday destination, but her Monster Ball tour schedule had landed her in the nation's capital for her 25th birthday. The gardens are home to a rainforest walk and that's where the dinner was held – among the tall trees and low-lying ferns in the dark of night. There was a long banquet table lined on either side with her friends, family and touring party. There wasn't a stage per se, so I decided the table was the best place for my rendition of 'Sweet Transvestite'. After dinner it was my job, with a tiki torch in one hand and the world's most famous human in the other, to lead Gaga on a late-night adventure down a rocky set of stairs through the rainforest. It was damp, slippery and she was wearing eight-inch heels. I was acutely aware that my queer life wouldn't be worth living if I broke Lady Gaga.

What took me aback was how present and earnest she was: we talked about identity and drag as we negotiated our way through the rainforest and to a clearing where the rest of the crew had already assembled. They were reclining on picnic blankets and watching a pre-release copy of *Avatar* on a 50-foot (15-metre) outdoor movie screen. A string of personal videos from family and friends was also played. It was a privilege to see the star's grandmother on the big screen. 'I'm so proud of you, Stefani,' she said, adding a human side to this pop fantasy.

Now, back at the club in 2011, Gaga took over our little Disgraceland stage with nine dancers and gave one of the most electric performances I've witnessed. This boutique club licensed to hold 340 people was absolutely rammed to legal capacity. Seeing such a big personality on such a small stage made it a memorable night for everyone in that room – it will go down in infamy in Sydney nightlife.

Whether it was walking her through the Botanic Gardens, hanging out backstage at Nevermind, or any of the other times I've had the pleasure of being in her company, Gaga fortifies my faith in artistry and gives meaning to the often vacuous concept of celebrity. She's the real deal. She's also a bisexual woman; aside from her banging pop tunes and avant-garde looks, Gaga is often forgotten as a member of the queer community. As a drag queen it's clichéd to say, but I'm inspired by Gaga. *Chromatica* dance breaks were essential parts of writing this book. Many amazing celebrities and artists had stood up for queer rights before Gaga was on the scene – Madonna, Liz Taylor, Princess Diana, to name but a few – but when Gaga burst onto the scene she forced a conversation that no one else was having at that time. She was the first mainstream artist of the new millennium to be actively talking about and celebrating queer people and culture. These days pop stars use drag queens and LGBTQ+ people as props as a matter of happenstance, but I'll always be grateful to Gaga for the space she created in the mainstream for our voices, and the strength and sense of inclusion she gave so many young, and not so young, queer people.

Infused with the spirit of Gaga, I moved to America. On 22 August 2011, I boarded a flight from Sydney to LAX. I was about to begin my new life in the land of opportunity as an alien of extraordinary ability.

Act III

16

'But pink is a girl's colour!' The tone of my voice unironically went up an octave as I exclaimed my opposition to Miss Bradley's idea.

'What on earth do you mean "a girl's colour", ya fag?' His Southern twang arced up from a 6 to a 9, with a hint of aggression in it.

'I just don't know if I feel comfortable having pink draped all over my kitchen. What will people think when they come over?'

'It will confirm what they already know: that you're a flaming cross-dresser!'

'I want it to be gay, but not *too* gay.'

'I'm going to slap you in a minute.'

'What?! Pink is a girl's colour! I feel uncomfortable having it in my home.'

Miss Bradley and I had only just met and he'd offered to help add a little glamour to my new West Hollywood studio apartment the cheap and effective way – the drag way – with a bolt of fabric, a staple gun and some cable ties. Fifty-two years old and from Lexington, Kentucky, Miss Bradley was 21 years sober and always the most interesting person at any party. He decorated events for a living, and not just any events: Elton John's Oscars party, Barbra Streisand's wedding and Dita von Teese's bedroom. And now he was twirling pink and purple organza around my humble abode. He never bothered with a drag name; his real name is Bradley Picklesimer and he said that was about the best a name could get.

Even though I'd made my living as a drag queen for the previous ten years, I was genuinely afraid to have pink in my home or wear it as a boy. Shane was on one side, Courtney was on the other, and never the twain shall meet.

It all came back to sex. I was as far from attracting the gay gaze as one could be without being female. I didn't have pecs and a six-pack, I did drag for a living, was barely five foot eight and weighed 56 kilograms wet. I didn't need to exacerbate the issue by living in Barbie's Dream House. It was hard enough picking up a guy at a bar, and if I did manage to fool a handsome suitor with my masculine peacocking, I felt the whole charade would be ruined by some pansy pink poly-chiffon window treatments. Miss Bradley won the argument, however, through sheer force of will, and proceeded to drape the fabric around the kitchen window and secure it with cable ties. I lived in opposition to the pink chiffon the whole time I was in that apartment.

I'd landed in Los Angeles on a Tuesday. By Thursday I'd found my new home on Sweetzer Avenue, and by Saturday I was at a pool party in the Hollywood Hills. I'd hit the ground running. Like most mansions in the neighbourhood, the venue for this party had an uninterrupted view of LA, alongside luscious green lawns and a massive pool. The backyard was full of beautiful people – beautiful men mostly, with beautiful bodies, their oiled-up muscles glistening in the sunlight. I felt out of place, a skinny little twink in a sea of Muscle Marys, but I was content with the access to this fantasy world, even if I was an observer and not a participant.

A lady on a li-lo floated past me. She was wearing an oversized black-and-white floppy hat, big black sunglasses and a bikini.

'My name is Triana Lavey, and I'm a reality TV producer. What do you do?'

'My name is Shane Jenek, and I'm a reality TV star.'

We both chuckled. Triana introduced me to her gays and we kiki'd together all day. As much as this was her crowd, we were both outliers. We swapped numbers and made plans to have lunch and talk shop. I've since learnt that people in LA often flake on plans, but Triana and I made it to Veggie Grill on Sunset and Crescent and enjoyed a Santa Fe Crispy Chick'n Burger, sweet potato fries and an iced tea. Triana must have seen real promise in me, because in the days afterwards she took me for 'go-sees' with all the production companies she had connections with to pitch me as new talent. I had only been in this city a couple of weeks and I was already in meetings with major global production companies. LA was full of promise and potential.

Back in my apartment, as I flipped between channels on the TV, I saw a show called *Hillbilly Handfishin'*. If there was a place for that, I knew there would be a place for me on TV too. It was just a matter of time.

I had a $40,000 business overdraft and a dream! I've never been good with credit, and spent it as if I'd saved $40,000 to bankroll my relocation. Not quite what the ANZ bank had in mind, I'm sure, but I *was* in LA on business… technically.

I didn't work for the first few months, convinced I would hit it big before I ran out of money. This notion was supported by the collective psyche of the city: everyone around me was trying to make it too.

Much like when I arrived on Oxford Street all those years before, LA felt like a homecoming, but instead of slowly defining my queer identity I was longing for mainstream success as Courtney Act. The industry of LA is entertainment, and to live inside that bubble was thrilling and soothing. In Sydney, my friends had nine-to-five jobs and the tall-poppy syndrome, the Australian cultural insistence to stay humble or get mocked, kept everyone grounded. In LA, everyone was on the same hustle, having moved from all around the United States in order to live their Hollywood dream, and everyone was busy creating content and going to auditions, meetings and classes, on the brink of getting their big break. You legitimately might be waiting tables one day and get cast in a network sitcom the next. The pulsating, galvanising energy of the city meant that our – my – dreams felt within arm's reach.

'We have more go-go dancers per square mile than any other city in America, and it's time we celebrated their efforts and hard work!' announced Mayor Duran of West Hollywood. And so the first Go-Go Dancer Appreciation Day was declared on 29 October 2011.

I'd only been living in the US officially for two months, and I was fast falling in love with America's first gay city (incorporated in 1984). I was also fast falling in love with its go-go dancers, always performing my civic duty to 'celebrate their efforts and *hard* work', as the mayor had exhorted me to.

I was beguiled by the bold and beautiful Adonises who adorned the pedestals of WeHo's gay bars. I usually use the world 'queer' when describing bars where LGBTQ+ people gather, but West Hollywood feels capital-g Gay to me. While there are Black, Latinx, Asian, trans and girls' nights in the bars and clubs that cram the barely half-mile along Santa Monica Boulevard and North Robertson, WeHo is pretty homonormative, replicating some of the bias and prejudice you see in the straight world. It's predominantly white, male and muscular: the epicentre of the flesh-industrial complex.

Except, that is, for the go-go dancers, who are a United Nations of aesthetically perfect men gyrating in their swimwear, the lining cut out to reveal the outlines of their engorged penises. The epitome of unrealistic body image, they stand high above the crowd for you to worship with your eyes, or by slipping a $1 bill into what little clothing they are wearing. I was always amazed at the brilliant value of being able to run my mitts across the coconut-oiled skin of a beautiful man for just one dollar – even the 99c Store charges tax! I was stimulating the economy and stimulating myself.

When I first got to LA I used drag as a social lubricant; it was a great way to make friends. My nightlife gaggle included Rhea Litré, a drag performer and WeHo party girl who introduced me to Marco Marco, a celebrity costume designer who'd dressed J.Lo, Shakira and Britney, but had a passion for dressing drag queens. I dreamt of being worthy of his outfits one day – of being the Cher to his Bob Mackie.

Once the bars closed at 2 am, we would find an afterparty and I would stick to the Sydney rule – 'nobody gets out of drag' – because being Courtney made me stand out. I was like a glamorous jester holding court, just as my medieval counterparts would have – although I doubt they did as much ketamine.

People can find LA a lonely place where it's hard to make friends, and I was so glad I had found this gaggle.

I affectionately referred to another crew I hung out with as the Mean Gays. Each one more genetically blessed than the last, these WeHo party boys had bodies that would make Michelangelo weep. Every one worked in showbiz, doing hair, makeup and fashion styling for the Kardashians, Madonna, Fergie, Miley, Katy Perry… I was two degrees from pop-culture royalty. One of the boys, Simon Sherry-Wood, was an Irish expat and therefore an instant ally because we were both foreign. Simon and I became friends, hanging out by day at pool parties and Runyon Canyon Park and by night at the bars. (He would later be a member of the Pit Crew on my season of *Drag Race* – but more on that soon.)

My overdraft was getting close to its limit, so it was time to go to work. One of my first regular gigs was at Rasputin, the name of the club night established by Luke 'The Ass' Nero. After the epic production of the shows in Sydney, with choreographed dancers and custom soundtracks, in WeHo my job was to turn up at 10-ish, look fabulous, have fun and still be there at 1.45 am to collect my paycheque. No performance, just paid to socialise, to be the life of the party.

Rasputin was a really fun time and showed me more of the queer side to West Hollywood than I had been privy to. If I was wearing something high cut, which was often, I would tape before leaving home at 10 pm. If I forgot to pack a spare roll of tape I wouldn't be able to pee until I got home at 2.30, for fear of the tape not resticking properly, leaving me with an unsightly bulge. This four-hour no-pee zone wasn't helped by the 80-centimetre-tall fishbowl I drank from throughout the night.

It wasn't always drugs and booze, though. Often my glass would be filled with fruit juice, and I'd have a few squares of dark chocolate tucked in my handbag for when I needed a buzz. When I first got to town and had no commitments I was living my best party-girl lifestyle, but now I was working I needed to be a bit more realistic with my substances. I'd learnt from my misspent Sydney youth that nightlife can suck you in, so unless there was clear fun to be had, I'd stay sober. The good thing about the LA scene was that the drugs of choice were coke and weed. Crystal meth was never done socially; it had a dark reputation as something shameful that other people did behind closed doors. When I told Marco and Rhea I used to do meth, they were shocked I had made it out of that experience alive and asked how I still had all my teeth.

Between the go-go dancers and the jacked-up men in the bars, a skinny little twink like me didn't get much attention. The boys in West Hollywood were interested in muscle. A motto of the gay scene I often jokingly tout is 'pecs get sex', and in WeHo that motto was on steroids (often literally). To me, muscles were a symbol of success in one's gender. I still didn't feel I was passing as a man, though I hadn't yet acknowledged that feeling to myself or tried to understand the source of my discomfort. In Sydney I'd grown up in the gay scene so this disconnect hadn't felt as apparent, but as a transplant in West Hollywood I became more aware of this sense that I was 'failing' at being a man.

As Courtney, though, I was able to borrow confidence. People looked at me and treated me differently. Gay men who had no interest in sleeping with me would treat me like a princess, a courtesy not afforded to other drag queens (back then), or even the occasional cis woman who frequented the gay scene. I think it was the high-femme beauty I could achieve that drew them in. LA has a passion for superficial beauty. It *appears* to have a deeper side – with the organic-eating, kombucha-drinking, fitness- and yoga-obsessed lifestyle of many of its residents – but really this is performative too. It's all underpinned by a desire to be beautiful. A desire to be loved. As Roxie Hart reminds us in *Chicago*, everyone in showbiz is trying to make up for love or approval they didn't get in their childhoods. Even though I had been loved by my parents, their love was undermined for so long by the fear that people were loving someone I wasn't: a straight man.

Despite my limited means, every Saturday night at Rasputin I would wear something new and exciting. I rolled out my good-as-new back catalogue of costumes from Sydney. But whereas before I would just throw on a dress with a wig and generic makeup, at Rasputin I was inspired to come up with head-to-toe looks. Surrounded by the Club Kid culture, I was WeHo's shiny new toy and loved flexing my creativity.

One week Marco Marco let me borrow a dress he'd made for Paris Hilton. It was bright pink, with a giant three-dimensional daisy built out of the skirt. I glued daisy petals and glitter around my eyes, with my hair in an updo into which I pinned fresh daisies. It was theatrical, but also very soft and girly.

At 2.15 am I was standing at the end of a line of people waiting to pick up my car from the car park. This guy who was obviously straight joined the line next to me and I went weak at the knees. I struck up a conversation, began flirting furiously and he reciprocated. Turned out he was a Marine. I love seamen! There we were, an active US Marine and a passive Australian drag queen – what were the odds? To paint the picture, Channing Tatum (in his G.I. Joe era) will play him in the future daytime telemovie about our lives together. He had that polite, disciplined military charm and would reply 'Yes ma'am' as if I were his superior in uniform.

There was a real spark, and neither of us was being coy about our attraction to the other. He commented that my outfit was 'out there' and I told him I was a hostess at a nightclub. I gave a little shiver, 'cause the night air was cold. As he wasn't wearing a jacket he offered instead to put his arm around me to keep me warm. I accepted. His big strong biceps wrapped about my shoulders, and I felt so small and safe. I fucking swooned. This is the stuff fairytales are made of. Everything was beautiful at the valet.

I was so swept up in the moment I forgot about the implications of him not knowing I was a drag queen. I was imagining what he looked like under his polo and khaki slacks, a military-fit body to go with his short back and sides. But if he was also imagining me naked, I am pretty sure his fantasy didn't include boobs made of foam latex and an inflated *membrum virile* taped to my bum crack. But as we stood there staring into each other's eyes, it felt as if we were just a girl and a boy experiencing love at first sight.

'So, what are you up to now?' I asked.

'I'm actually staying off-base for the night at my little brother's place. It was his 21st, so we decided to hit up some clubs.'

'That's so cute!'

'Yeah, but I lost the little shit and his battery died. I don't actually know where he lives, so I'm not sure where I'm gonna stay tonight.'

Was he really trying this story on me? Here I was trying to construct a storyline where I'd ask him back to mine, but he beat me to the punch. The valet pulled our cars up to the kerb.

'Perhaps you can stay at my place? Follow me home?'

His eyes lit up, we exchanged numbers, I jumped into my car and he closed the door for me like a gentleman. I wound down my window as he bent down and gave me the softest, sweetest kiss on the lips.

'Text me your address,' he whispered, then he winked and walked off to his car. I sat at my steering wheel, high on young love and the possibilities of the night.

Shit! I'd forgotten I'm not a woman! And that, more importantly, he didn't know that. I suspected that the nuances of my gender, and the conspicuous presence of my penis, might prove a fistful for me to try to explain once we got back to mine. I thought I'd best disclose this to him before it went any further, and before I gave him my address. How to put all of that in a text?

Hey, I just want to check... you know I'm not a real girl, right? *Send*

It was an approximation, but felt like the most tactful way of describing the situation. I wasn't trying to be anything other than me, so it felt strange explaining my existence, but I knew it had to be done. I drove off down Robertson and turned left onto Melrose so that I would be far enough away by the time he read it.

I glanced down at my phone while stopped at a red light on San Vicente. No response. La Cienega. No response.

Finally, as I turned left into Sweetzer, the screen lit up and I pulled my car over to the side of the road.

What do you mean?

How could I explain this? I didn't want to say 'drag queen', 'cause that wasn't really what was going on. I didn't want to say 'I'm a man', 'cause that wasn't it either. With the limited language of 2011 I decided a picture would speak a thousand words.

Sometimes I look like this, I wrote, and sent him a picture of me dressed as a girl from earlier that night. And sometimes I look like this. I sent a cute but not too masculine photo of me dressed as a boy.

Retrospectively, sending him a boy pic was a misstep – knowing that under the makeup I was a boy was one thing, but seeing what I looked like out of drag was another entirely.

I sat there waiting in my car, just staring, as the iPhone ellipsis taunted me with a reply. The three little dots would pop up, then go away, then pop up again. What was he thinking? Did he already know? Was he shocked? Was he angry? Did he feel deceived? I hope he didn't. I wasn't deceiving him; if anything I felt more authentically me flirting with him as Courtney than if I was dressed as Shane and flirting with a gay boy. I hoped our brief but thrilling connection might transcend my biological sex.

It wasn't my intention to deceive you or anything. I was just totally caught up in the moment. Sorry. Are you OK? Do you have any questions?

I drove up the road and parked at my building. Defeated and deflated, but still eager to pee, I ran through the front door, peeled back the tape and sat down on the toilet, waiting for a response. Silence. No ellipsis. I started tidying up my room optimistically, waiting for him to respond before I admitted defeat, had a shower and washed the makeup away. No response. Oh well, maybe he was that boy. But I wasn't that girl.

Aside from my Marine who never was, there were many boys, always straight-identifying, who did hook up with me – but always when I was dressed as Courtney. I'd had experiences procuring men when I was in drag back in Sydney, but I'd never been around such a concentration of hot, sexed-up, let's-call-them-heteroflexible guys before.

COURTNEY FACT

Heteroflexible is a word I use to describe the men I have sexual relations with who identify as straight. You might argue that if they're having sex with me, someone with Mummy's features and Daddy's fixtures, then how can they be straight? Most people would call them closeted, and some might pop them in the bisexual box. I like to think of the world as queer until proven otherwise; if people want to come out as straight, they can. These men usually just call themselves straight because they don't have the language or the tools in them to say otherwise, but as long as they have their tool in me, I'm happy.

Let me flesh this out with a little data. In a recent survey performed by YouGov, a British market research company, respondents were presented with the categories of gay, bi and straight to describe themselves, and 86 per cent of them self-identified as heterosexual. However, when plotting themselves on the Kinsey scale from 0 to 6, where 0 is completely heterosexual and 6 is completely homosexual, the number of exclusively heterosexual people fell by 20 per cent. Interesting, right? Now get this: when asked, 'If the right person came along at the right time do you think you could have sex with, or fall in love with, someone of the same sex?', only 46 per cent of hetero-identifying peeps answered 'absolutely not'.

Does this mean that more than half the straight people in the world are *at least* heteroflexible?! When I performed an excited follow-up survey, the results were even more astonishing: after respondents were asked if they would like to have sex with me, 30 per cent of straight men said 'yes', while the other 70 per cent said, 'What, again?'

OK – those last two stats are jokes, but the others are real.

When the respondents of the YouGov survey were asked who had actually had a same-sex experience, 28 per cent of people aged 25–34 said they had. That figure accounts for many more people than just the Ls, Gs and Bs, so what's going on? Lots of straight people are having same-sex experiences, that's what!

Having sex with more than one gender doesn't make you straight or gay. Technically it's bisexual behaviour, but that doesn't quite seem accurate either. Maybe the label of 'heteroflexible', originally cooked up by marketing departments, will help to tease out the edges; we only achieve a sense of personal authenticity when our desires reflect our behaviour, and when our behaviour reflects our actual identity. Or maybe we just need to debunk the stigma and embrace the full spectrum of our sexuality. Baby steps.

Many of these heteroflexible guys came in the form of the go-go dancers who worked at the gay bars in WeHo. Their honest living was made being ogled at and groped all night by gay men, and my presence always seemed to be a welcome reprieve. I would get the affection from the go-gos that the gay men fantasised about. Being Courtney gave me access to a whole different class of men.

At Rasputin one night I went behind the shadow-box screens with the go-go dancers. Men's hands would reach through the cut-out hole to slip dollar bills into the elastic waistbands of the dancers' underwear (if they were wearing any). I joined one of the boys I'd been flirting with in the dressing room and we put on quite the show for the people on the other side watching our silhouettes. At first I just danced up against his body as I felt his already engorged penis grow hard. I got down on my knees and took him in my mouth and put on a Shadow Puppetry of the Penis show.

On another night at Stripper Circus, a weekly club night with strippers galore, I found myself crammed into a toilet cubicle with a straight go-go dancer, asking him to hold my hair back while I did a line of coke off his erect penis – which you really only do to write about in your memoir, because in practice it's clumsy, and then the dick tastes awful when you put it in your mouth shortly after. There was a security guard who came back to mine after work one night, and then the next week and the next. Not a go-go dancer, but one of these straight-adjacent men who find themselves working in queer spaces. I still message him when I am in LA for a booty call, and if he doesn't have a girlfriend he'll come over and we have some fun. I think he appreciates how much I love sucking his dick. Comedian Michelle Wolf says, 'Gay guys talk about dick the way (straight) men wished women talked about dick. Straight men, if you want someone to love your dick, be gay.' It's true.

Big Gun Fridays was the strip's newest night, and boasted a plethora of really hot go-go dancers and your hostess Courtney Act. It attracted a manly crowd with lots of muscles and facial hair, and there was always a line down the block. Inside, men would be shoulder to shoulder, drinking and shouting over pop remixes, with music videos playing on screens around the bar. I'd spin around the crowd saying hello to people, buying them drinks, looking glamorous and having fun.

As the hostess I shared a dressing room with the dancers. Although I would come from home fully dressed, I was always sure to pop down there every few hours to touch up my lipstick and look for opportunities to smudge it up straightaway.

The boys would get ready for their go-go sets by 'fluffing' their members, by jerking off to straight porn. Once they got some blood flowing, they would pop on a cock ring and head upstairs to earn their tips. (For the uninitiated reader, a cock ring is a rubber, metal or leather ring that goes around the base of the penis and balls to help maintain an erection once the penis has filled with blood.) I was always happy to offer a hand or lips as an alternative fluffing service – surely more helpful than straight porn on a lubey Android? I lost my gag reflex in that dressing room trying to leave my lipstick ring on the depilated skin at the base of each penis.

That's where I met Diego. One night when I walked into the dressing room we locked eyes, and it was lust at first sight. We giggly-smiled at each other like kids in the schoolyard, and as I walked towards him we didn't break eye contact.

'I'm Courtney.'

'I'm Diego,' he said, and we both leaned in and started kissing. Diego was in his early 20s and had dark hair and brown eyes. He had sexy tattoos, and he wore these steel-blue cotton Lycra bike pants his mom had made him. They had a penis pouch sewn into them, quite a large penis pouch – designed like a glove, but for just one finger that was about eight and a half inches long. I thought it was quite grotesque… at first, but came to appreciate it.

Each week Diego and I would flirt outrageously. Our eyes would always light up when we saw each other, and one night he offered to take me for a ride on the back of his motorcycle. Not to anywhere in particular, just for the fantasy. He brought a spare helmet and I wore appropriate hair, wrapped my arms around him and lived that bad-boy heteronormative fantasy of sitting on the back on my boyfriend's motorcycle. We rode up to the Sunset Strip and I felt like I was in the movies. The cold wind beat across my face as I nestled into the shoulder of Diego's leather jacket, and the glowing neon sign of the Body Shop strip club whizzed by: *LIVE. NUDE. Girls. Girls. Girls.*

Past the Mondrian, past The Viper Room, past Sunset Towers to Whisky a Go Go and then down San Vicente and back to Revolver.

Diego and I decided that after work the following Friday we should consummate our dressing-room romance with a night of love-making at my place. I spent all day 'preparing the corpse'. I shaved, clippered, plucked and douched. Even though I usually dressed quite vampy on Fridays, I picked a virginal white girl-next-door dress and put on creamy-blond bouncy human-hair curls. I wanted to look special for him, and couldn't wait to walk in the dressing room and see his face light up. But when I did, it didn't. He was buried in his phone looking stressed. His motorbike had been confiscated by the police and he was not at all interested in the virgin-bride fantasy standing before him. That was the night I realised men wanna fuck the fantasy and marry the girl next door. I think if I had been wearing black fishnets and red lingerie – straight men universally love black fishnets and red lingerie – I would have been able to draw just enough blood away from his brain and down to his groin to get his attention. But alas, I was left at the altar.

I was waiting in line for a stall in the all-gender bathroom, recounting my frustration with Diego to my Irish friend Simon, when the door of the toilet cubicle opened and another one of the straight go-gos, Rob, walked out. Diego had a boyish charm, but Rob was a man – actually, he could play He-Man in a movie. He was wearing Speedos, boots and muscles. So. Many. Abdominals. He had a handsome face and short blond hair. I saw a glimmer of an opportunity and grabbed it with both hands (and my mouth).

I pushed Rob back into the stall and locked the door behind me. We started passionately kissing as he lifted me onto the marble basin, my hands pressed against the walls to support myself. I wrapped my legs around him and he picked me up again, this time placing me on the toilet seat and pulling down his pants. I impressed Rob by getting my mouth all the way down his penis, though my eyes did start to water. I pulled a condom and my purse-sized pack of silicone-based lube out of my handbag, determined not to let my colonic cleansing go to waste. Usually getting any penis in my butt was a slow process, but this time I really wanted it, had had a few libations and I managed to fit a big thing into a small place.

'HURRY UP!' someone called out as they banged on the door. Ripped from our fantasy, Rob and I quickly fixed ourselves and exited the stall. We were both so flustered and unsure what had just happened, but we swapped numbers and arranged to finish what we had started in the privacy of my bed later that evening.

Rob would come over occasionally after work on different nights and we would flip-fuck, taking turns at being the top and the bottom. He loved bottoming. He said he was straight, but told me I was the exception. Sometimes I believe it when guys say this, and sometimes I think it's a line. I think Rob might have had more than just one exception, but was still very much into girls, whether they had a vagina or a penis. One night Rob asked if I wanted to go on a date. He suggested we go to the gun range and go shooting. Guns are certainly not a part of Australian culture and the mere thought of them scared the shit out of me, let alone being somewhere in drag where straight men had live ammunition. I dramatically considered that this might be a plot for Rob to 'accidentally' shoot me, to keep his 'dirty little secret' from ever surfacing. There wasn't anything in my experience with Rob that suggested he would be capable of that, but the threat of violence is always so close to the surface when it comes to having sex in drag. I suggested to Rob that we go instead on a date somewhere with food and no semi-automatic weapons.

I'm more familiar than I'd like with the look a trick gets in their eyes right after they come – that 30 seconds of the day when a man isn't thinking about sex and you don't know if he's going to get aggressive or throw up. I remember one night back in Sydney when I brought home a bouncer from the Midnight Shift with me, and we started getting hot and heavy in my bathroom. There I was with this big straight guy, his pants around his ankles, bent over my basin as I topped him. I looked up in the mirror and was so bewildered by what I saw: me, a woman, fucking this man from behind. The visual confused my poor little brain. Moments later he started to groan and I knew I was doing my job right; before I knew it he was cumming everywhere.

Once the bouncer finished he turned around, and as our eyes met I saw disgust, confusion and shame swirling around in this expression. The look of disgust manifested literally as he threw up into the toilet. I popped out of the bathroom to let him gather himself and touched up my lip liner. Apparently the disgust left his body along with the contents of his stomach as he then tried to kiss me again. Not after he'd just vomited. Gross.

The date with Rob was the first time I'd actually gone on a date in a public place in drag. I'd certainly met guys out in public places, and I'd got into drag a few times when guys were coming over to mine for sex, but I'd never got dressed and gone on a dinner date. Rob said there was a place up on Sunset that he loved called Aromas. I mean… I'm not sure it's where I would have chosen for a first date, but it was adequate. It was basically a Coffee Club, and the date was cute.

A few days later, I got a text from Rob: What are you up to, cutie?

Nothing much. Just lying in my bed. Under draped purple organza.

I'm just around the corner. I'll pop in.

WAIT! I'm not… dressed. Rob had never seen me out of drag before, and I knew he liked women. I couldn't let him see me like this.

Even better! I'll be there in five.

No! I mean… How could I say this without ruining the fantasy? I knew from my experience with the Marine not to send a pic of me as a boy this time. I'm not 'Courtney' right now.

Yeah, I know what you mean. I'll see you soon.

Wait, what? *I am not presenting as the appropriate gender for your sexual pleasure, sir!* This sent me into a tailspin. I was sure Rob thought he knew what I meant, but was he actually prepared to see me as a boy? I wasn't in hair and makeup, and was wearing shorts and a T-shirt.

My phone rang. Rob was at the front door, so I pushed the buzzer to let him in. My mind was racing. Usually I was a girl around him, so I acted soft and feminine. But now I was presenting as a boy, so I wondered whether I should act as I normally would if I was dressed as a boy in the bedroom with a guy. What if he was disgusted by the fag who answered the door and beat me? As a boy I would normally code-switch and be as masculine as possible around a straight guy to avoid aggression or violence, but Rob was attracted to girls, so I thought maybe I shouldn't try that. But because I wasn't in drag, it would've felt weird to be feminine.

Rob knocked at the door. My heart was beating fast, and I could feel my face flushing. My brain was short-circuiting because I couldn't work out which side of the binary I had to be on. These ideas of masculinity and femininity that had long been battling inside my head were colliding against each other, like in a superhero cartoon when the goodie and the baddie have their final showdown. The only thing I could do in that moment was be me and just see what happened. I took a deep breath and opened the door.

'Hey, sexy,' said Rob as he smiled and leant straight in to kiss me passionately. We'd clearly been thinking about different things in the lead-up to this moment. Rob had been thinking about sex while I'd been having an existential crisis about my gender presentation. But weirdly, once he started kissing me, none of that seemed to matter.

There were so many factors that had culminated in this moment. I had always felt I was performing a charade when I presented as one side of the binary, always coming up short: not feeling man enough as Shane or woman enough as Courtney. And the feedback I received from sexual partners, even if it was positive, only served to further invalidate whoever the real me was. Validation through sex only reinforced the insecurities I had been trying to cover up; when someone was attracted to the façade I displayed, that reinforced a feeling that I wasn't worthy of love.

Where did these ideas about myself come from? I'm sure Freud would say it had something to do with my parents, but I keep coming back to those early moments standing under A block, looking at where all the boys sat at lunchtime back in high school. *Why can't I sit with them? Why don't they like me?*

So the seeds were sown, and the narrative of my identity was formed. My sexuality had no chance of expression, no relative experience. Without a framework with which to understand these feelings of attraction, which felt quite wonderful to me, I was hearing a language I wasn't able to speak yet. I didn't know what 'gay' was; all I knew was 'faggot' and 'poofter' and the other names they would call me. I didn't know that boys could be attracted to boys and have healthy, loving relationships. And so that box of clutter containing my formative experiences of being attracted to men went into the attic in my mind, saved to make sense of at a future time when I had the language to translate it.

Was this that moment? Was Rob an unexpected interpreter? Something changed in me that night; I learnt I could be desirable just as I was. Not masculine. Not feminine. Just me.

Nonetheless, all of these experiences as Courtney, being fawned over by hot straight-identifying go-go dancers or being celebrated by the WeHo scene for my femininity and glamour, started to play on my mind. My look was getting more feminine – human-hair wigs, softer makeup, girlier looks – and I was always thinking about the straight-male gaze when I got ready. Unresolved feelings started to stir inside me. I could feel a discomfort growing, and I realised that those questions about my gender identity were back. Whereas before I usually would look in the opposite direction, now for the first time I was willing to have a glance. But I was too scared to go it on my own. I needed help.

The only person I could trust with this dark recess of my mind was Vanity. Since I'd moved to LA we would often fantasise on the phone about what our lives would be like if we were trans. Even though these fantasies didn't present an honest examination of our gender identity, they still pointed at a deeper issue. When Vanity was 20 she had begun to transition with hormones, but after two months she realised she'd entered into the process for the wrong reasons and stopped. Even so, I know for both of us our gender identity had always remained a question mark. I think Vanity and I were drawn to each other because we saw ourselves reflected in the other in so many ways. It wasn't just that we looked like siblings; our gender identity sat in a very similar band of the spectrum. We were able to share with each other the most intimate parts of our identities without fear or explanation.

In our phone conversations, Vanity and I often discussed how we were cut from the same cloth as many of the trans women we grew up with, but because we were from a different generation we had the freedom to make different choices – as if being trans were a choice. (Because I thought it was, then.) Vanity and I would text back and forth about how we loved the idea of being women, but we didn't want to suffer the way the trans women around us did. As long as the question was unexamined, I lived in a gender purgatory, and so the day came when the risk it took to be a boy was more painful than the risk it took to be trans.

Before I was even ready to admit the truth to myself, I had to say it out loud to Vanity to see how it sounded.

'I'm going to say something, and I'm not sure what it is, but I just need you to listen.' I didn't even give her a chance to respond. 'I think I might be...'

Too soon.

'I've been living in West Hollywood for a year and it's so different here. I go out looking all girly and people love it, and more than that, *I* love it. I just love being a girl. I think I might be...' Nope. Couldn't say it.

‘It’s just that in Sydney I was always being told I wasn’t draggy enough, I needed bigger hair, higher eyebrows, “and for god’s sake put on some pantyhose”. It’s so nice here being respected as a girl. I think I might be… I just enjoy expressing my femininity and not having to be the butt of the joke all the time. I think I might be…’

Tears welled up as I fought for the courage the end of that sentence needed. Vanity remained silent, holding space, knowing exactly what I was trying to say.

‘… But it’s not as if I don’t like being a boy. I just really like being a girl too.’

Hearing myself say this out loud for the first time gave my inner truth new meaning. I’d been aware of my desire for both masculinity and femininity since that night a decade before in Sydney, just after I’d come out to my parents, when I was at my friend Sarah’s place and began to seriously question my gender identity. But I always thought I would have to eventually pick a side – to be cis or trans. Man or woman.

I continued with what I recognised as a totally different tone in my voice. Where before there was fear, now there was wonder in the realisation that I did in fact enjoy being a boy too.

‘I think I might be… It’s not like I feel uncomfortable in my body. It’s just that there’s no place for me to express my femininity as a boy. But maybe it’s not about choosing. Can I be both?’

My words were an epiphany. *Can I be both?* In the act of saying all of this out loud to someone who received it with empathy – whose careful listening had allowed me to be honest – I found my sense of shame evaporating. I’d shone a torch under the bed and found there was no monster there at all: I didn’t need to live by someone else’s values. Maybe the real me didn't fit at one end or the other of the gender spectrum, but rather somewhere in between.

Things started to happen the week following this revelation. On Friday night I was working at Rasputin in drag and started chatting to this boy I had long thought was cute. I had talked to this guy before, but this time the conversation just flowed.

Eventually he said, 'Do you want to have dinner on Tuesday night? As Shane, obviously.'

I had never actually been asked out on a date by someone as Shane. It wasn't something people seemed to do in the world I lived in. I'd certainly seen these acts of courtship in the movies, but hadn't really seen them unfold in real life. I had definitely asked lots of people on dates, but never with success, and had never been on an actual date that wasn't just meeting someone drunk in a bar and going home to fuck.

Later that week I was out as a boy at Sunday Funday, the colloquial name given to Sunday drinks on Santa Monica Boulevard in WeHo, when another guy started chatting me up and asked if I wanted to go on a date.

How novel! I said yes to both suitors.

These two events could have just been coincidences, but I honestly think that while nothing about me had changed on the outside, a whole lot had changed on the inside. I had a new sense of resolution with my gender identity when I was chatting to people. I wasn't trying to be what I thought they wanted me to be, I was just being me, and that resonated with others in a subtle, subconscious way. I was being desired for me – and that is real validation, the validation I had been seeking, the validation we all are seeking. Being vulnerable enough to be seen for who I really was, even if it was just while flirting over a cocktail on a Sunday afternoon at The Abbey, was deeply healing.

17

'The winner of *RuPaul's Drag Race*, America's next drag superstar… is… Courtney Act!'

How humiliating. Who would have thought 12 weeks ago that hearing my name called as the winner of Season 6 could feel this horrible? I wanted to vomit. I didn't want to pretend in front of a room full of thousands of fans that I was a worthy winner. I mean, we didn't know who the winner would be, but we all knew it wasn't me. Even though I knew this would never go to air, I had to fake it. I took a deep breath and forced a smile. Just one lap of the runway and then we could all go home.

Because the finale of *Drag Race* is filmed in front of a live audience two weeks before it airs, they shoot alternative endings with each of the top three contestants winning to keep the real winner a secret. The rest of Season 6 had been shot about ten months earlier. When the finale aired, the producers would show one of the pre-taped endings and the winner would be revealed to the world.

And yet, in what was supposed to be a triumphant moment, all I could think was, *I made it. It's over. Now I just have to get to my hotel room so I can go to sleep and this day can be over forever.*

The floor manager interrupted my thoughts: 'OK, reset! Thank you, ladies. We have one more ending to shoot. Everyone back to one.'

Adore, Bianca and I all looked at each other, confused. What now? We had already filmed each of the three of us winning.

'Girl, what kinda stunt are they trying to pull?' Bianca asked.

'I'm scared.' A quintessential Adore response to anything.

I couldn't even talk, because I was so close to breaking as it was. I was just trying to remember to breathe.

'Quiet, please! Cameras still rolling, and… action.'

'The winner of *RuPaul's Drag Race*, America's next drag superstar… is… It's a tie! Adore Delano and… Bianca Del Rio.' RuPaul's voice echoed out across the auditorium and the crowd jumped to their feet, screaming.

Adore and Bianca both looked at me as if to say sorry then they joined hands and took their winners' walk down the runway. I stood there by myself, looking at the backs of their gowns and the faces of the thousands of fans filling the theatre at the Ace Hotel. I continued trying to take deep breaths to stop my body from shaking.

It's OK, I thought, trying to delude myself in order to maintain some face. *They're probably going to film a fifth ending with you in the tie. Just breathe, Shane.* I waited for the applause to die down and the floor manager to call reset.

'That's a wrap. Thank you, everybody.' The houselights of the theatre turned on. It was all over. I stood there frozen until my body involuntarily gasped for air. I had literally been holding my breath. I was wounded, and felt like I'd just been intentionally publicly humiliated.

I can't quite remember what happened next. I remember being with Simon at the top of a set of stairs that led to the afterparty in the Spanish Gothic–style theatre foyer. The high vaulted ceilings were lit pink and purple, and *Drag Race* superfans crowded the parquet floor below, ready to celebrate the night with the stars of Season 6.

'I can't do this, Simon. Isn't there another way out?'

'They said this is the only way back to the hotel. I've got you. Just stay behind me.'

'Please walk fast, like you're in a hurry, and please don't stop for anyone or I'm sure I will just burst into tears.'

This might sound dramatic, but I'm a drag queen; it's my M.O. to be dramatic. I felt like Whitney Houston in *The Bodyguard* when she's pulled from the stage singing 'Queen of the Night'. All of the crowd clings and claws at her, then Kevin Costner comes to the rescue and carries her to safety.

In my mind Simon was carrying me, but in reality I followed him with my hand on his shoulder, my head down. I wanted so badly to be invisible. My shoulder-length dusty pink hair was swept across my face in beachy waves, my floor-length transparent gown made of iridescent Mylar reflected all the light that touched it in beautiful shards of pink, purple and blue, and my six-inch aurora borealis–stoned shoes meant that I was a six-foot-three-inch woman trying to discreetly move through a crowd of people for whom she had just spent the previous few hours performing. Somehow we made it without a single person stopping us.

We got to my hotel room, sat down on the bed, and I noticed I was panting. I was trying to catch my breath but I couldn't because I was struggling to focus on reality. I looked around the room for microphones or cameras. I'd spent all day on stage in front of thousands of people, with TV cameras pointing at me as I smiled and pretended everything was OK.

Now I was in my hotel room with Simon, but I was struggling to understand what was public and what was private.

It's like when you've been on a boat and you get onto dry land, but you still feel the rocking. I had a weird, but justifiable, sense that I was being watched. I checked my cleavage to see if I was wearing a microphone and tried to tell myself that now I was in private and could let my real feelings show. I tried to tell Simon what was going on inside my head, but even then I was still afraid to speak freely because I was paranoid that World of Wonder, the production company, had bugged my hotel room.

'You think RuPaul has bugged your room?'

'I mean… no. And I know it sounds crazy. But also yes. Oh my god! I sound crazy. Am I crazy right now? I need to go home. I need to pack up my things and I need to drive home.'

The hotel was in downtown LA and I lived in West Hollywood, which was a 20-minute drive at that time of night. I had driven my car and was meant to stay overnight, but I was feeling so anxious that I just wanted to leave all of this and go to my home, to a place I could feel some sense of safety and security.

As I rushed around my room packing everything up, I recounted different stories from the day to Simon: 'I was sitting there on stage during a commercial break and Kylie's "Get Out of My Way" starts playing. I was grooving along, and then I glanced over and saw Ru bopping away too. Our eyes met and I mouthed across the stage, "I love this song."

'She smiled at me and mouthed back, "So do I," but then she stopped abruptly like she caught herself doing something she regretted and looked away. That's when I realised—' I stopped the story and jokingly ran over to a lamp as if to check it for a microphone before I finished in a whisper, 'that was the one and only human moment I've ever shared with RuPaul.'

When I'd first told Triana I was auditioning for *Drag Race*, around two years after I'd started living in LA, she gave me the 411 from her perspective as a reality TV producer.

'You have to know who your character is, and always be giving them story.'

'I'm not a character: I'm me. I've spent so much time trying to understand who I am in a world that would tell me otherwise – isn't that enough? Isn't the story just what happens when I'm there?'

'Oh, sweetie. You have to drive the narrative and create your own storylines, otherwise they will create them for you – and you don't want that. You're pretty, so they will probably cast you as the bitchy girl. And you have a British accent, which makes you sound more intelligent and less trustworthy. Why do you think villains in American movies so often have British accents?'

'My accent is Australian.'

'Yeah, but Americans don't know the difference. Think about it: Scar in *The Lion King*, Hannibal Lecter. Even Darth Vader sounded British. It's an easy character fit for a lazy story producer.'

'No! I don't want to be a bitch or a villain. I don't want to be one of those reality TV tropes. I want to show people you can go on reality TV and be rational, calm and kind.'

Triana let out a sigh. 'OK, where do I start? Reality TV is entertainment through conflict. If you are not creating drama or reacting to drama, you don't get any screen time.'

But Triana was missing my whole point. I wasn't there for the drama. I was there to do my best, have fun, make friends and become America's next drag superstar. The stakes were so high: apart from the US$100,000 prize money, the show was starting to swell in popularity. Fan favourites had lucrative careers touring around the country performing at gay bars, and doing well could even make my dream of being a pop music artist come true. Sharon Needles, the winner of Season 4, had released a pop album that charted on the Billboard 200. Her music videos were slick and glossy. I was so hopeful for the possibilities that lay in store.

I put together my audition video with photographer and friend Magnus Hastings, sent it off and awaited a response. I'd actually been asked by World of Wonder to submit an audition tape in early 2012, but they'd told me a few months later that my O1 Work Visa made me ineligible to enter the show. This time things looked more positive; I got a call about the background check and psych evaluation, standard procedure in US reality TV, which meant I had made it onto a shortlist.

I got some index cards and started Blu-Tacking costume ideas onto my bedroom wall. Rhea mentioned an idea for a drag look based on the image of Klaus Nomi, the German singer. I stuck that up there. There was a look that referenced a design by Viktor & Rolf, the avant-garde Dutch fashion house, where the model looked like she was walking down the runway in a bed. I stuck that on the wall too.

Then I remembered a pair of wings from a Divastated show in Sydney. One of the male dancers wore them in an X-Men show as Archangel, and Ashley Swift had worn them in a big group Mardi Gras show we did in 2008. They were massive mechanical wings that expanded to a span of eight feet. I called up Ashley and he said Abbey had them. I called up Abbey, who now lived an eight-hour drive from Sydney in Byron Bay, and he said he would drive them down to Chelsea at House of Priscilla in Sydney if I could work out how to get them to LA. My friend Mitch bundled them up so they were packaged for flying and I called Penny Tration, who worked as a flight attendant; she arranged to have them flown in oversized baggage. I was so mad at myself when I had to wake up hungover at 4 am to drive to LAX and collect the wings, cussing non-4-am me as I tried to wedge these giant mechanical wings into the tiny trunk of my Jetta. I didn't even know if I was on the show, so I felt this was probably a total waste of time.

When the call to confirm my place on Season 6 came I was at home. I had three weeks to pack. This was it; I was going to be a part of the legacy. *Drag Race* felt like my second chance after *Idol*, and this time I would do it even better.

The producers gave me a list of possible looks we would need for the show:

Black and White
Crazy, Sexy, Cool
Red Carpet
Best Drag
Animal Kingdom
Executive Realness

and so on.

I started matching all of the costume ideas I had on my wall to the list, then called some costume designer friends, Perry Meek and Shokra, and asked if they could help. I asked Dallas Dellaforce if she could make me a gown that incorporated the Australian flag and the Aboriginal flag; I had seen her wearing this design and thought it was the perfect homage to my homeland. Vanity flew over to LA for a week to help me prepare and style my wigs, and it felt like the good old days making costumes for a Divastated show. We bounced ideas back and forth and watched Season 5, paying closer attention than ever before. In particular we both noted how we didn't really like Alyssa Edwards at the beginning and then somewhere mid-season she had morphed into our favourite. It was fascinating watching the narrative unfold, knowing I would soon be in that same workroom.

I didn't tell anyone except Vanity that I was on the show. The contract made it clear it was top secret, and I didn't want to jeopardise my chances. *Drag Race* alum Willam, from Season 4, had previously told me all about the process, including the fact that you are allowed five bags, but because they don't specify size or weight I would be best to get 90-gallon storage tubs from Home Depot. When the day arrived and the production assistant knocked on my door I had five trunks filled to the brim, a giant foam Priscilla-style wig made by Maude Boate on my head, and the massive mechanical wings on my back. I figured it was like at the airport when your bag is overweight and you put on your heaviest boots and biggest jacket.

'This is just what I am wearing on the flight,' I said cheekily, hoping she would let the wings not count as one of the five bags. I asked her when the truck and removalist crew would be arriving to collect everything. She seemed confused. She was a small woman with a Prius and was somehow expected to get a drag queen and bags on their way to the *Drag Race* studio into an eco-friendly car. Even if I'd had five regular-sized suitcases we would have only been able to fit two into her car, and I thought it was really strange they weren't better equipped. As it was we couldn't even fit one of the tubs in the boot of her hybrid. I reluctantly agreed to give her my house keys so production could send people to collect everything.

'Can I also have your phone, please?'

'Oh, I'm going to leave that here.'

'Sorry, you have to give it to me.'

'I am not going to take it with me. I am going to leave it here.'

'That's not an option. You must surrender your phone to me now. It might be required during filming, if you need someone's number or something else. It will be kept in a safe place in the production office and you will get it back once the show is over.'

I knew I wouldn't have access to my phone, but my preference was to leave it at home. The idea of handing it over to the production crew raised suspicions. I had just signed a contract, which I read cover to cover, that explicitly said I had no right to privacy, so I was feeling a little wary. I had two choices: give her my phone and house keys, or not go to 'summer camp'.

Contracts for these sorts of shows state that they have the right to videotape, film, portray, photograph, otherwise record me, my actions and my voice (and other sound effects) on an up to 24-hours-a-day, seven-days-a-week basis, whether requesting me to wear a microphone or not. There are also clauses allowing them to bug your home without your knowledge, and allowing producers to make certain misrepresentations of you, or to reveal information about you that is private, personal, sexual, surprising, defamatory, disparaging, embarrassing or unfavourable.

When I was in my hotel room during the filming of *Drag Race* I felt nervous about getting naked in the shower for fear that I was being recorded. I didn't think it was likely, but according to the contract it was allowed. I even masturbated under the covers, fearful that this season things might be done differently.

Reading through the contract stirred up all the fears that would be fully and finally realised in my hotel room at the Ace on the night of the finale taping. But at the beginning of filming, as I ran into the workroom for the first time, I was full of hope and innocence, ready to work my way to the top of Season 6.

'Is this *America's Next Top Model*?' I chirped as I ran into a big open-plan pink room, with worktables and makeup stations, surrounded by brick walls. It was just like on the TV, only it felt bigger. I was greeted by Joslyn Fox, Trinity K. Bonet, Milk, Magnolia Crawford and, last but not least, Bianca Del Rio.

Bianca and I gave each other knowing looks and were thick as thieves from that moment forwards, developing a mutual respect. We'd grown up on opposite sides of the world but in a similar era, in similar drag scenes. Bianca reminded me of the drag queens I'd grown up with in Sydney – old. Kidding. She had a razor-sharp wit, giant eye makeup and a heart of gold. I was always inspired by her work ethic; she is such a polished drag queen and I worked hard to keep up with the pace she set.

I had first met Bianca when I interviewed her at the premiere of *Priscilla* on Broadway, and we'd hung out in a bar once or twice since. We had actually been messaging on Facebook early in 2013 about me doing a guest spot at Hot Mess, a show she hosted at XL Nightclub in New York. Rhea Litré had heard Bianca was going to be on *Drag Race* and messaged me about it in the wee hours of Thursday morning, 6 June 2013. I was being sequestered the day after, so I sent Bianca a message:

Hey
See you Friday *winky face*

She replied:

Oh god
You ready?

It was such a comfort that I at least sort of knew someone who was going to be part of the Season 6 cast. We didn't know each other well, but I knew Bianca was good people.

Right after my entrance into the workroom we heard footsteps coming down the hall. Bianca announced, 'I hear a Clydesdale.'

In bounded the irrepressible Darienne Lake, smiling all over her face. Like Bianca, Darienne felt like someone I was already friends with but just hadn't met. She stood out. She looked stunning in burgundy hair and a royal-blue dress, but more than that, her personality shone. Bianca, Darienne and I clicked instantly, and made each other laugh. We were the three oldest of the group – though *obviously* they are *significantly older* than *I* – and we all just made sense to each other. I enjoyed hanging out with the other girls too, but there was something special about the connection Bianca, Darienne and I had.

What we didn't know at this point is that Adore Delano, BenDeLaCreme, Gia Gunn, Laganja Estranja, Kelly Mantle and Vivacious had already entered the workroom and filmed an entire episode. After my group filmed our episode we were introduced to the other group of Season 6 queens, and that brought in a real sense of competition.

Adore and I didn't get off on the right foot.

'I'm glad I'm not the only *Idol* contestant here. I was on *American Idol*,' she said to me, prompted by a story producer.

'You're on Season 1?' I asked, trying to make conversation.

'No!' Adore exclaimed. 'Oh, we're playing that game, bitch?'

To this day I am not sure why my question was offensive; I recently asked Adore and she wasn't entirely sure either. I think it was because she would have been about 11 years old when Season 1 of *Idol* aired, and thought I was insinuating she was older than she was.

In any case, after that little hiccup Adore and I got on well during filming. One moment captured on film that always makes me chuckle was in an episode of *Untucked*, the backstage companion show to *Drag Race*. We were all in high drag, having just come from the black-and-white runway, and Laganja was rabbiting on about something when Adore and I, sitting together on a couch, caught each other's eye and were unable to contain our smirks. It was one of those little moments shared between friends, when not a word needs to be spoken to know exactly what the other person is thinking.

Together, all four of us were dubbed by the *Drag Race* fandom 'the ABCD of drag': Adore, Bianca, Courtney, Darienne. Eight years later, it's rare a day goes by without our group message buzzing. Our friendship circle is a real safe space to share ridiculous memes or have intensive conversations about what we're going through. We are often in different parts of the world, but depending on the time zone, Darienne is usually the first to reply to a late-night message, on her way to the loo at 6 am when she wakes up in Rochester, New York. Bianca joins the conversation mid-morning with caps lock on, and Adore rolls out of bed a little later and we chat about whatever is on our minds. Their friendship has been the greatest gift to come from *Drag Race*.

The actual six weeks of filming *Drag Race* were an amazing time. Every day I walked into the workroom and wondered what exciting challenges we would be handed, trying my best not to feel the pressure, despite knowing that what took place inside those walls would one day be seen across the world by millions of fans. For those six weeks our whole life was living and breathing performance, which is what makes me tick. So much of my previous experience fed into the challenges we had to do, starting with my first drag pageant at Mr Tiny Tot 1987. My years at Fame, competing in talent quests, soaking up everything I could performing in drag shows on Oxford Street, being on *Idol*, releasing music with Sony – my whole life had been leading to this.

There were some surprises during filming. For one, the brick walls of the workroom weren't even brick! They were fabric drapes with brick walls printed onto them. I don't know why that was such a shock the first time I saw them blowing in the air conditioning; I guess I had taken TV at face value, and had always just thought *Drag Race* was filmed in RuPaul's basement! I know that sounds totally dumb now, but the way he enters the workroom feels as if he's coming down from his living room to say hello. I had never thought about the fact that it was all just a make-believe TV set inside a big Hollywood sound stage. On *Idol* I had no preconception because it was the first season, so I'd never seen the show before, but I had watched five seasons of *Drag Race* and had an expectation about what it was going to be like.

The mini-challenge on the first episode was a photoshoot in a bed involving the Pit Crew and a pillow fight. It was so lovely seeing Simon there, although we couldn't interact as normal because we were 'on the job', so we just gave each other knowing smiles. In the photoshoot I had an opportunity to be silly, and made RuPaul laugh by clucking around like a chicken, Kath and Kim style.

In the next episode, Bianca and I had so much fun putting on campy British accents in a horror-movie spoof called *Drag Race Me to Hell.* Then came something I could really shine in – *Shade: The Rusical*, a musical theatre challenge. This was playing to my strengths: I had played Angel in *Rent*, and had written and produced my own cabaret shows and performed them around the world. The musical episode was my first win, a very big achievement. I felt as though I was in the game. After years of hard work and perseverance, I was finally able to shine.

Having worked on Australian TV I felt like a bit of a pro: I was familiar with the crew, cameras and lights, and with directors calling 'action' and 'cut'. But this was much more intense, because we were sequestered away and had no contact with the outside world. If we weren't on camera and mic'd up we weren't allowed to interact with each other, because the producers wanted to capture all of the magic on camera. Even though that might seem harsh to the uninitiated, I understood the rationale behind the rule. It's human nature to resolve issues in private, but that doesn't make for good TV. There were a few times you could sneak a conversation off camera when a producer wasn't looking, but that just meant there was no resolution to a story that had started on screen.

At the end of a long day filming, we were piled into a minibus and taken back to the three-star glamour of the Beverly Garland Hotel in North Hollywood. On the bus they would only let us talk about a subject that wasn't related to *Drag Race*, like volcanoes. Darienne would sit in the front seat jabbering away and distracting the production assistant, while Bianca and I sat on the back seat whispering.

'So you know how Visage keeps going on about my makeup being too big?' she said, referring to Michelle Visage, one of the judges and an old friend of Ru's. 'Tomorrow in the workroom I'm going to ask you to help me dial it down a bit. OK?'

'But that's your makeup. And besides, you know how to wear less makeup – why would you ask me how to do that?'

''Cause that's what they want. They want to see you listening to their feedback and acting on it.'

I was so confused by what Bianca was telling me. Producing yourself seemed counterintuitive – or, even worse, to me it seemed like a lie.

At the hotel we were sent straight to our rooms, where the producers would put a piece of blue masking tape across the doors so we couldn't sneak out. I believe this is thanks to Season 4, when the girls *would* sneak out of the hotel when no one was looking. There was a hotel-room-cum-production-office on the floor, with a production assistant always on watch. If we had any requests we would write them on pieces of paper and slide them under the door. For me at least, the solitude was actually quite lovely because it was the only alone time I had all day. As much as I would have liked to kiki with all my sisters off camera, I understood why we were kept separate and cut off from the outside.

The biggest surprise of all was RuPaul himself. I had heard a few negative stories from people who'd had interactions with him over the years, including the year before, in 2012, when he had performed at the Sydney Gay and Lesbian Mardi Gras Party. Sydney Mardi Gras is famous for its massive shows in the Royal Hall of Industries (RHI) with teams of dancers and lavish costumes and production, and over the years I have seen

Cher, Cyndi Lauper, George Michael, Olivia Newton-John, Sam Smith, Dua Lipa, Pabllo Vittar and more perform in them.

I'd heard stories that something was awry with RuPaul's show the day before, when his management announced he wouldn't be leading the huge production show that had been months in the planning. Instead, on the night the 40-dancer number happened on stage without him, and then the stage cleared. Ru sang 'Supermodel', his hit from the early 90s, alone on stage, wearing the gold Season 4 promo catsuit. He finished up by saying, 'Thank you! Happy Pride, happy Smardi Gras.' Then, mimicking the Australian accent, 'Good on ya, mate. Don't come the raw prawn with me. All right?'

He turned and walked off the stage. No pyrotechnical finale, no huge ovation, not even a lighting cue for his exit. The crowd was confused, and the hundreds of queer artists who had invested so many hours in a show that was a celebration of RuPaul were so disappointed; this wasn't the spirit of Mardi Gras at all. Aided and abetted by booze and ketamine, I tweeted @Rupaul disgusted and hit send.

When I came to, somewhere in the daylight hours, I saw that tweet. I was shocked; usually I'm such a good drunk! I quickly deleted it and tweeted a decoy – @RuPaul disgusted I couldn't push my way to the front for ur RHI show, but glad I was front row in Hi-Fi! Chookers for tonight – and hoped she hadn't seen it already.

When I entered the workroom for *Drag Race* I was experiencing a mild fear that a giant novelty printout of my tweet would be unfurled and that RuPaul would interrogate me about it. I tried to write off the stories I'd heard so I could go into the show and have my own first-hand experience. Everything I'd heard was second-, third- or fourth-hand, and people love to slag off a celebrity. They misconstrue events, take things out of context and extrapolate things when you're in the public eye. I felt it was best I make my own judgement.

I had been excited to meet the warm, fun man and to be welcomed into his family, as I'd heard him welcome queens in previous seasons. I had been following and admiring RuPaul since my early teenage years, from that 'Supermodel' cassette shown to me covertly by the older boys at Fame, to saving photos of him in a folder on my desktop computer is the early 2000s, or reading his self-help book *Letting It All Hang Out*. I'd watched every episode of *Drag Race* in the previous five years. I was excited about everything I'd seen of RuPaul – I couldn't wait for his energy to inspire our journey week to week.

But the only interaction we had with Ru was when the cameras were rolling. I was surprised there was no introduction beforehand: 'Hi, how are you? Thanks for being here.' No moment where he shook each of our hands or gave us a hug or even looked us in the eye. It was like we, the cast of Season 6, were actually audience members watching at home on TV. Ru never broke the fourth wall with us. Messages like 'Everybody say love' and 'I am your family. We are a family here,' are consistent hallmarks of the franchise, but they never felt authentic in real life.

Even so, I tried to brush my reservations about Ru aside; I figured that maybe, since he was the host, this was his way of preserving professional boundaries. But it was disconcerting. I think we all felt a bit disillusioned, but I did my best to ignore it as we had to spend the next six weeks as subjects on his game show. A contestant on Season 7, Pearl, later famously said that in response to her thanking RuPaul for the opportunity of being on the show, Ru turned to her and said, 'Nothing you say matters unless the camera is rolling.' I think that sums the experience up. People often ask what it was like to meet RuPaul; despite spending six weeks in the same room as him, I honestly never felt like I did.

Vulnerability and authenticity are what Ru, the judges and the producers constantly tell you they want from you, and so we all dug deep and gave it in spades, which can be hard when it doesn't feel reciprocated. We were there to perform, and I had gone into the show wanting to be genuine and to connect with others and the experience, but there were some structural reasons that made that almost impossible to achieve. For example, before we met Ru for the first time, we were told that he often wouldn't look at us when talking because of 'sight lines'; this isn't something I have come across in television since as a contestant or host.

In one of the episodes Ru came over to me in a workroom walkthrough and, after hitting the story points they were following, as he stared past my left shoulder he said to me in a Kath and Kim-style tone, 'I have one word for you, Courtney: humanity.' I was confused; I felt that I was trying to bring exactly that to *Drag Race*, so the suggestion I was lacking humanity perplexed me. I have since learnt that when story producers and hosts of reality TV start asking questions or making statements that don't make sense, it's usually an indication of the story they are going to tell on television, despite what is going on in real life.

18

Season 6 of *Drag Race* aired ten months after we had filmed the show, and I was in for a rude shock.

It started well, at least. An early highlight was watching *Shade: The Rusical* on Episode 4, the musical-theatre challenge I had won. Online, people were praising my performance. Everything was going really well; my social media followers were ticking up, my calendar was filling with high-paying gigs all around the USA, and at those gigs I felt really loved.

A turning point in my 'narrative' on the show occurred during Episodes 5 and 6. Episode 5 was the infamous Snatch Game; my Fran Drescher impersonation was by the by, and I was somewhat absent from the episode. I wasn't really featured much in Episode 6, the rap challenge, despite thinking I had done really well. No storyline, no confessional quips, just the bare bones of the performance. It was like I disappeared for two episodes.

When I returned in Episode 7, the Courtney I saw had a totally different vibe from the Courtney of the first few episodes. In particular, there was a whole narrative that was fabricated between Joslyn Fox and me that turned me into a cold, mean and bitchy character who I just didn't recognise.

Joslyn is an adorable queen from Massachusetts who is four years younger than me. She knew of me before walking into the workroom, but they set up this storyline that she was a Courtney Act fan and I was being dismissive of her. If Joslyn had felt hurt by me this was never something she or a story producer mentioned, but it became one of my main storylines in the second half of the show.

In Episode 7, Joslyn and I were paired together for the maxi challenge. We had to create a beauty advertorial for a range of makeup. During the planning process, Joslyn set me up for a playful dig: 'Imagine if you were the before...'

'But the problem is no one will ever believe that you're the after,' I quipped back. In real life we both chuckled, but on TV it cut to a shot of Joslyn looking dejected, with me laughing loudly at her face, and a metallic sound effect to really drive home how much I had offended her.

I was portrayed as being mean to a fan, and the online world of fans read into this interaction as if I was being mean to one of them. After that episode aired, I received a lot of comments on social media asking me why I had been mean to Joslyn. Years later, comments still pop up about this interaction.

Another comment I often hear from fans of the show is about one of the few bright spots in the second half of the season. In Episode 9, the runway theme was Animal Kingdom Couture, and I strutted in thigh-high boots, a moulded plastic bodice, feather hackle pads on my eyes and slicked-back hair, all in a light blue-grey. When I got to the end of the runway I pressed down on a lever behind my back that expanded the pair of mechanical wings I'd gone to such lengths to procure from Australia. With the eight-foot wingspan, I created an iconic moment in *Drag Race* herstory. (If I do say so myself; I mean, it was immortalised in *The Simpsons* and everything!)

Nonetheless, it was in the second half of the season that I started to feel the show's presentation of me diverge quite a lot from my recollection of the filming. I had felt that, by the time ABCD made it to the final four, it had been smooth sailing. We were all getting along so well and there was no conflict to speak of. I remember Adore, Bianca, Darienne and me making jokes about it being a very different kumbaya end to the season. It felt special, and so different from what I had seen before on *Drag Race*. In fact, it was my ABCD sisters who helped me through the tough time I went through as the later episodes of the season aired and in the immediate aftermath.

I'd gone into the experience of filming the show bright eyed and excited about delivering a new kind of narrative on reality TV. Rather than starting fights or being bitchy, I was going to show the world that being rational, kind, calm and non-reactive was also a possibility. I thought there were so many negative examples of how to act on reality TV and I wanted to add another archetype I hadn't seen before. I had found myself in a mediator role on several occasions when I could see conflicts emerging, but I remember at one point a producer asked me to not defuse situations. Even though that was so counterintuitive to my approach in real life, I tried my best to step back.

Although I had been working in TV in different capacities in Australia for the previous ten years, I didn't realise how naïve I was about the process of making reality TV. I genuinely believed they were making a documentary of actual events that occurred in this manufactured world. But when I saw it on-screen, I was heartbroken to see that the show exaggerated my cattiness instead of my attempts at kindness. The best way I can put it is that the producers and editors took 10 per cent of my character and turned it into 80 per cent of my storyline.

When someone on reality TV blames the edit, people often respond, 'You said it; those words came out of your mouth,' but so much of our interpretation of dialogue and action comes from the context: the mood created by music, sound effects, reaction shots and, of course, which parts the editors choose to show or not show. There are usually two parts to reality TV: the action they are filming on set and the commentary given after the fact in a confessional-style interview. Story producers use these interviews to craft the narrative around each contestant/ character.

In hindsight, part of the problem with my 'character' on *Drag Race* was that the show doesn't foreground experience and confidence: the producers want relatability. Ru and the story producers kept hinting at this on the show – as when Ru had said to me, 'I have one word for you, Courtney: humanity' – but I couldn't understand what they meant. It's only years later, as I write this, that I think I've identified the issue with my character and narrative: if they were looking to draw entertainment from me out of moments of weakness, they were simply looking in the wrong place.

In American drag culture there is a real theme of being your own cheerleader, because the rest of the world isn't. This cultural norm only works in practice when your capacity to let everyone know how fabulous you are is underscored by deep vulnerability. The problem is that I wasn't vulnerable, at least not in any way the producers could readily recognise. I had told them tales of teenage struggle, the drug years and my battle with crystal meth, of my confusion about sexuality and gender, but among my peers that was all par for the course.

Despite my various struggles, I was very privileged, generally speaking, but especially in the world of drag. I'd had a pretty charmed life: I had parents who loved and supported me, I was

Ian 'Dicko' Dickson (with me *above*) was a champion of mine on *Idol*. The show brought me to national recognition alongside characters like Mark Holden (*left*), Rob 'Millsy' Mills and Shannon Noll (*below*).

Belinda Rolland

After *Idol* I walked every red carpet I was invited to. (*Clockwise from top left:*) Wearing a dress made of photos of TV icon Bert Newton at the 2003 Logie Awards; at the ARIAs, wearing a dress that paid tribute to Delta Goodrem, who at the time was suffering from cancer; at a party with Paris Hilton and 'blonde bombshell pop singer' Sophie Monk. (Technically I'm Sophie's doppelganger, because *Pop Stars* predates *Idol*.)

Belinda Rolland

The early years in Los Angeles, where I moved in 2011.

Above: With the affectionately named 'Mean Gays', featuring future *Drag Race* Pit Crew member Simon Sherry-Wood, second from left.

Left and below: Some of the looks I turned at Rasputin, the WeHo club night put on by Luke Nero.

Below left: Luke with me and my fishbowl glass.

Roy Martin Photography

Two of my most memorable looks from *Drag Race*, photographed by my friend Magnus Hastings after the show.

Left: The look inspired by German singer Klaus Nomi.

Below: Wearing those wings, perched above the City of Angels.

Santiago Felipe

The ABCD of drag: Adore, Bianca and Darienne, my Season 6 sisters, have been a source of friendship and support since we filmed the show back in 2013.

Voss Events

With my fellow top three finalists Bianca Del Rio (*above*) and Adore Delano (*below*).

Rachel Murray/Stringer/Getty Images

Chaz Bono is another friend who I met while filming *Drag Race*. I'll be forever grateful to Chaz for the conversations we've had through the years about gender and identity.

Mike Marsland/WireImage/Getty Images

My infamous entrance on *Celebrity Big Brother UK*, when my skirt fell off on live TV.

With Wendy Richards, my friend and long-time manager. We've been at this together for 15 years, and I couldn't have done it without her. It's wonderful to know that Wendy's in my corner in the wild and crazy world of showbiz!

Mitch Fong

Above: With Mum, Dad and Kim in 2019.

Below: My parents have been my biggest supporters throughout the years. Whether it was at one of my early shows at Stonewall or the filming of *Dancing with the Stars,* it's always such a joy and a privilege to have Mum and Dad in the audience.

thriving in the competition, I was the walking embodiment of the unrealistic beauty standard forced on women. And no one wants to hear a pretty, privileged girl talk about how good she is or how good she's had it. For this reason, any quips about my success, or barbs towards other contestants, had nowhere to land but in Unrelatable Town.

'You don't have a chip on your shoulder. There is no dark motivation to your drag. You just do it because you love it,' Mathu Andersen, RuPaul's hair and makeup artist, told me not long after *Drag Race* aired. As we ate lunch at Café Gratitude in Larchmont, with Mathu speaking in his diluted Australian accent and stroking his luscious grey beard, he tried to pinpoint what had gone 'wrong' with my edit. Before the show he'd told me I was the 'heir apparent to RuPaul'; he'd seen big things in my future. But in the wake of the show he told me I'd come across as 'frozen Barbie fish sticks'.

I'm revisiting all of these memories to explain why I felt so terrible at the filming of the finale, which took place after most of the season had aired. When the 14 of us were whittled down to the final three, the sentiment in the fandom was clear: Adore and Bianca were loved and Courtney was third. Which, looking back now, I am so grateful for and proud of, but at the time the experience was marred by the on-screen Courtney and online reaction. It was reflected in followers, attendance at my live gigs and the applause when we taped the grand finale.

The reason I was so distressed wasn't because I didn't win, or because Adore and Bianca were the favourites to win. It was because in the experience of watching the show, I was starting to question my own memories. The main events were all the same, but all the nuance was skewed. The Courtney I saw on TV wasn't horrible: she just wasn't me.

The first sign that my edit wouldn't match my experience of filming the show had been when I was talking to a couple of guys at The Abbey in West Hollywood before *Drag Race* started airing. I was out of drag, and a few sentences into our conversation one of the guys had suddenly clicked: 'I've been staring at your face all day. I'm one of the editors of *Drag Race*.'

'Lovely to meet you. I can't wait for it to go to air!'

'You probably won't feel that once you see it,' he'd said with a chuckle that I hoped was sarcastic. I was slightly taken aback, and that little fear inside me was tripped. Now I was watching those fears unfold in real time each week.

Reality TV of this nature is reductive by definition. Producers and editors take two or three days of filming and chop it down to the most sensational 42 minutes. The characters need to be clearly defined and separate. Each portrays a familiar archetype that audiences can latch onto and champion or rail against. That process, while by no means exclusive to *Drag Race*, is literally dehumanising, as a complex individual is distilled down to a set of catchphrases and extreme behaviours for the purpose of entertainment.

I understand that the simplicity of those now two-dimensional characters is what endears them to the audience, because it makes them accessible and tells a story, and you need that to make the show work. *Drag Race* is one of my favourite shows on TV; I love watching every episode and texting my friends and other *Drag Race* sisters to discuss, dissect and disseminate the happenings. I love being inspired by the creativity and character of each of the girls on the show. I am forever grateful for the platform the show, World of Wonder and RuPaul have given me, and I am forever grateful for the way the show has influenced the mainstream and progressed queer visibility. But I can hold all of this love and gratitude towards the show while also knowing that I was hurt by my portrayal – and, if I am honest, I know I was also let down by the difference between my high expectations and the actual result.

The term 'gaslighting' wasn't in the vernacular then like it is now, but that term describes my experience of watching the show back on TV: a kind of psychological manipulation in which someone is made to doubt their own memory, perception or judgement. This can often result in a sense of cognitive dissonance and/or other changes such as low self-esteem. I don't think that anyone involved in the production of *Drag Race* set out to gaslight us contestants, but it is how I was left feeling in the aftermath. I guess that's just the collateral damage of reality TV – the cost of doing business.

Then there is the online world, the comments, the followers, the trolls. You get a slanted view when you go online. A very vocal minority takes up most of the digital oxygen, and it's hard to gain any perspective. I remember becoming obsessed with what people were saying about me online. I would spend the first and last hour of every day, and every spare moment in between, scrolling through the comments. Looking back, it was really unhealthy to bookend my day with digital dribble, because it's impossible to stop the comments influencing your self-perception in some way. I would reply to as many as possible, trying to convey a warm and friendly persona. I would follow back anyone who left a nice comment on Twitter, hoping to win their love with my follow. I was overcompensating for the Courtney on TV who was seen as being mean to Joslyn Fox.

Michelle Visage, one of the judges on *Drag Race*, always tells the girls on the show not to blame the edit, and consistently shames them for doing so. RuPaul and Michelle even devoted a whole episode of their podcast *What's the Tee?* to the topic 'Don't blame the edit'. But in the first string of tweets she made when evicted as a housemate from the *Celebrity Big Brother* house in 2015 she wrote: good LORD. i am now hearing about all of the edits. i am now one of 'them'. i only WISH you could've seen what i TRULY said #CBBUK. Funny how the story changes when the heel is on the other foot.

It wasn't that I was salty about losing; it was why I lost and how that impacted my life and my livelihood that upset me. If I had seen myself reflected back on the TV, plus or minus 20 per cent of what I understood to be accurate, I would have been fine with accepting that people didn't like me, or that I didn't have as many followers or that fewer people showed up to my gigs. But everyone having an opinion on someone else's constructed reality of my experience was hard. I felt ashamed wherever I went.

I've been rewatching *Drag Race* while writing this chapter. It still doesn't ring true to my experience, but it's not nearly as bad as I remember, and doesn't hurt nearly as much to watch. With seven years' distance from the show I'm able to feel some resolution; life has gone on and I know how that chapter of my life ends. Even to this day, when someone says they loved me on *Drag Race* I cringe a little, because I didn't love the person I saw. But most people don't remember that. They just remember the fun and the camp, and maybe that I wore a big set of wings.

In the immediate aftermath of *Drag Race* I felt cracked open and I was struggling to put the pieces back together. I didn't enjoy doing the gigs; I felt anxious that the audience didn't like me, and I got stuck in a world of comparing myself to the other queens, to their Instagram followers and likes. Despite having more commercial success, more money and more opportunities than I'd had before the show, I was miserable.

Try as I might I couldn't get out of my funk, and I knew I needed to take drastic action or I would slip deeper into depression. Of all the self-help books and fads I have tried over the years the only method I still hold on to today, the one that actually works for me, is meditation.

After I broke my heart and my leg in 2008, still on crutches, I'd hobbled off to a ten-day silent Vipassana meditation retreat in the Blue Mountains, just outside of Sydney. For 11 hours a day I sat completely still and silent. It was the hardest and most transformative experience I have ever had. The purpose of this meditation was to see reality as it is, not as you want it to be, and I was left with a profound sense of peace that had remained with me until the wheels started to fall off the proverbial *Drag Race* cart.

That peace was still MIA eight months later. I booked myself into a three-day Vipassana retreat in Joshua Tree; this would be the longest I'd had off since the *Drag Race* juggernaut started rolling. I needed to hit the reset button, because being on reality TV had caused me to lose touch with reality.

Through meditation I let go of the habitual negative self-talk. Those three days brought me back to my senses, and I don't mean that as a platitude; in Vipassana you are made to focus on the sensations of your body.

It was exactly what I needed to shake off the *Drag Race* juju, and I once again felt connected to myself rather than all the noise.

I got a call from Wendy.

'I'm back,' I proclaimed. 'I don't know where I went. But I'm back.'

'I'm so glad. You were gone for a while and I was worried you weren't coming back.'

Neither of us was talking about my return from the Vipassana retreat. I had clawed my way out of the deep, dark hole of my post-*Drag Race* mind: I had returned to the present moment. I wasn't 'cured', but the intense meditation had turned me around and pointed me back in the right direction: I became determined to take my broken heart and turn it into art, as Carrie Fisher famously said. I needed to show the fandom who *I* thought I was.

19

One of the maxi challenges in an episode of *Drag Race* had been hosting a chat show that included an interview with Chaz Bono and his grandmother Georgia Holt. Chaz is an actor, author and trans activist who also happens to be the son of Sonny and Cher. I actually won that challenge; hosting my own chat/variety show has always been a dream (one that has come true a few times since), so it was a good test of my skills. I loved the glory of winning, but the more lasting impact of that day has been my friendship with Chaz.

Chaz got in contact with me after *Drag Race* because a live show he was working on, called *30 Minute Musical*, was looking to cast a drag queen who could sing. I joined the Christmas season, had a lot of fun and met a really lovely bunch of folks. Through the process Chaz and I started hanging out, having dinners and watching movies. It became clear that my knowledge of American cinema was limited, so Chaz educated me in some classics including *The Godfather*, *Gandhi* and *Sophie's Choice*. We would order in then sit and talk for hours, which I really appreciated because I had very few straight friends and even fewer straight male friends. I had recently vowed to make more straight friends; the cultural tide was turning in the big scary heteronormative world, and I felt safe enough to venture out of my protective queer bubble.

Chaz has such a unique understanding of the queer world and gender. Our friendship was a place where we could have intellectual conversations that made me feel supported, but also challenged me in ways that I didn't experience with my gay male friends. Chaz had the unique viewpoint of a straight man with none of the fragility of a cis straight guy.

I suspected Chaz might have a little crush on me; he had been flirty on *Drag Race*, which might have just been for TV, but I also got a sense when we were hanging out that there was something more there. I think he was confused by this because he's attracted to women, and he later said he had always preached fluid sexuality but never experienced it personally until meeting me. He described me, as a boy, as having a feminine side, which I knew wasn't intended to cause offence – but I felt my feathers ruffle up nonetheless. However, because of the person who said it and the context, I could see I was reacting to something that wasn't in the room.

In our conversations about gender, drag and sexuality, I told Chaz about the trans women I had grown up with on the drag scene in Sydney and described my understanding that most trans women had been gay men who did drag before making the decision to transition. Chaz looked a little confused by this, then told me that is not the experience of most trans women at all – that the majority of trans women don't have a background in performance or drag. Because Chaz has long been an advocate for the trans community, and I knew he was more knowledgeable than I was, I trusted what he said even though it was contrary to my experience. I definitely knew a lot more trans people than most, but I could see how it was possible that I only knew a sample of one kind of trans people.

In our safe space of curious inquiry I decided to ask Chaz a question I'd been asking myself since the Sydney years: 'Do you think that one day in the future trans people will be so accepted in society that they won't have to transition medically or surgically?'

Chaz's response was unequivocal: 'No. Absolutely not. My top surgery was absolutely necessary to me being authentically me.'

Not the answer I was expecting. But through that conversation with Chaz, I was able to finally understand the trans experience in greater depth, despite my presumed proximity to it most of my life.

'So you don't think that the reason you had to have surgery to feel like yourself was because society wasn't accepting of you as you were?'

'No, Shane, not at all. You think that because it's not your experience. You can't understand the experience because it doesn't apply to you, but my transition had nothing to do with how the world saw me and everything to do with how I felt inside.'

Chaz was right: I didn't understand his experience. But I knew he was a smart, assured, compassionate, insightful guy who was in tune with himself, and he was being generous with me as his friend by letting me know such deeply personal feelings. Because of his work as an activist and advocate for the trans community, Chaz was also well equipped to articulate the complex and nuanced experiences beyond his personal journey. With the benefit of hindsight, I can also see that it might have been easier for me to accept what Chaz said because he was a guy; I wasn't able to overlay his experience as a trans man onto my own old anxieties about whether I was a trans woman. It's also important to note that

Chaz's identity is unique to him, as is every transition. Some people feel surgery is right for them and some don't.

And so something magical happened: I simply trusted and believed what Chaz said, even though it contradicted my prior understanding. This was a big moment for me: responding with empathy to what Chaz was telling me, and letting this new information change my perspective.

Before this moment I'd thought empathy just entailed understanding someone else's experience, but there is more to it than that. Empathy is defined by the choice to understand someone else's experience not through your own lens but through theirs. It means letting go of our own worldviews in order to believe someone else's. Before this pivotal conversation I'd filtered my understanding of the trans experience through my own experience, but now I could see I was really just projecting my values onto people who had their own personal experiences.

The world was starting to change. Chaz had been on *Dancing with the Stars* a couple of years prior and had published memoirs about his experience. Around this time I read Jennifer Finney Boylan's autobiography *She's Not There*, about her life as a professor at Columbia University, her wife and two kids, and her transition. Kate Bornstein's *Gender Outlaw* was full of queer theory that broke down the old paradigms and explained the system. Facebook brought in 50 different classifications for gender. Laverne Cox was on the new hit Netflix show *Orange Is the New Black*, and in January 2014 when she was being interviewed by Katie Couric she was asked her about genital surgery.

Laverne put Katie in her place: 'I do feel there is a preoccupation with that. The preoccupation with transition and surgery objectifies trans people. And then we don't get to really deal with the real lived experiences.'

Laverne was calm, concise, powerful, and she didn't make a joke. She didn't apologise for being there and she held Katie to account. This was a pivotal moment in the public image of trans people. Laverne owned the interview and commanded respect, and it was powerful.

The next month, Janet Mock appeared on *Piers Morgan Live* to promote her book *Redefining Realness*, an honest and beautiful memoir. I was in awe seeing a trans woman on such a mainstream show. I was inspired by how Janet spoke in the interview, but when the show aired she tweeted a series of criticisms tagging the show's Instagram account, including a reply to a tweet of theirs that read:

> How would you feel if you found out the woman you are dating was formerly a man? @JanetMock shares her experience now. #RedefiningRealness

Janet replied:

> .@PiersMorganLive I was not 'formerly a man.' Pls stop sensationalizing my life and misgendering trans women. #redefiningrealness

I'll be honest: at the time I didn't quite understand why Janet was upset. I was so used to the language of the tweet, as I'd heard the trans experience framed in these terms by the media all the time. In fact, I thought that Piers inviting Janet on to talk about her book was a huge step in the right direction. And it was, but representation matters and I now understand why this language was so problematic. Time for another Courtney Fact.

COURTNEY FACT

The tweet from the *Piers Morgan Live* account frames trans identity as something that is used to deceive others. The idea that trans women are 'formerly men' reinforces the categorically false notion that trans women are men. When someone says a trans woman was 'born a man', we need to reflect on the fact that no one is born a man; we are born babies, unaware of the gendered world already swirling around us. Yes, our sex is observed at birth, defined by our genitals, and for most people that categorisation fits with our gender, but not for trans folk. It wasn't a name, clothes, hormones or surgery that made Janet a woman; she was always a woman. When Janet had agency over her life she changed her name, clothes, hormones and body to align with the woman she always knew herself to be.

This isn't semantics: it's a really important paradigm shift from the reductive understanding of 'formerly a man'. Language is important, especially when talking about marginalised communities who have been historically misrepresented. There is a documentary on Netflix called *Disclosure* that beautifully articulates through the voices of trans interviewees the nuances of trans representation in the media. I recommend everyone (especially Piers) check it out. For trans allies in the media, it is incumbent upon us to understand these nuances and lead by example, using language correctly.

Following a huge furore that emerged on Twitter in response to the tweet from the show, Piers invited Janet back on the following night. He opened the interview with a 90-second rant about why he was upset, then asked Janet questions with language that fixated on her assigned sex at birth, gender affirmation surgery, when she changed from her birth name to Janet, and the disclosure of her trans status to her partner. She remained calm and stated her case, but Piers didn't listen to what Janet said, talking over her and failing to hear what she was really saying. By reducing Janet to the most basic media tropes of the trans experience, Piers' interview questions and commentary were transphobic. You could see Piers probably wasn't trying to be offensive, any more than Piers ordinarily is, and I don't think he was out of step with any other interviewer of the time – but that doesn't mean he didn't get it wrong.

Between Laverne and Janet schooling Katie and Piers, a precedent was set for how to talk about and to trans people in the media. Trans people are no longer here to answer your invasive questions; they are no longer going to be sensationalised. They are real people, with rich experiences worthy of respect and airtime. Even if the media wasn't capable of understanding these shifts in language and framing, trans people were no longer waiting for false allies to catch up. If someone was truly an ally, they would do the work to understand beforehand. Is giving someone a slot on your TV show and ignorantly exploiting them with puerile questions being an ally?

I am glad that Janet and Laverne, two exceptional women, spoke up back in 2014. Having them as strong role models certainly had an important impact on my own ability to understand my gender identity when the time came. Visibility matters to those who are reflected, and influences worldviews at large. That said, visibility without protection is a trap. We are seeing anti-trans laws and violence towards trans folk skyrocketing all around the world as a form of cultural backlash. Visibility needs to be backed up by allies and laws ensuring the safety, dignity and respect of trans people.

It was around this time that Season 6 of *Drag Race* was airing, and after one particular episode aired on 17 March 2014, a debate about its mini-challenge erupted online. We contestants had been given paddles that on one side read *Female* and the other *Shemale.* We were shown close-up photos of cis women and drag queens and had to guess which group they belonged to by holding the paddle up.

The term 'shemale' became associated with trans women through the porn industry, and has become a pejorative term often used to belittle or fetishise them. The meaning of words change over time, but even by 2014 standards this term shouldn't have been included in the show. Tbh, when we filmed the show in the spring of 2013, I wasn't enough of an ally to twig that there was something wrong with the term. I wish I had been aware and spoken up on set.

The use of the slur fanned a flame already burning within the drag and queer communities. Near the top of each *Drag Race* episode there was a voice-over saying, 'You've got she-mail', which is a spoof of 'Tyra Mail' from *America's Next Top Model* with Tyra Banks and the iconic AOL inbox greeting. The first season of *Drag Race* was filmed in 2008, when the phrase might've been seen as a cute play on words, but as the years went on and trans visibility in the media increased, people raised questions about whether the trivialising use of this slur was appropriate.

When Viacom, the broadcaster of *Drag Race*, did eventually decide to remove the slur from future airings of the show, Ru made it known it wasn't his choice. 'You'd have to ask [the network] why they did it,' he told *Vulture* in 2016, 'but I had nothing to do with that.' Ru also stated in an interview with the *Guardian* that trans people would 'probably not' be allowed on the show if they had begun to transition, and in 2018 he drew a peculiar comparison in a tweet (which he later apologised for): You can take performance enhancing drugs and still be an athlete, just not in the Olympics.

Ru's past brushes with transphobia, coupled with his repeated use of the T-word at that time, meant that I didn't want to remain silent on the matter, especially as I was on the episode that had initiated this latest conversation about transphobia on the show. I wrote a Facebook post and sent it to Wendy to read over, as I usually do before I post something that I know might be sensitive. She gave me some very good feedback on how I was framing the post and made suggestions on how to make it less inflammatory. My goal wasn't to fight. I thought the argument about the words was missing the real point: that trans people are the most marginalised in the queer community, and we should be listening to them and lifting them up, not telling them how they should feel. On 26 May 2014, I made a post online to this effect – here's an abbreviated version:

> I'm a little surprised by @rupauls recent reaction to trans issues. I understand and apply in my own life the logic about not giving other people power over how I feel, but I am not 1 in 12 trans people in America who will be murdered...
>
> What would be energy better spent right now is focusing on helping trans people improve their quality of life. Here

are some facts I'm sure we all can agree are not acceptable and that we need to come together and bring about positive change:

TRANSGENDER FACTS

1 in 12 transgender people in America is murdered. (This one fact alone is more than enough.)

Although social acceptance for transgender people is growing, parents continue to abandon youth with gender-identity issues when their children need them most, advocates say.

49 per cent of transgender people attempt suicide.

Transgender youth account for 18 per cent of homeless people in cities such as Chicago, but researchers estimate fewer than 1 in 1000 people is transgender.

Transgender youth whose parents pressure them to conform to their anatomical gender report higher levels of depression, illegal drug use, suicide attempts and unsafe sex than peers who receive little or no pressure from parents.

Sources: Guidelines for Transgender Care (2006), Gender Spectrum Education and Training, Families in TRANSition (2008)

At the time I thought that this status was going to earn me RuPaul's respect. I wasn't attacking him, like so many were; I was trying to refocus the conversation on our trans siblings and the horrible realities they faced. I guess I was wrong, as a short while later Ru blocked me on Twitter. At first I couldn't work out what was going on; I was trying to tag him in a tweet and the platform wouldn't let me. When I clicked on his profile

I was greeted by the message, @rupaul has blocked you. I was kinda gagged; in fact, I felt shamed at first. I didn't tell anyone for a while, and then just some friends, and about a year later I talked about it publicly.

My point in including this story is not to grandstand or to brag, but to show that my personal understanding was changing all the time, and it's important to have these hard conversations as an ally in order to try to change people's minds. Sometimes it doesn't work, and sometimes it comes at a cost, but these conversations are worth it because they're a sign of respect for the trans and gender-diverse people in my life. It has also been wonderful to see *Drag Race* expand its view on which kinds of drag are valid over the seasons. These days we see out trans men and women, non-binary folk and AFAB queens competing, and in the most recent season of *All Stars*, Kylie Sonique Love, a trans woman, took home the crown.

On 29 May 2014, just a month after the online backlash about the *Drag Race* episode, Laverne Cox appeared on the cover of *Time* magazine with the headline 'The Transgender Tipping Point'. Slowly but surely, the world was changing.

20

'No sleep! Bus, club, 'nother club, 'nother club, 'nother club, plane, next place. No sleep.' Lady Gaga's immortal words from an interview describing her life on the road perfectly described ours in the wake of *Drag Race.* Now that the weekly trauma of the show airing on TV was over, I was in four or five cities a week, and often away from home for months at a time. There was no logic to the touring geography; I remember in one day I flew from Provincetown in Massachusetts six hours across the country for a lunchtime meet-and-greet at an American Apparel store in Portland, before flying another five hours back to NYC that night. I basically went to whatever gig was booked. There were silver linings to the schedule, though; after the previous few years of making a modest living in LA, and seeing that looming overdraft still sitting there, I was now making bank. I was a Ru girl, and I was touring the world.

Much of this post-show touring phase passed by in a blur. I would average four hours of sleep a night in an actual bed, and the rest of the time I would sleep in the back of a car, against a plane window or on the airport floor during a layover. During the filming of *Australian Idol,* I remember Marcia Hines giving her pro tip for our new lives as touring artists: sleep whenever you get the chance. It was true and good advice.

When I would arrive at my hotel room in the next city, there were usually two or three hours till I had to be ready for the show that night. Sometimes I would opt for an hour nap there, and during that time Moses, my friend-cum-assistant, would find a local vegan haunt to get us some takeaway that I would eat while beating my face.

The Four Points by Sheraton, the DoubleTree by Hilton, the Country Inn by Raddison – the hotels we stayed in were never the actual luxury brand, but rather a budget spin-off. I started to think that many US city centres consisted solely of a Walmart, because we would often be staying next to one. We didn't get to see the actual city, just the airport, the drive to the hotel, the view of the Walmart car park out the hotel room window, and the drive to and from the venue. (Incidentally, I sit here writing in a similar three-star hotel in Sydney's Olympic Park. This time, though, I am here for two weeks, quarantining on my return to Australia during the Covid pandemic. These hotels are fine for a fleeting layover to do makeup in and have a nap; not so thrilling for two weeks of solitary confinement. But I digress…)

We always had two rooms when on tour, one for Moses and one for me. There would usually be two double beds in each room, one I designated for eating and one for sleeping. The sleeping bed was used as labelled, though the eating bed was more versatile; it could also be used for unpacking drag and counting tips and the fee from the gig. In the US it's customary to tip drag queens while they perform, which I found quite confusing when I first arrived; it can feel a bit cheap and interrupt any magic you are trying to create during a number.

In the beginning I would resist collecting the bills offered my way, but that just felt rude. I came to understand that an audience member giving me a tip was less about the value of Washington, Lincoln or Hamilton's cameo and more about the audience member's ability to connect with me. Tipping in the service industry is an essential part of the US economy, and the same goes for drag queens performing in bars and clubs, who get a small fee for doing the show while the main portion of their loot is made in tips. The magic queens create is always over and above whatever they are paid.

The equation was different for *Drag Race* queens, however. We were getting large sums of money for these gigs, so I didn't like taking the tips. It felt as if I was taking money from the local girls. Sometimes I would try to give my tips to the local queens in the lineup after the show, but it would always cause a fuss and often seem grandiose and patronising.

Doing these club shows wasn't really the best use of my skills, either. Some queens are masters at a slick lip-sync, whipping the 1 am gay bar crowd into a frenzy, the audience making it rain dollar bills. These girls would do three-minute numbers with costume reveals, death drops and jump splits, and I would watch in awe. Singing live on a gay bar sound system, on the other hand, is fraught with danger, and more often than not the set-up didn't allow me to deliver my best.

Also, to be honest, I was still struggling a bit. Added to the stress of travelling, I started experiencing anxiety at gigs thinking that the audience didn't like me. Every time I would take to the stage I tried to shake the feeling that the audience would have preferred to see Adore or Bianca, and when the crowds were thin I would blame myself, knowing that all the gigs of my top three sisters would be sold out weeks in advance. And if the crowd *did* like me, I couldn't connect with that either, because I felt they liked a Courtney from TV who wasn't me.

June rolled around: Pride Month in the US. At the beginning of June I was actually in Vienna, Austria, kicking off the celebration in the best possible way. I spent those first hours of Pride Month shuffling a man out of my hotel, frantically trying to pack for my flight back to New York, while scrubbing the night's outfit – gold glitter adhered with surgical adhesive – off my body. The evening before I'd been at the famed Life Ball, a huge celebration that has raised over $45 million for HIV/AIDS charities. It was a star-studded event, and the man I was ushering out of my room was one of the celebrities in attendance. (I didn't actually know who he was until the flight home, when I shared a photo with a queen sitting next to me. I would tell you more about him, but I wouldn't want to kiss and tell.)

From Vienna to JFK to LAX, a day off to do laundry, sleep in my own bed and re-pack, then it was off to Chicago. Pride Month was packed: that first week alone I would be at Roscoe's Tavern in Chicago on Wednesday; Thursday was a travel day; Friday was Pride in Indianapolis, Indiana; Saturday we were at the Town Dance Boutique in DC; and Sunday was Capital Pride, a huge outdoor festival stage with the United States Capitol Building providing the backdrop. In the weeks after, I would be in LA, San Francisco, Pomona, Denver, Detroit, LA again and Chicago again. Then I would head to Toronto for World Pride for four nights with Darienne, Bianca and Adore, and then we would all travel to NYC to march in the Pride Parade.

One small memory I hold on to of ABCD during that hectic touring time is when we landed in NYC to find our hotel rooms not ready. Having not slept during our red-eye flight, all four of us planted ourselves on the floor in the lobby of the Hudson Hotel and fell asleep. Adore and I snuggled into Darienne, with Bianca perched in a chair next to us until check-in.

In spite of some anxieties on tour I really appreciated the opportunities that were presenting themselves to me, and this new lifestyle felt so rockstar, flying around the country and the world doing gigs. And part of this lifestyle was the sex: leaving boys in hotel beds, having boys in different ports. It didn't feel as slutty as it sounds when you hear someone say 'a boy in every port'; I had repeat romances with a couple of boys in a few cities, and formed unique connections with them too. OK: I was totally being slutty. I just called myself out as I wrote that; I was having as much sex with as many people as possible, and it was really fun. No self-slut-shaming here. My lifestyle was spinning so fast that having one boyfriend in one place didn't make sense. My on-the-road romances felt practical and thrilling, and enough to make me feel satiated while on this crazy tour schedule.

One of the first boys on tour was Evan. To set the scene: I'm at a meet-and-greet with my Season 6 sisters at Roscoe's in Chicago. A six-foot-three blond walks up to me wearing only black-rimmed glasses and a pair of boxer briefs. He would have caught my eye in the line anyway, but this near-nudity really made sure he stood out.

At a meet-and-greet you're lucky to get 30 seconds with a person: you say hello, take a photo and then it's on to the next in line. In this instance there were ten other people in the photo lineup – no, not just people, drag queens! Evan walked past all of them, came straight up to me, said hello, we posed for a photo and then looked at each other and started making out furiously.

The other girls started whooping and heckling. My lipstick was smeared all over our faces, and I was smiling from ear to ear. I heard Bianca say in a loud and commanding tone, 'All right, queen, we got a meet-and-greet to do, keep it moving,' so I grabbed Evan's phone and put my number in it. He said it was his birthday, and I told him that I had a present for him.

By the time I got back to the hotel and had a moment to myself to check my phone, I was too late: Evan was home already. Damn.

But it's your birthday and you haven't unwrapped the present I got you! I wrote.

Let me jump on my skateboard and I'm on my way.

Ahh, my sk8er boi was on his way. I needed to prepare the corpse, and quickly! Some mouthwash, lip liner, a little lip gloss, good as new. I decided I'd better wash my junk too; they'd been tucked away all night long and I was sure they didn't smell cute, let alone taste cute.

I decided to put my meet-and-greet outfit back on because it was kinda skater girl vibes: a pair of black pleather American Apparel overall shorts, a hot-pink bra with a cage detail on the bottom of it and a black pleather cap to one side and a low pony to the other. Once the music and lighting were cued I plonked myself down on the bed and waited.

After 30 minutes I sent him a text. You still coming?

No reply. Ugh. I figured he'd flaked. I took off my overalls and cap, almost ready to admit defeat and have a shower. I kept my bra on, though, and threw on the grey hooded robe I'd mopped from the Ace Hotel when we were shooting the *Drag Race* finale.

I didn't want to just sit there all pathetic waiting for a boy who probably wouldn't turn up, so I started packing up my makeup to buy some more time.

I zipped up my makeup bag and checked my phone. There was a message! Yeah, sorry, I fell off my skateboard when I was changing trains. Busted my knee open.

Completely ignoring the fact that he was injured, I responded, Changing trains? How far away do you live? Where are you now?

At the station.

Send me the address. I'll send a car.

I felt so pimp. This was the first time I had ever sent a car to bring trade to me (wouldn't be the last time though). Because it was Evan's birthday I splashed on a black SUV.

Twenty minutes later he turned up at my front door, skateboard in hand, blood dripping from his knee. It was so hot. I cleaned up his knee and popped a bandaid on it then proceeded to explore the tattoos on his body. As I did, he told me how he worked in a steel factory. I felt like several porn fantasy plotlines were playing out at once.

I wasn't quite sure what Evan's experience was with boys, or with boys dressed as girls. I presumed that because I was in drag he was straight, but then why would he have been at the meet-and-greet? Not that straight men can't be fans of *Drag Race*, but the usual meet-and-greet demographic is two-thirds women, predominantly straight, and one-third younger queer guys plus a smattering of bears. Not to reinforce a stereotype, but you don't get many single straight men waiting in line to meet a bunch of drag queens. It turned out Evan had been watching *Drag Race* with his ex-girlfriend, her brother and his boyfriend, and he'd commented a few times that he thought I was really cute. As a joke they bought him meet-and-greet tickets for a show, which coincided with his 22nd birthday.

In any case, Evan was into me and I was into him. He seemed pretty comfortable with my penis, so I guessed he'd had some experience in that department. His penis, on the other hand, seemed to be a new member of LIMP: Ladies Impeded by Malfunctioning Phalli.

A few weeks earlier in Saskatoon, Canada, I'd had my first experience with post–*Drag Race* trade. Another boy in a meet-and-greet had been very familiar, amorous and forward; I started to think this must be part of the new rockstar life. This guy, though, was gay and interested in having sex with me as a boy, so we swapped numbers and I went back to my hotel, showered and waited for him to arrive.

Once he was there we got into it. He was very enthusiastic at first, but when I went south with my hands I couldn't feel any… firmness. We were both naked: me rock hard, him limp. He said he'd had half an ecstasy earlier with his friends, and this was probably why he couldn't get it up.

A hard penis is a yardstick for sexual desire, and on this occasion it was 32 inches short of a yardstick. Although I was aware that erectile dysfunction was a thing, and that drugs can affect one's wood, I'd never experienced it myself. I also know that a hard penis isn't an imperative for sexual pleasure, but its absence left me feeling insecure. When this guy left after our encounter I felt a bit weird about his flaccid penis, and my head was filled with all sorts of questions: *Is it me? Was he attracted to me? Am I hideous? Am I too girly? Why was he here if he's not attracted to me? Why doesn't he like me?* This guy had seemed so sure of his attraction, but either he was deceiving me, or his penis was deceiving him.

There was a distant but familiar feeling that I couldn't quite place my finger on. I'd felt like this before, but not for a very long time. Post *Idol* I remember a spate of deflated members coming (or not coming, as it were) into my experience, and the fact that they had returned a decade later in the wake of my second reality TV appearance led me to think that maybe there was a correlation.

I messaged Willam, who had been on Season 4 of *Drag Race* so would have had some post-show notches on her belt. We had worked together a couple of times, and I knew she would be comfortable talking about sex. I ran her through what had happened. I felt embarrassed to even admit that the guy couldn't get it up with me, but I was hoping for some insight.

Has this ever happened to you before?

OMG! Yes! But I thought it was just me. I figured the guys just weren't that into it. Do you think this is a thing?

I messaged Adore and she confirmed it had happened to her, and Willam messaged a few girls and confirmed more cases of this limp-dick epidemic. Later, when Willam and I were discussing the phenomenon with Alaska (the drag queen, not the state), we decided to give the syndrome a name: LIMP, Ladies Impeded by Malfunctioning Phalli. There was also an east coast chapter, SOFT, Sisters Opposed to Flaccid Trade.

We spread the word to our *Drag Race* sisters and there was a strange comfort in the solidarity. We had all been suffering in silence that whole time, thinking it was something unique to us, when it seemed that if a male had seen you on *Drag Race* it rendered his penis debilitated. Ladies, I've just inducted a new member of LIMP is a message Willam, Alaska and I have sent several times to our group thread over the years.

Back to me and Evan in the hotel room in Chicago. After the guy in Canada this was only the second time in recent memory this had happened, so I gave Evan the benefit of the doubt. I asked him if he wanted me to fuck him, but he said he only topped. Evan told me he identified as bisexual, but lived a mostly 'straight' life as he wasn't really out. He'd been with guys, trans girls and cis girls, and enjoyed all of those experiences.

These non-normative sexual experiences always led to the most interesting conversations, when I would lie naked in bed with a stranger hearing the most vulnerable truths about their sexuality and attractions. Even though Evan wasn't out to everyone, he seemed quite resolved in his sense of who he was and who he was attracted to.

Eventually we got back to sexier talk, and we started making out again. I could feel some blood flowing down below and we both managed to finish what we had started. I said good night, called Evan an Uber home, and saved his number in my phone with the note Pashed at Roscoe's meet-and-greet. Bi. Tats. I had another gig in Chicago in 20 days' time, so hopefully I'd get to see him again.

I knew he would be cute, but I didn't expect there to be an instant connection the moment our eyes locked. More than any form of verbal communication or body language, I remember staring into Taylor's eyes as a distinct moment in time. We had both stopped to look at each other against the backdrop of the bustling dressing room, and were abruptly snapped back to reality by the promoter making an announcement to the room: 'All right everyone, let's clear out and give these two some privacy.' As he walked past he leant in and whispered, 'See, I told you Bianca picked out a good one.'

This was all so weird – like an arranged marriage, but we were standing in the basement of a gay bar in Indianapolis, Indiana, smack bang in the middle of the three-day Pride festival. Bianca had performed there the night before and had already flown out to her next gig, so we didn't get to see each other, but she had sent me a text: Girl, there is a boy there I picked out for you. His name is Taylor, he'll be your security guard... Don't say I never give you nothing. This was by no means a common practice; in fact, Bianca is usually the opposite to a catalyst for romance or sex. Not just because of her giant clown makeup; it's almost like she disapproves of such shenanigans. But clearly this time Taylor was an exception to her rule.

Taylor and I now had the dressing room to ourselves, and I was still staring into his big blue-grey doe eyes that were turned down slightly at the corners, which made him look innocent and vulnerable. His hair was brown and floppy, and he had lovely full lips and a strong jawline. He was an all-American corn-fed white-bread midwestern boy, the kind you might see on an Abercrombie & Fitch bag. As it happened, when he wasn't protecting drag queens, he was in fact an Abercrombie catalogue model.

'Hi, I'm Courtney,' I said coyly.

'I'm Oscar,' he said with a slight grin.

'I thought your name was Taylor?'

'That's my work name. I also dance here on other nights.'

'Oh, I get it. I have two names too. I'm Courtney, but sometimes I'm Shane.'

We still hadn't broken eye contact, so I snapped out of it with a cartoon-style head shake. Oscar told me he was a stripper and offered to do a number in the show, and I told him

I would love that. I was trying to be my usual flirty self, but there was an obvious mutual connection and attraction here that made our encounter more innocent, almost schoolyard.

Later that night, after my second number, it was Taylor's turn to take the stage. The room was packed with screaming straight girls and queer people, extra busy 'cause it was Pride and there were Ru girls in town. Usually the crowd in a queer bar like this would have patrons crammed standing-room-only in the front of the stage, but this place had strip-club vibes, with chairs circled around little cocktail tables and raised seating around the edges of a dance floor. There was a long catwalk off a raised stage area, along with lots of club lighting and a big LED video wall. It felt cosy, but very high-tech for a regional bar in Indiana.

The drag queen host announced Taylor as the next performer and the locals got excited. I was excited too, and a little nervous. I didn't have Magic Mike expectations for the show, but as Taylor unbuttoned his light purple business shirt with a navy pinstripe to reveal the Abercrombie body that went with his Abercrombie face I went from being lost in his eyes to lost in his abs. He kept glancing across at me and smiling while doing his number, and after he peeled his shirt from his body he swung it in the air and threw it my way. I caught the shirt and theatrically pulled it to my face, taking in all the pheromones. The people in the crowd were cheering and throwing dollar bills at the stage.

After Taylor's number we continued our coy flirtation backstage. He said I could keep the shirt he threw at me. I still have it in a box in storage in LA; I can't wait to rummage through that box when I'm 70 or 80 and remember that night.

I was excited by what the rest of the evening might entail. I didn't want a quick fumble in the dressing room, but I was also aware that Oscar identified as straight, had only ever been with cis girls before, and was a gentleman. But I was only in town for one night and had to be ready to go to the airport at 6.30 the next morning to fly to Washington DC to perform at Capital Pride. But you make hay while the sun shines, and there was a lot of sunshine and hay being made in Indianapolis. The sun had gone down, but I was hoping I might get to see it come up with Oscar.

I was trying to work out the best way to ask him if he wanted to continue the evening with me somewhere more private when he beat me to it.

'Excuse me, Courtney – I was just wondering if you would like some company this evening in your hotel room?'

'Why yes, Oscar, I would.'

There was something so simple and sweet about Oscar; he was only 21 and seeing the world for the first time. He hadn't seen *Drag Race*, and didn't know anything about me beyond what he had seen that night. In a world where I felt everyone had a preconceived notion about who I was, it was refreshing to meet a stranger.

After a cloak-and-dagger operation to get Oscar into the car – to allow him to be discreet in this small town – we got to the hotel. I kept the lighting as dim as I could muster, with just a single lamp providing enough illumination to blur the mundane surrounds into the background and bring Oscar's eyes into focus.

We started very slow and sweet. Soft kisses, and a lot of eye contact. As we slowly peeled off each other's clothes, I checked to see he was comfortable with the pace and with everything that was going on. It wasn't my first time at the straight-boy rodeo, and I was aware it was all very new for him. Not to sound perverse, but there is a unique enjoyment in sleeping with someone who's never before been with someone who has the same parts. It's usually a less rigid world; my feminine presentation and male anatomy allows some fluid exploration of my mate's sexuality in turn.

I was now in a bra and undies, and Oscar was in only a pair of white jocks. I ran my hand down his hard body to his crotch. 'Is this OK?'

'Yes,' he whispered. I continued to trace the path my hands had explored with my lips and tongue. While I was exploring Oscar's body, specifically his penis, with my mouth, my own penis was still safe and sound in my tucking panties, uncharted territory for him. As he was a newcomer to fellatio performed by a person with a penis, I gave him the full-service experience. You can't forget any of the anatomy; you gotta get those balls in your mouth and use your tongue on the taint while you work the shaft.

I rolled Oscar over and rimmed his hole. I was almost certain this was the first time Oscar's arsehole had been touched with anything other than toilet paper. There was something thrilling in knowing that no person had ever got their mouth this acquainted with this part of Oscar's body before.

It's easy to make a straight guy come from oral, but I wasn't ready for it to be over that quick, even though at 21 I'm sure Oscar had more than one round in him. I eased off as his breath grew heavier and slower and his yelps got louder, and I worked my way back to his mouth. Then he nervously slid his hand down my body and around my cock. He seemed to enjoy it enough that he decided to go down for a closer inspection and taste.

'How's that?' a muffled voice asked from down below.

'Great,' I answered. In truth it was a little toothy, but that was to be expected from a first-timer. As Oscar came back up to kiss me I rolled him onto his back and straddled him, gyrating on his crotch with mine. I grabbed the lube, rolled a condom on his rock-hard cock and slathered it and my hole with lube. We stared deep into each other's eyes again as I slid him inside me.

There is something transcendent about penetration; it's the closest two people can ever get to being one. I started sliding up and down quicker and quicker, still staring into Oscar's eyes as we kissed, then I got up on my feet, rested on my haunches and made the pace even quicker. His breath turned into groans and so did mine. I could feel sweat lubricating our bodies as Oscar let out a groan; knowing his load was inside me, I ejaculated all over his stomach and chest. I fell down in a heap on top of him.

After a few minutes of lying in the silence of the afterglow, Oscar started to stammer something he'd been working up to.

'I don't know when I… I'll be in this position again. Do you want to put it in me?'

'Why yes, Oscar. I do.'

I really admired his pragmatic thinking and zest for new experiences. What a turn-on. It didn't matter that we had both just come; I was up again and ready for it. I engaged the Courtney Act Patented Lubing Technique: lots of silicone-based lube, and not just slapped around the hole; more like you're trying to grease the inside of a bottle rim, slowly and gently and all the way to the second knuckle. First with one finger and then with a second, taking it nice and easy. Some first-timers think they can just sit down on a penis and are quickly shocked by the pain. I always find the best position is for the top to lie on their back, so the bottom has all the control.

Oscar was about to experience a whole new level of pleasure in his hole. He slid down my cock inch by inch as I jerked off his penis. I knew it wouldn't take long for climax; often on a first time there isn't much thrusting back and forth, and just getting it in is enough of an accomplishment for one night. We rolled over so we were both lying on our sides facing each other as I gently thrust myself inside him. I continued jerking him off until I could feel his hole spasm on my penis, and his whole body start convulsing.

Oscar rolled off me and onto his back, and clasped my hand in his. We both lay there staring at the ceiling, catching our breaths, with smiles on our faces. In a perfect world, we would have woken up and gone for breakfast or maybe we would have stayed in bed all day snuggling and fucking. But alas, I had to shower, pack and hopefully get a few hours of sleep in before my flight.

I didn't want him to leave, but I did need to shower. Even though we'd just experienced a most intimate act, there was still the artifice of drag between Oscar and me. I was wearing a bra, wig and makeup – at least from my nose up; the makeup from my nose down was somewhere between Oscar's legs. I told him that when I got back from the shower I wouldn't look like a girl any more; he looked confused, but said he would stay.

After the shower I styled my wet hair and wrapped the towel around my waist, getting myself as cute as possible for Shane to meet Oscar. I felt nervous. Would Oscar still want to kiss me as a boy? Or would he put on his clothes and politely say goodbye?

After a moment's hesitation, there was a smile of recognition as Oscar realised it was all still me. He leant in and started to kiss me, which was the greatest relief – and turn-on. I instantly became hard again. The kisses got faster and the towel came off as we did it all again, but this time Oscar made love to Shane.

At 5.30 am we were rudely awoken by my alarm, having had about an hour of sleep. After hitting the snooze button a few times to nuzzle back into Oscar's arms, I frantically got up and packed my suitcase. Oscar's boss from the club drove us to the airport, and Oscar and I took the back seat. I had the biggest smile on my face. I felt Oscar's hand slide on top of mine, and in the rear-vision mirror I noticed his eyes looking at me. He put his head on my shoulder.

At Indianapolis Airport we had our goodbye kiss. I wondered whether, once I got out of the car and he drove off into the distance, and once the intoxication of the previous hours had worn off, he would return to his heteronormative world, where boys fall in love with girls, and forget all about me. Then again, I hadn't expected Oscar to come in the car to the airport, to be so affectionate in the daylight, or to kiss me in front of his boss. Usually these straight guys would scamper off before the sun came up.

Maybe Oscar would be different. But would I ever see him again? When would I even be back in Indianapolis? No point wondering about a future that hadn't happened yet. I would just have to wait to find out.

Throughout Pride Month, Oscar and I texted and FaceTimed a bunch, and I was smitten. We'd been talking about when we could meet up again; not overly familiar with the geography of the USA, I started google-mapping my upcoming gigs and their proximity to Indianapolis. Two weeks after our first encounter I was going to play a gig in Detroit, only a four-and-a-quarter-hour drive away. Oscar said he could come up to spend the night. I was so excited to see him again, and nervous too. How would he feel when he saw me again? Courtney had been his gateway drug to Shane last time, but this time I would be dressed as a boy. In broad daylight.

When I met Oscar again I could tell we were both feeling a bit awkward, but we fumbled our way through hello and talked about what to get for dinner. This wasn't going to be the long romantic dinner I had planned for our second date, but in some way the haste was a blessing; it didn't give either of us much time to think about our insecurities or my gender presentation. We just had to find somewhere to get a feed. Our best options were Wendy's, Panera Bread or Chipotle. We opted for Chipotle (I know: rookie mistake eating a burrito before anyone bottoms) and went back to the room to eat, on the eating bed of course.

Once we finished our food we rolled around and messed up the sheets – but not too much, because I had to start beating my mug for the show.

I felt a little weird with Oscar being there while I transformed. Having someone watch the process, especially when I'm rushing, takes the magic out of it; they're able to deconstruct the illusion into a linear series of perfunctory steps. I had always liked the theatre and the element of surprise of being a boy or being a girl, and I still didn't feel quite comfortable in between. Also, it should be said that there is nothing sexy about getting into drag; at times in the process I look feline, at others alien, but never sexy. The glamour forms right at the last minute. There is no moment before completion that I am 'in drag'; it's the very last step that brings it all together, and that's usually something as simple as lip gloss, a touch more blush, or earrings. I just don't feel right as Courtney otherwise.

I was still only starting to understand that, while my gender presentation oscillated from one end of the spectrum to the other, my identity, who I am, was always consistent. I always feel like me; there is no point where Shane ends or Courtney begins, as we are two ends of the same stick. The world looks the same to me regardless of how I am dressed; it's the world that looks differently at me. All these thoughts were going through my mind as I got into drag in front of Oscar. I just wanted to present as Courtney as quickly as possible so he didn't get confused by the in-between phase.

In the car to the venue, I felt the full effect of my transformation into Courtney. I said hello to Oscar as if I'd just arrived. I became more girly and flirtatious. Being Courtney allows me to be soft, and in that moment it made me more comfortable because I felt I was presenting in the way Oscar would find most attractive. As a girl I have the confidence of a universal appeal, while I know my appeal as a boy is more niche.

Let's just say I shouldn't have worried so much. It was 3.30 am when we stumbled back to the hotel room after the gig, which gave us five hours before my wake-up call to consummate our second date, shower and sleep. Once we'd finished our shower we took to the sleeping bed and broke the bedding designation rules. Our sex was wet and drunk and fun.

Afterwards we fell asleep, and two and half hours later my alarm woke me up. This time I left Oscar in bed to sleep, kissed him softly on the cheek and snuck out as quietly as possible.

I was back in Chicago at Roscoe's Tavern, but this time just with Adore, Bianca, Darienne and BenDeLaCreme. We were all in the dressing room catching up when we heard a knock at the door and were delivered a copy of *Billboard* magazine. The official US music rag is known for its charts including the prestigious Billboard 200, which ranks that week's most popular albums in the nation. We all gathered around as Adore flipped through to reveal that her debut album, *Till Death Do Us Party*, was at number 59.

I have to admit that, in the moment, I was conflicted seeing Adore's music career take off, because she was living my dream. On 14 May I had released a song and music video called 'Mean Gays'. It got heaps of attention, including tweets from Kylie and Gaga, and the video racked up a quarter of a million views in the first week. Then Adore released her first single, 'DTF', followed two weeks later by her amazing single 'I Adore You' and her album. People were in love with her music, and she had the metrics to prove it. My modest success now felt insignificant, especially because Adore and I had been compared on *Drag Race* for our singing ability, as the two former *Idol* contestants.

But in that dressing room, I took the road less travelled. I chose to put my insecurities aside and refuse the dark lure of jealousy. Something transformative occurred; I was overcome with excitement for my friend and, instead of feeling spiteful, I felt inspired. Adore was living a dream we shared, and I couldn't be happier. This is just one reason that those dressing room times spent with my sisters were so grounding for all of us. Being around each other felt healing; it took us back to a simpler time when we were unknown to the world and in a Hollywood sound stage slapping on makeup to strut down the runway.

A healing of a different type came later that night, as I writhed around my hotel bed with Evan, who was now a proud graduate out of LIMP.

Over the following months, Oscar and I would see each other in different cities whenever we could. Our next trip was to The City: New York City! I was going to be there for a month performing my show *Boys Like Me* at the Laurie Beechman. I was staying at the home of my friend the composer and music director Lance Horne while he was out of town. I evolved from sending cars for boys and booked Oscar a flight to NYC. We had a fairytale time enjoying the city and each other's bodies, especially since Lance's bedroom had mirrored walls and ceiling.

One afternoon Oscar and I had sex in the bathtub, and I felt for the first time that we were making love. As I lifted my body up and stared into his eyes, all that was running through my head was, 'I love you'. I wanted to say it out loud so bad, but my rational mind interjected and overrode the impulse. Probably for the best, since we weren't at the stage of our relationship for me to say those words, but in that moment I was in love.

I learnt a lot when I was with Oscar, most of which I wasn't really cognisant of at the time. Allowing myself to be seen by him was scary and hard, but his attraction to me in spite of the fact that I wasn't masculine as a boy was palliative. I still experienced that lingering fear in allowing myself to accept his attraction to me as a boy, but each day I leant into it and slowly began to undo those years of conditioning. Although I doubt whether Oscar and I would have ever got to 'love', this connection was certainly an evolution from the platonic one-way bromances I was used to finding myself in.

I'd spent most of my sexually aware life in unrequited relationships with boys who were never going to love me back, starting with Ritchie in high school; there are a number whose stories I haven't shared on these pages. I'd spent so much time struggling to find myself desirable, feeling I was inadequate as a man, unable to be loved as I was. This experience, of being with Oscar and him reciprocating my feelings, challenged everything I'd held to be true about myself and had spent years, with the exception of the time spent in my relationship with Jack, reinforcing. I'd had glimpses of a different reality when I was with Rob, and now with Oscar, and those glimpses were like breadcrumbs leading me to authenticity. Who would have thought that procuring sex while dressed up in women's clothes could lead to such enlightenment?

Oscar headed back to Indiana and I stayed in NYC to perform *Boys Like Me*. The show was inspired by different sexual and romantic encounters I'd had over the years, each reflecting the full spectrum of the Kinsey Scale. Spending that week with Oscar felt like the happy ending to all of those forlorn dalliances that I'd spun stories about in my cabaret.

I decided to call Chaz to tell him all about these realisations. I'd been keeping him abreast of the romance with Oscar and, as often happened in our conversations, we traipsed down the deep and meaningful paths of gender, sexuality and identity. I was telling Chaz how I felt so comfortable with Oscar because, even though he was currently dating me, Shane, a boy, he was otherwise attracted to girls. With Oscar I could be soft, emotionally and physically, in a way I couldn't with gay men.

I love to pace when I am on the phone, and I was doing laps of Lance's apartment as the full moon watched over the New York City skyline.

'Why do you think you do drag, Shane?'

''Cause it's a job. I put on a uniform and I go to work. Nothing funny going on here.' I went into automatic defence mode.

'Is that why?'

The trans women in my life had always asked questions that felt like they were suggesting I was trans, trying to lead me in that direction. It always made me feel uncomfortable. I thought that's where Chaz's question was heading.

'That may very well be, but have you ever considered why, out of all the possible styles of drag, you have chosen to present in a binary-passing, hyper-feminine way? Do you think there could be more behind "why" you do drag?'

Even though I was inclined to get my defences up when my gender was questioned, I trusted Chaz and kept listening.

'Have you heard of the term gender-fluid?'

'No.'

'Gender-fluidity is the idea that it's OK for boys to be feminine and girls to be masculine. Gender isn't binary, it exists on a spectrum, and you can occupy any positions along the spectrum and express your gender in any way you want.'

I stopped in my tracks, staring out the large arched window.

'Hello? Shane? Are you there?'

Chaz's words were like poetry to me in that moment. To borrow from Audre Lorde, these words *gave name to those ideas which are – until the poem – nameless and formless, about to be birthed, but already felt*. I was finally seeing what Chaz and the world had been pointing at this whole time; there was the full moon staring right back at me.

Where I'd always been afraid of the dark, this big, bright, gender-fluid moon bathed me in its golden light. I felt so validated just knowing that this concept and label existed. For the first time I had language to describe how I felt on the inside, and it all made sense. This seems so obvious now, but at the time it was a revelation. I had been so ashamed that the ideal of binary gender didn't fit me that I just pretended it did. I thought there was something wrong with me, but it was the system that was broken. I had pretended I was a man and compartmentalised my femininity by doing drag, but now the charade of binary gender was up.

I had been carefully peeling back the layers of conditioning for years to try to discover this truth inside me, and the label 'gender-fluid' created such an instant sense of clarity, connection and belonging in me. Unbecoming who the world had told me to be, I was finally able to become myself.

COURTNEY FACT

Remember how back in the Courtney Fact on pages 112–115 I talked about gender being a construct? I want to add to that idea. I think we can all agree that if you took a woman or a man from today and time-travelled them back a century to the 1920s, they would be totally out of place, especially in terms of their gender presentation and expression. Women weren't even allowed to wear trousers back then; when Katharine Hepburn started doing this during her rise to fame in the 1930s, it caused a huge stir. Even in 1951, by which time she was well and truly a star,

Hepburn wasn't allowed to enter the lobby of Claridge's Hotel in London because she was told that women weren't allowed to wear slacks there. (She chose to use the staff entrance instead.)

Judith Butler writes that *the social meanings of what it is to be a man or a woman are not yet settled. We tell histories about what it meant to be a woman at a certain time and place, and we track the transformation of those categories over time. We depend on gender as a historical category, and that means we do not yet know all the ways it may come to signify, and we are open to new understandings of its social meanings.* One of those new understandings in contemporary Western society comes in the form of non-binary gender identities – though it's important to note that these identities have existed in First Nations and non-Western cultures since time immemorial. Historically, institutions of colonial power such as the Church enforced the idea of a rigid gender binary, man/woman, as a way to have greater control and power over people (though ironically the Church's traditional depiction of Jesus seems pretty androgynous to me). This gender indoctrination by Church and state simply does not serve men or women well at all, and non-binary folk are here to liberate us all from that.

A non-binary person identifies outside the traditional, socially constructed gender binary. Non-binary folk define their gender based on their own internal sense of identity rather than the dated gender ideology most of us have had forced on us since before we were born ('Are you having a boy or a girl?'). Non-binary is an umbrella term that includes people whose gender differs from the expected gender identity and/or presentation of what contemporary Western society typically refers to as a woman or a man. There is no correct way to be non-binary, no specific look, just as there is no correct way to be a woman or man (or at least there shouldn't be). Some people might look femme or masc or neither. The term non-binary can include people who are gender-fluid, genderqueer, agender, androgynous and gender non-conforming, and some transmasculine and transfeminine people identify as non-binary too.

Non-binary identities are commonly spoken of in the media as something new or even strange, but make no mistake: this is a form of gaslighting. The gender binary is itself a relatively new concept within the broader timeline of humanity. And when you take a moment to consider what it means to live your life against the grain of the constructed gender binary, you can see it really is the most natural expression of gender there is.

Pronouns

A while back I was reading an in-depth article about a non-binary artist named Dorian Electra, whose pronouns are they/them. I was already on board with the idea that using the pronouns that feel right to you can be validating and liberating… but as I was reading the article I became increasingly obsessed with whether Dorian had a penis or a vulva. I couldn't tell just by looking at photos of them online, and my brain wanted answers! Then it occurred to me that the reason I wanted this information was so I could filter my understanding of Dorian through the lens of how a man or woman should act. (And as you'll recall from the Courtney Fact on pages 164–168, a fixation on the genitals of trans and gender-diverse people is dehumanising.) This was a real moment of self-awareness and learning for me, because I recognised how my own unconscious bias and misogyny was playing out. This realisation gave me a newfound understanding for just how punk they/them pronouns can be in breaking our thinking out of gendered expectations.

If you're not familiar with the concept, I'll explain they/them pronouns. Some people are not 'he' or 'she', but instead have the non-gendered pronoun 'they' to signify their non-binary identity. People love to get their knickers in a twist, claiming that 'they' can only be used as a plural pronoun rather than for just one person, but we actually use 'they', 'them' and 'theirs' in singular form on the regular. Let's say you found a backpack that someone clearly forgot in a café. You'd say to yourself, *Oh no, someone forgot THEIR bag… THEY are gonna panic! Glad I'm not THEM, I'd better give it to the manager. THEY'll be able to return the bag to its owner.*

We learn a whole new name for every person we meet, so learning just one of three pronouns doesn't seem like a huge ask. It can require a bit of a paradigm shift to start using 'they' for just one person, but that's the point: we do need to change our thinking about gender and language. Also, for the record, they/them pronouns are not only 100 per cent correct according to contemporary linguistics, they have been around a long time. Since about the 16th century, to be precise. To give you some perspective, that is around the same time the letter 'J' was added to the English language. Do you seriously want to be the person who's just catching up to using J's in your words?

We all want to feel like ourselves when someone is referring to us. It's the bare minimum to ask that we care for each other in this simplest of ways. So if someone tells you their pronouns, their name, or anything about how they identify, think about how you would feel if you told someone your name was Christopher and they said, 'Meh, I don't buy it. I'm calling you Christina. Because that's how I see you!' See what a jerk that person sounds like? Well… I guess we'd have to call them an 'erk'… since the letter J didn't even exist at the time they'd formed their opinion.

My pronouns, in case you were wondering, are 'he' when dressed as a boy and 'she' when dressed as a girl – and 'they' works however I am dressed!

I'm now at the stage in my life where I'm able to reflect on how this journey towards understanding my gender identity unfolded, at first in flashes of memory and then with increasing force: as a teen, realising I wasn't like the other boys at A block. In Melbourne, wearing my red turtleneck jumper, being mistaken for a girl while shopping with Mum. Dressing as a girl and lip-syncing to 'I Don't Care if the Sun Don't Shine' at the wrap party of a Fame tour. Arriving in Sydney and meeting drag queens and trans women, and having my eyes opened to the possibilities of gender. Katherine's mystic prediction that I would one day be a woman. My drag debut on New Year's Eve; the birth of Courtney Act. My uncontrollable kicking and screaming in Sarah's apartment when I first expressed my failings at being a man.

In my song 'In Between', I reflect on the impact of all of those years of searching and questioning myself:

Why can't I see my reflection?
Frightened to look at my face
What will I see – in my complexion

That I can't bear to give space?
When I reflect back on that time, oh I, I wish that I could see
If I looked into the mirror I could find who I'm supposed to be
I'm in between
Living in the middle, in between
Never really knowing how I'm seen
Terrified of where there's no returning
Looking in the mirror, who I see
It's not the only person I could be
But I know for now I'm on a journey
'Cause I'm in between

I know now that the space in between is so much more expansive than you could ever imagine. But during my years in Sydney, when I'd first started questioning my gender identity, I thought I needed to stick to one side of the binary. Growing up in a world with such limited conversations and understanding of life outside that binary meant travelling all that way with no light to guide me, with no map to follow; just fumbling around in the dark, feeling objects to try and understand their form.

Why can't I see my reflection?
Clouded, unclear, unclean
Trying to find a connection
With all this space in between
When I reflect back on that time, oh I, I wish that I could see
The person in the mirror wasn't me, who I'm supposed to be
I'm in between

When I arrived in West Hollywood, I thought I had to make a choice. I remember so well that phone call with Vanity, when I was ready to come out as trans, but my loving friend held space for me. In this moment of deep empathy, for the first time I understood I didn't have to choose between man or woman. It wasn't about choosing. Could I be both?

Now I can see my reflection
Still asking, 'What does it mean?'
Walking without a direction
Accepting that I'm in between
When I reflect back on that time, oh I, I'm glad that I could see
The person in the mirror was just me, that's who I'm supposed to be
I'm in between

My realisation that my gender was fluid wasn't because I sometimes wore girls' clothes and sometimes wore boys' clothes; it emerged from a deep sense of who I was, and I now saw that identity reflected back in a label. From the day I talked to Chaz over the phone in NYC nothing drastic changed on the outside, but so much changed on the inside. I was making peace with my 'masculinity' and my 'femininity'. I was able to just be, instead of always trying to live up to an expectation of gender. I'd never lived up to that expectation anyway, but had spent so much energy trying.

I will be forever grateful to Chaz for being such an amazing and supportive friend, and for the many hours of conversation that enabled me to understand and accept my gender identity. He later admitted that when we first met he thought I was transphobic, which I was, but he realised that was a reaction to the world I'd been brought up in. I am so glad that he saw through that and through my confusion, and that he listened and guided me. With Chaz's empathy and compassion, my shame couldn't survive.

Now I can see my reflection
Finally I know what I see
There's no such thing as perfection
There's not one reflection of me
Shatter it to pieces, let it fall, the mirror breaks apart
One million tiny broken shards, they all reflect a different part
A different part of me
Yeah I'm in between
Living in the middle, in between
All I know is I'm a fucking queen
And I don't know it all but yeah I'm learning
Looking in the mirror and I see
I'm exactly who I'm supposed to be
And I had to find them on that journey:
I'm in between

I wasn't cured in an instant. It's not as though I haven't since struggled with or questioned my gender identity, but now that my internal sense aligned with an external definition I was able to recognise what was intrinsic and what was imposed. Any time I notice I am code-switching I just try to sit with the feeling and remember that who I am is enough.

21

With the ever-looming question of my gender identity resolved, I hurtled forwards into my career with renewed clarity. My 15 minutes of post-*Idol* fame had slipped through my fingers without being fully realised, and now I was in the rare position of being given a second 15 minutes, I wasn't taking it for granted.

While I was on tour I'd begun filming my adventures and putting them on YouTube in a travel vlog series called *Courtney Chronicles*. It felt empowering getting to tell my story, and while my videos didn't have the reach of *Drag Race*, the making of them certainly helped to placate my anxiety. These videos were one way for me to take back the narrative.

I expanded my YouTube credits to a living-room chat called *Courtney Talks*. Each week I filled my lounge with YouTubers and drag queens like Miranda Sings, Jackie Beat, Davey Wavey and Jinkx Monsoon. I wanted to host my own talk show, so the best way was to try it. Collaborating with creators who had different audiences also meant I could expand and define my own. To further build my online repertoire I also tried my hand at being a beauty vlogger with a series called *Chapstick and Mascara*.

Then American Apparel called and asked me to be in a new advertising campaign as their latest American Apparel Ad Girl, along with iconic *Drag Race* alumnae Willam and Alaska. I have always been a hustler, creating opportunities and keeping my face out there, but working with Willam I saw someone who took it to a whole new level. She had been in a girl group called DWV who'd had huge success with their track 'Boy Is a Bottom', a parody of 'Girl on Fire' by Alicia Keys, and she asked Alaska and me if we wanted to sing a track together. Willam wanted to turn our American Apparel photoshoot into a full-blown pop culture moment.

Willam, Alaska and I wrote and recorded a parody of the Capital Cities track 'Farrah Fawcett Hair' – which was to be simply titled 'American Apparel Ad Girls' – then hired a studio, got a whole lot of lewks sent by the company, and asked Mathu Andersen to beat our mugs and style our hair, which was a real honour and career highlight for all three of us. We released the track to a great fan response, and so our girl group, the AAA Girls, was born. We toured the US doing in-store signings, embarked on a European tour and released a Christmas single, 'Dear Santa, Bring Me a Man'. Being associated with Willam and Alaska felt like another step in shaking off *Drag Race* Courtney. They were such well-established and loved fan favourites, and our power of three seemed to be a winning ticket.

That New Year's Eve I had a gig in Austin, Texas, and invited Oscar along. I thought we could go on an adventure, meeting up with some friends in Vegas on 1 January, before heading back to LA for a week. Oscar had never been, so it would be fun to introduce him to friends and show him around. When I said goodbye to him at LAX after a really wild seven days, though, I didn't know that would be the end of our relationship.

After that week in LA, Oscar became distant with me. We still texted and chatted, but I could tell something had changed. Leading up to Valentine's Day I was in Australia and was subtly trying to ask for his address so I could send some flowers, but he never replied. The best I could do was a 'Happy Valentine's Day' text message. No response. I was feeling a little emosh and started writing a song about the situation; throughout the day I would add lyrics by recording them into my phone, and the story in the song would unfold. I sat in Hyde Park that afternoon crying as I realised it was over with Oscar. The last line of the song is 'I guess you didn't wanna be my Valentine.'

Being ghosted really sucked, but I had my suspicions as to why it had happened – the same reason trysts like this had always ended. At the beginning of these romances with heteroflexible guys, infatuation acts like a buffer to their default reality. But as time goes on, the outside world creeps in and they have to ask themselves all sorts of questions that challenge their views about sexuality and gender. Try as I might to reassure them that their attraction is valid, that sexuality is a fluid thing, my voice alone is nothing compared to a lifetime of conditioning. There is no space in their world to fall in love with a boy like me without telling their tribe and risking the loss of social ties, so they go back to their heterosexual lives and I become that 'phase' or 'experiment' they never talk about again, but hopefully will always remember fondly.

As part of the writing process for this book, I reached out to Oscar and had a really nourishing conversation. Unprompted, he stepped up and showed how that 21-year-old I met had grown into a man.

'I never did apologise for just ghosting. I know it's old news, but for what it's worth, I'm sorry for doing that,' he told me. He went on to explain how the experience we'd shared had gone against all the negative bullshit he'd grown up hearing about queer people, and that eventually the pull of his reality had overwhelmed our bond. Oscar said he was grateful, and he thanked me. He said our time together taught him so much and still teaches him today. That it teaches his fiancée, too, because when he'd told her about us, she hadn't reacted so well – at first. But now she accepts him and celebrates the queer community too. (Oh, you thought I was joking when I said at the beginning of the book that I've been changing the world one straight-identifying man at a time?)

Inspired by the success of the AAA Girls, I began working on my lifelong dream of writing my own solo pop record. I wrote tracks with Sam Sparro, Jake Shears and LA producers The Prodigal, slowly crafting pop tracks that would become my debut EP *Kaleidoscope*. Inspired by Kylie's *Impossible Princess* album, I wanted the front of my album to be a hologram (or lithograph, for those who want to get technical). Continuing the Kylie theme, William Baker, her long-time collaborator, directed my first video, for my song 'Ecstasy', in London.

The next single was 'Ugly', the video for which I co-directed in LA. The narrative was loosely based on meeting Oscar, but rather than a hotel in Indianapolis it featured a desert motel just outside LA. The third single, 'Body Parts', was probably the slickest track, and I was honoured when The Squared Division said yes to directing the music video. I'd performed alongside and worked with this creative duo, Ashley and Antony, back in Sydney, but they had since blown up into go-to creative directors for stars like Katy Perry, Cardi B, Ariana Grande and Sam Smith.

All of this art didn't come cheap, and after reading Amanda Palmer's book *The Art of Asking* I decided to ask my audience to help me fund the production on Kickstarter. The campaign achieved its goal of $20,000, going on to raise more than $37,000 in total. The traditional model would have been to make money off the release after the fact, but Kickstarter enabled me to involve my audience ahead of time to help pay for the album before it came out, thereby also involving them in the creation process. In reality, I spent several times that on the project using the money I had earnt from touring and maxing out that overdraft after I had finally paid it off. I really put myself in a financial hole, but it was worth every cent as I got to create the album and music videos of my dreams.

Before the album launch I felt so content with everything I had produced. The production process was what drag had always been about: I had hustled so hard and called in so many favours to make everything as professional as possible. I imagined my music climbing the charts around the world and crossing over into the mainstream pop world. The first single, 'Ecstasy', got a lot of pickup in the press. Billboard.com exclusively premiered the track, and the early feedback was exciting: these were bona fide pop bangers, rather than the niche genre of 'drag queen music'.

We did a massive album launch concert with Live Nation at The Gramercy in NYC. I performed with a live band, and it was my first time using in-ear monitors. I felt like a pro. On the west coast we launched the record with an acoustic show at Bardot in Hollywood.

Despite all of this hype, though, the numbers didn't live up to my expectations. The YouTube views were decent, but nothing runaway. The songs skipped around the iTunes charts a little, but didn't make it onto Billboard. It was nothing compared to Adore's success. But I didn't feel defeated or deflated; I was so happy with the quality of what I had created, and that was enough. Yes – obviously it would have been wonderful if my music had gone number one around the world, but I now felt such an unexpected sense of satisfaction that the external validation didn't actually matter that much.

Because my aspirations of being a pop star were fizzling, and I wasn't enjoying the club shows as much as I had before, I returned to an artform and environment that would showcase the best of me, and in which I would feel most comfortable: cabaret. On stage, singing live with good sound, in a theatre, with a seated audience who were there to see a show. I love storytelling and live music, lighting cues and costume changes. The money in performing cabaret was nowhere near as good, and I had to work a lot harder, but I knew it would be rewarding. I toured my cabaret show *Boys Like Me* and *The Girl from Oz* around the US, UK and Australia in those post–*Drag Race* years from 2014 to 2017. I started with smaller venues of 100 to 200 seats, and slowly grew the audience, going on to perform long summer seasons in Provincetown, a queer destination at the tip of Cape Cod off the coast of Boston. A career highlight was performing at the Edinburgh Fringe Festival in 2017.

Another feather in my (wig) cap came when I started making explainer videos for Australian website Junkee.com. Tim Duggan, my friend from the Sydney days who I'd started the Disgraceland parties with, was the publisher at Junkee, and we were talking about the confusing American political system. It was early 2016 – that big election year spawning Brexit and a Trump presidency. Not that we knew that yet, but it was going to be a game-changing year in politics. I created a video explaining the US primaries system; the idea was to demystify the process for Aussies. It quickly got a million views, and I knew I was onto something. People really connected with the way I broke down a confusing subject and explained it so that they could understand. It turned out that quite a few Americans watched the video and now understood their own political process a little better too. Not long afterwards I was on a tour bus with Adore, and she told me she'd watched the whole video and felt smarter because of it.

So began the *American Act* video series for Junkee. I followed up with an explainer on the US Supreme Court and a plea to the Australian government on marriage equality; this was the year before the divisive postal survey that was designed to measure support for it. The next logical step, while I was wading into this difficult territory, was to get in drag and interview people at a Trump rally. Clearly one to put myself in harm's way, I also went to that gun range the go-go dancer Rob had wanted to take me on a date to in LA – in drag – and fired a few rounds for a video about gun control. I went to a Hillary rally in Massachusetts, the Trump Inauguration in Washington DC, and the Women's March on Washington too. That amazing display of solidarity gave me hope, knowing the dark days that were coming.

Drag is not just for the gays any more. When I'd picked up drag all those years back, I loved it in spite of the messages I received from the outside world. Drag empowered me and gave me an outlet to express my creativity and my femininity, but in the early 2000s no one 'got' drag except for us drag queens. And even if people enjoyed watching the shows we put on – the nightclubs that went from empty to packed because of our shows were testament to that – our choices were never seen as aspirational. We were glamorous jesters on stage and at the afterparty, and there was a fine line between laughing with and laughing at us.

I worked hard to be taken seriously in the Australian entertainment industry and slowly chipped away a career and a space for myself, but in those early years I felt like a gimmick. At the time I was fine with that because I didn't know any different, and while I remain grateful for these opportunities, it's only now that I can recognise they often came at the expense of my own humanity. I don't blame any particular TV network, record company or journalist; I know it was much worse and much harder for those who came before me, and we can't go from zero representation to perfect representation overnight.

I was lucky to have the opportunities I had, even if I had to assimilate and behave in ways that made me 'acceptable', and I think I was granted access to the mainstream because I blended in. I was accessible to everyday folks. Think of the optics: I was a pretty, blonde, white girl on the TV, and if you didn't think too hard about who I really was you could just be entertained. I was cheeky, but not grotesque. My binary presentation made me palatable. Even though I subvert heterosexual culture by presenting my male body as an object of straight male desire, it works because I pass as a straight woman, and a leggy blonde one at that – the expression of femininity that is most valued in mainstream Western cultures.

Perhaps because I never expected the drag community to be accepted and celebrated as we are in the *Drag Race* era, I am more grateful for how far we have come than bitter about how long we were oppressed. And despite having some negative experiences on the show, I can recognise that it was a pivotal moment in my life and career, and that it speaks to a loyal cult audience. *Drag Race* fans love the show, they love the queens, they come to our gigs, they listen to our music and they love interacting on social media. In fact, just as at the gigs, two-thirds of my audience on social media are women, most of whom are straight. The *Drag Race* fanbase has grown and expanded to the point that we now see drag queens everywhere in mainstream media.

Drag Race helps convey to people why I love drag so much – why I kept doing it during the early years in Sydney despite the warnings about how it would harm my career. Recently I was reading a book about Andy Warhol and wondering where and when the next iconic era of pop culture would be, and then I realised we are living in the middle of it. There are drag queens in business class, at Paris Fashion Week, running for office, on the Billboard charts, drag queens with million-dollar homes, with makeup and beauty empires and with wig companies (wigsbyvanity.com – that's wigsbyvanity.com).

RuPaul and *Drag Race* gave me an opportunity on the world stage in an arena filled with the most wonderful and enthusiastic audience, and I really am grateful for that. I've loved touring the world performing, and I've loved the opportunities I have had to write and release music, and to make a living doing what I love. It has been a privilege to have fans welcome me – the entirety of who I am – into their lives.

22

In early 2017, I was using a location-based dating app called Thrindr, which was used to facilitate couples seeking a third – although the name has since been changed to Feeld, I assume after a cease-and-desist from Tinder. I wasn't specifically looking to be a third, but I also wasn't against the idea. I was using this particular app because I had found there were a lot of open-minded single guys seeking… whatever. On this app you have to select how you identify your sexuality and which genders you're interested in seeing. I had set up a banging Courtney profile and would receive many messages from men who described themselves as straight, bisexual, pansexual and heteroflexible.

One day Julius sent me a message. He identified as pansexual. Where lots of guys sent dick and hole pics as a greeting, he was really sweet and interested in getting to know me. I felt respected and treated like a human – which, in this context, came as a shock.

Time for another Courtney Fact.

COURTNEY FACT

The attraction to trans and non-binary bodies is largely a taboo subject for those in the constructed heteronormative world, especially for straight guys. Their sexuality and identity can become threatened if they find themselves attracted to anyone who isn't a cis woman.

Many straight-identifying guys who are attracted to trans and non-binary people are on the DL (down-low); they're discreet. They don't want to take you on a date or be seen in public. This repression of the emotional or romantic side of desire can often lead to a fetishisation of trans and queer bodies. Hooking up and dating these guys can also be fraught with danger for their partners, as these men are often conflicted by the disparity between the desires they feel and what society has deemed 'correct'. This mismatch can result in aggression or violence. The man is overcome with the social conditioning that projects disgust onto the sexual act he's just performed, and he directs that self-loathing at his partner, sometimes violently.

Trans and non-binary folk are not just at risk in the bedroom. Many experience aggression, violence and legal and social discrimination at the highest rates of anyone in our society. Black and brown trans women and femmes are some of the most marginalised and at-risk people on the planet. Too often they experience risk and danger because of the fragility of straight men who are undone by their own desires.

I don't want to make any wild claims and suggest that I single-handedly invented video dating back in 2016, but I am pretty sure I did. I always video-chat with a guy before I meet up with them: it's safer, and there is only so much you can tell from a few curated photos and some text chat over the apps. When Julius and I (as Courtney) chatted on video, there was a real spark. His smile drew me in. He was a man, to be sure, but something about the smile behind his eyes told me about the cheeky boy inside. He was super smart and switched on, with a straight-boy charm that didn't seem repressed. He had recently moved to LA to pursue his dreams of being an actor, and in between acting jobs worked as a personal trainer. We decided to meet up.

Because I was using a Courtney profile, I figured it was best to be presenting 'as advertised' when he arrived at my place. His photos were cute, but they didn't do him justice, and our chemistry was instant. I would say that the sex we had that day falls into the category of top three all-time best sex ever. Lying in bed after we had done it in the vestibule, on the kitchen counter, the couch, the floor, the hallway, against the window and in the shower, we talked about the fact that he had dated cis girls, trans girls and cis men. He was totally open and comfortable with his sexuality. I related to the idea of being open to sex or a relationship with someone regardless of their gender; although I'm mostly attracted to guys, I had certainly had quite a few experiences with women, both cis and trans. I decided the label of 'pansexual' better described my sexuality too. Pretty soon Julius and I were dating, and I was smitten. That first time was the only time I was in drag while we had sex, and my presentation as Shane didn't seem to affect Julius's attraction.

In early 2017, I got a message on Facebook from a friend I had met in Sydney a few years earlier. She was casting for an MTV show called *Single AF*. Basically the premise was that a whole bunch of single 'celebs' would fly around the world going on dates, before picking a favourite and taking them back to live in a chateau in France for a week. I was really excited about the opportunity.

The slight issue was that I wasn't actually single. I'd been dating Julius for about four months, which was long enough to feel serious, but not long enough to divert major career opportunities because of our relationship.

Julius and I were in an open relationship, so I figured I could just pretend I was single on the show. Also, over the course of my career Wendy had taught me it was best to keep saying yes to an opportunity until the point you have to say no. I'd been so focused on my career, and a new TV show would be a huge opportunity for me, but who knew if it would even come to pass.

Six months into my relationship with Julius, Wendy told me I was confirmed to be on the show. If you're going to tell your boyfriend you are going on a dating show and pretending to be single, you should probably do it with a little more tact than I did. I didn't see that being a cast member on *Single AF* and being in a relationship were mutually exclusive, and to his credit neither did Julius, but I kinda phrased what should have been a question and a conversation about his thoughts and feelings on me doing the show as a statement that I was doing it regardless of what he thought.

Julius was hurt, understandably so, and over the next two months that breach of trust seemed to undermine everything. We broke up. My words and actions about *Single AF* had showed both him and me where he stood on my hierarchy of values. I do wish I'd been less thirsty for my career and more compassionate for a person I was falling in love with. Julius was the first guy since Jack who I believed loved all parts of me, a person I felt so comfortable with. I was devastated it was over and I was so angry at myself. I wished that I could have turned back time on that conversation and said things differently.

Even though Julius was pretty clear that the relationship was over, that didn't stop me turning up at his house unannounced like a crazy ex-girlfriend the day before I flew to the UK to start filming. I wrote a letter, bought some flowers and printed an album of cute photos of our time together. But Julius wasn't interested in hearing my excuses or apologies; he had clear boundaries and I had crossed them.

I woke up in my hotel room in London ready to start my makeup for the first day of filming. Lorde had perfectly timed the release of her breakup album *Melodrama*, which I put on; I cried so, so much to that album. I couldn't do my makeup for all the tears running down my face. I felt so heavy, and the last thing I wanted to do was slap on a face and be the life of the party. But I had to go to work. I put on 'Wannabe' by the Spice Girls and listened to their first two albums. It helped a lot, at least in that moment.

I hadn't dealt with my feelings about the breakup with Julius, but I resolved to push them aside for now and focus on the job: flying around the world going on dates. I genuinely hoped I might find someone, too. I now realise that is the furthest thing from the reality of a reality show about dating.

I was going to go on dates as Shane and Courtney. I explained to the producers the nuance of attraction. As Courtney I don't go on dates with gay men: they are attracted to men, and Courtney doesn't look like a man. For Courtney they would need to find guys who were attracted to… femininity. I described the types of guys I dated as Courtney – bi guys, pansexual guys, straight-identifying guys on the DL – but either the nuance was lost or it was an impossible task, because only men who were gay were cast to date me as Courtney. It didn't really make sense to me or them, but… it was TV.

I kissed every boy and the one girl I went on a date with on that show, and I even kissed two boys at once on a double date. To come live with me in the chateau in France I chose a Brazilian guy called Lucas who lived in Sydney.

The first part of the show – the journey around the world to go on dates – was quite wholesome and fun, but when we got to France it went full-hilt MTV reality drama. The first night people were smashing things and fighting. Lucas started crying because it was so unhinged. I knew about two hours into our stay that Lucas was not there because he was attracted to me, so the rest of the week was spent making awkward conversation. I took a fancy to one of the other girls' dates, Kyle, and started flirting with him, which caused Lucas to get jealous. In a drunken rage Lucas stormed up to me with a glass of white wine in his hand, yelling, 'COURTNEY ACT – IT'S ALL AN ACT!' I grabbed the glass of wine out of his hand and threw it onto the grass. It was so dramatic, and my heart was pounding in my chest. I'd crossed over into reality-TV land.

Even as recently as 2017, it wasn't really common to have a queer person on a dating show. I was happy that I got to be on TV kissing boys and girls, getting to include a queer narrative. Always one to make the juice worth the squeeze, I also pitched an idea to MTV that I could make a bunch of explainer videos to run on socials as a compendium to the show. They were about all sorts of topics, from consent to lube, and I made a video called 'Gender 101' that got millions of views. Even these days I'm often sent a photo of a university lecture room or a boardroom where people are watching this video as part of their sensitivity training.

Single AF didn't make much of a splash, but one of the girls on the show, Marnie from *Geordie Shore*, said to me that I would be great on *Celebrity Big Brother*. I thought she grossly overestimated my level of celebrity, but the popularity of *Drag Race* was growing all the time; the current season had begun airing on Netflix in the UK, and all the previous seasons were also available to watch.

Even though living in the *Single AF* house for just a week had been such a horrific experience that I genuinely did not want to be locked in a house for a month, Marnie set up a meeting for Wendy and me with her agent, and next thing I had an interview with the producers of *Celebrity Big Brother*. They loved the content I had been making in recent years: the gender video, for example, along with some of the greatest hits in the *American Act* series like the video I filmed at the Trump rally. The producers also wanted this season of *Celebrity Big Brother* to have a different tone from those of previous years. 2018 was 'Year of the Woman', and that was the theme for the house. They wanted less conflict and more conversation, which made me feel better about the prospect. They assured me that it was going to be a more respectable affair.

On New Year's Eve, Willam, Alaska and I performed as the AAA Girls at G-A-Y in London, and the very next day I went into lockdown for *CBB*. In the leadup to production there is a lot of secrecy around the cast, and the producers said that if my casting was leaked I would be cut. I didn't want to risk it, so I didn't tell a soul. Telegram, telephone, tell Willam… But I didn't. Willam and Alaska were plucked and pressed when I got out of the house because I had been with them the night before I entered, drunk at a house party, and hadn't said a word.

The cast of *CBB* were divided into men and women, with the women to enter the house first before the men followed a few days later. I felt a bit weird entering the house as Courtney in the men's group, as I don't see Courtney as a man, but then

I didn't want to take up space in the women's group either, not that it was my choice. That's the limit of binary categorisation I guess. I wasn't familiar with the women before going in because they were British celebs, but I had 48 hours to watch and google everyone. Perhaps most noteworthy among them was Ann Widdecombe: a Conservative politician who in 23 years of parliament had voted against every single piece of pro-LGBTQ+ legislation that ever came before her.

I tried to read as much as I could about Ann. She was 70 years old. She had left the Church of England and converted to Catholicism when the former started ordaining female priests. She is against abortion, denies climate change and is pro–capital punishment. She has consistently voted against an equal age of consent for same-sex relationships; opposed the repeal of the controversial Section 28, a Thatcher-era law that prohibited the 'promotion of homosexuality' by local authorities; and has voiced support for conversion practices on LGBTQ+ people. And the list goes on.

Before going into the house there was a tabloid article that reported Germaine Greer was going to be there. I wanted to anticipate some of the criticisms Germaine might have of drag, so I told a friend of mine, Calpernia, that I was doing a panel show in the UK and asked if she would be up for having lunch with me where she role-played Germaine. I knew and admired Germaine as one of the major voices in the radical feminist movement, but she had made despicable transphobic comments in the past and might also see what I did as an attack on women. I wanted to focus my thoughts before I got into the house. Calpernia pointed out at lunch that I probably wasn't going to change Germaine's mind on anything, but to remember there would be people at home watching. This was good advice.

While Germaine wasn't in the house in the end, the conversation I'd had with Calpernia kept me grounded and focused on being effective when having conversations with Ann. I'm pretty even-keeled anyway, but it was so helpful to make sure I was remembering the people at home. When I approach these conversations about gender and sexuality, I always think about how I can be most effective rather than how I can be right. Telling Ann why she was wrong would have been easy, but engaging her in conversations about marriage equality, a woman's right to choose what happens to her body, climate change and other hot topics was going to be a more effective way to make my case.

I entered the house with a bang. My skirt fell off on live TV and I flashed my tuck to the world.

As I walked down the stairs waving to the crowd the pop studs on my skirt flew open, exposing my meaty tuck and bare bum. The cameras cut to a wide shot. I panicked and ran across the gangway, past all the media, and frantically fumbled with my skirt trying to find which direction was the right way up. There are some brilliant photos of the moment the skirt drops; the look on my face is priceless. These photos were on the front page of newspapers and featured in memes. It was a great way to get the nation's attention on me from the start of the season, although I didn't know I had because I was about to enter the *Big Brother* bubble.

In that moment I gathered myself, got my skirt back on and walked down the steps into the house. As I was telling the housemates what had just happened my skirt flew off again, this time in front of Ann. If she was wearing pearls she would have clutched them.

Then down the stairs came Andrew Brady, a handsome and cheeky lad who caught my eye immediately. Andrew and I hit it off instantly; I definitely batted my eyelids and let my glance linger a little too long. That first night, and pretty much every night after, I would end up outside with the lads, Andrew, Dapper Laughs and Jonny Mitchell, drinking until the chirps of the dawn chorus. It was strange because I always gravitate towards women over straight men, but I found myself having the best time with the lads. I felt like one of the boys and I quite relished that. I finally got to sit with the popular boys at A block.

When I was Shane, Andrew and I would get up to all sorts of mischief, and when I was Courtney there was some sexual tension. I think Andrew was a bit confused whenever Courtney appeared. I wanted something to happen between us, but I didn't think a straight guy was going to start making out with a drag queen on national TV. We did have a lot of fun: we had a secret handshake, we shared a bed, we shared a bath, and I put Andrew in drag one night and showed him how to tuck. The intimacy of our friendship was appreciated by everyone except for Ann, who called us 'disgusting'.

Part of me wishes I'd taken Ann to task more for a lot of the things she said. I knew my limits back then, and I wasn't as confident in speaking about issues, and with her decades of debating experience in parliament she had watertight, well-argued answers for everything. I wasn't completely aware of the full depth of her bigotry at the time either. At face value she was a nice older woman who was actually one of my favourite housemates despite our clear differences, but on a very real level she had spent her career legislating against my right to exist.

I also attribute my ability to remain calm when talking to Ann to meditation. I would often take myself to the bedroom and sit and meditate for a while to centre myself. In a house with so many hours to fill, it's easy to turn to destructive behaviours to pass the time. People try to push others' buttons for amusement.

Near the end of the competition Andrew, Dapper and Jonny all got evicted from the house in one go. I was left without my core friend circle and felt really isolated. A peculiar alliance formed when two older gay housemates, Amanda Barrie and Wayne Sleep, started turning on me because they said I was trying to turn housemates against their friend Ann. I found it so weird that these two housemates, who were 82 and 69 respectively, had sided with a woman who'd made a career out of oppressing them. When I pointed out to Amanda that Ann had actually voted against her civil partnership with her partner, Hilary, that somehow became my fault.

At one point I was feeling really down and I couldn't snap myself out of it. I went to the bedroom and meditated, and when I was done a thought flashed through my mind: what would Bianca, Adore and Darienne think about all this? I thought of Bianca's strength and confidence, Adore's sense of fun and loyalty, and Darienne's heart and humour. I thought about how proud they would be of everything I had done over the previous few weeks, and how they were in the outside world cheering me on. I always find that after meditating I don't need to try and think of the answers; I get out of my head and I just know what to do.

My gratitude journal is the only thing I have really carried forward from the time in which I was into self-help books. Each night before bed I like to write down five things I was grateful for that day: *Thank you for the delicious dinner, Thank you for the FaceTime with Vanity*, etc. Some days I write more than five. There is something really powerful about recognising the good in our lives, and over time I've found it has helped to skew my confirmation bias more towards the positive end of the spectrum. As we didn't have any reading or writing materials in the house, I think my little exercise of thinking about Adore, Bianca and Darienne was like my brain reminding me that there was lots to be grateful for.

Slowly the other housemates were evicted, and it came down to Ann and me sitting on the couch on the night of the finale. I didn't go into the house thinking I could or should win because it was 'Year of the Woman', but when it was just Ann and me left I really hoped it was me; Ann's views on gender are regressive, and I am 100 per cent committed to allyship with women. When Emma Willis, the host of *CBB*, called my name as the winner, I actually didn't know how to react. I felt really calm and silent. I remember thinking, *Shit… Put on a show. Show people you are happy about winning* – which I was of course, but I guess I had no context for why I won or of how people had been receiving my stint in the *Big Brother* house in the outside world.

What I do know is how my life has changed since leaving the house. All of a sudden everything was different; people were interested in what I had to say. Instead of the same reductive question like, 'How long does it take you to get into drag?' people were asking me to explain the difference between sex and gender, or between the drag and trans experiences. People wanted to know my thoughts on politics, the environment and race. I was on the BBC talking about the NHS and commenting on Brexit!

This was a dream come true for me. I'd been talking about these things on my socials and YouTube for years, but interviewers in the mainstream media were never really interested in what I thought. Being a young(ish) queer person and having a voice that was respected in the mainstream was so cool. It was validating. I was being respected and celebrated as me.

Part of the reason I think people responded to me on *Big Brother* is because, in an increasingly polarised and heated political climate in the UK after the Brexit vote, I was able to calmly explain different topics to my fellow housemates, and I spoke to political opponents like Ann pleasantly and with compassion. Even Ann appreciated that. When we finished the first conversation about 'Marriage equality, as you call it', Ann paused and said to me, 'Thank you for that conversation. Most people would have raised their voices, stormed off, or called me a homophobe.' That was a clue to me that Ann wasn't used to being heard or having a respectful conversation with opposing views.

I knew I wasn't going to change Ann's mind in the house, but I hoped to understand a little more about why she held the views that she did. And I did understand, but maybe in a way I hadn't expected to. People who have different views don't hold them because they want to be bigots; they think they are right, that they are doing good in the world, and they think of themselves as good people. I don't need everyone to agree with me, but I would like a world where people can hold differing opinions and still respect one another.

That said, the thing about Ann's views is that they aren't just about her and her beliefs; they also dictate what I can and cannot do and be. Although I think Ann liked me as an individual, her views are essentially evidence of a lack of respect for and understanding of who I am and the people in my community. Such people actively try to oppress us, make us less visible and take away our rights as humans. I think the real issue lies with giving Ann a platform to be likeable, even lovable. We give divisive people platforms because they make for good TV, and we don't often pair them with a capable partner to refute their arguments. I wasn't a capable opposition to Ann, but I knew what my limits were and I tried to stay within them. While I did win the competition, I still don't think I did the best job of addressing Ann's really damaging, anachronistic bigotry.

It's a vicious cycle. The producers' decision to put people like Ann on mainstream reality shows like *Strictly Come Dancing* and *CBB* results in sensational coverage of her appearance; in turn, the viewing public is sidetracked and entertained by the outrage that ensues, driving up ratings and social media reach. Outrage culture plays into the audience's desire to have a voice, but people like Ann – who enact tangible harm through their views – are rarely 'cancelled'. In part, her popularity as a 'character' on TV has allowed her to attract press and attention. In 2019 Ann was once again elected to political office, to serve as a Member of the European Parliament for South West England for Nigel Farage's right-wing populist Brexit Party.

When I got out of the *Big Brother* house I was excited to see Andrew Brady as Courtney in private, when the cameras weren't rolling. We were both infatuated with each other, this much I knew, and I thought there might be fun to be had with less clothing on. After the cast party I got back to my hotel room and had a debrief with Wendy, who had flown all the way from Australia a couple of weeks earlier when she saw everything taking off in the UK. I really wanted to sit with her and get a trustworthy blow-by-blow of what had unfolded on screen.

By the time Wendy and I finished catching up, I messaged the boys to see where they were at and… they were asleep! There I was, winner of *Celebrity Big Brother* 2018, with my pink-and-purple unicorn side pony, blue glitter brows and metallic gold dress, sitting on my hotel bed listening to the dawn chorus all by myself. I wasn't ready to go to sleep; I wanted to kiki with the lads now we were back in the default world. And I especially wanted to see Andrew. I sat there for about half an hour grappling with the reality that it was over for the night, then I got out of drag and went to sleep.

The next day I messaged Andrew to see if he wanted to have dinner on Sunday night. I asked my friends for impressive, romantic date ideas. One suggested dinner at Berners Tavern and a room at the Sanderson. Done! Andrew was in. The plan was to go in drag, of course.

Then Wendy told me that, due to the visa I was currently on in the UK, I had to catch the train to Paris on Sunday and re-enter the country on a new visa. This piece of bureaucracy has always seemed so stupid to me, but I have followed the rules and caught the train to Brussels and Paris several times, and even flown to Milan or Berlin during a global pandemic to fulfil this immigration obligation. I would still make it back from Paris in time for dinner, but I wouldn't have time to get into drag.

I was kinda livid. My perfect plan had been foiled. In fear of sounding like dirty old Uncle Courtney, there was no deceit going on here; Andrew clearly knew Shane and Courtney, but I was just pandering my aesthetic to his tastes as a straight guy. I was 'peacocking', if you will. Some guys go to the gym and get a cute haircut to attract guys, and sometimes I get in drag to do it.

The dinner with Andrew was my first chance to properly celebrate my win in the outside world, so when the Champagne cart came around I said yes. We drank and ate and had a lot of fun catching up, trying to keep our voices down while we bitched about other housemates, but not doing a very successful job of it. We left the restaurant quite plonkered and headed back to the hotel bar, where we had another drink and then went up to the room. We raided the minibar fridge, where we found some minis of Famous Grouse, Ann's favourite tipple, then cheersed to Ann and continued to drink away. I had to be up in the morning for a live TV interview on *The Wright Stuff* on Channel 5 – as Shane, thankfully.

Andrew and I climbed into bed as we had done in the *Big Brother* house most nights we were there, but this time it was different because there were no cameras. I wanted so badly to instigate physical contact, a stray hand on a shoulder or something that would cross the line from friend to lover, but I was just too scared. I didn't want to embarrass myself or make Andrew feel uncomfortable. I was also aware that I wasn't dressed as my superpower. I set an alarm for a few hours later and we drifted off to sleep.

When the alarm woke me up I was still drunk, so a hangover wasn't an issue yet. I figured I would get a Black Taxi to the studio, do what I thought was a quick ten-minute interview and then race back to bed.

No. At the studio, a producer told me, 'Here are the articles for today's show,' and I was handed a folder with printouts in it. It turned out that the 'interview' was a two-hour-long live panel in which I would have to discuss Brexit and the NHS. *Holy fuck!* I was leaking tequila out of my pores, and I was sure I reeked of it.

My hangover slowly started to creep in, so I asked for some painkillers and a coffee. Sitting on the panel I somehow managed to keep it together, constantly sipping from the glass of water in front of me. I was quite impressed with myself. Andrew texted: he wasn't even able to stand up yet, so he had no idea how I was able to discuss the details of UK politics on TV.

'Now can I go to bed?' I asked Wendy afterwards.

'No, Shane – I told you this several times but we have a full day of meetings.' I am absolutely sure Wendy had told me all of this, but I guess I'd just drunk all memory of that away the night before. We went from the network studios to the offices of various production companies, traversing London. We had back-to-back meetings and even a few hours of phone press to squeeze in while we travelled.

The meeting with one production company, Monkey Kingdom, actually led to me hosting my own big-budget variety Christmas special on Channel 4, and hosting *The Bi Life* on the E! Channel all around the world. Despite my out-of-character hangover on a work day, I was so grateful for Wendy; she had made some really good career calls for me while I'd been in the *Big Brother* house.

23

I was snuggled up with Asaf in the back garden of a friend's house where I was staying. It was a small city oasis: the concrete walls and stone-tiled floor were littered with lush foliage. Long, elegant fronds and large, glossy leaves emerged out of big potted plants. Against one wall, bamboo trees grew out of a planter that doubled as the large bench we were reclined on.

Although the heat and hustle of the late-summer day had finally given way to the cooler, calmer ways of the evening, there was still a buzz in the air. It was the week leading up to the Mardi Gras parade, and the streets of inner-city Sydney were vibrating with anticipation. That weekend we would celebrate 40 years of Mardi Gras. This was also the first parade since marriage equality had passed in Australian parliament a few months before, so now it was time to party. To top it all off, Cher would be performing. It doesn't get gayer than this, friends!

Asaf was tall – six foot four – and I fit perfectly into his armpit. My back was nestled into his strong torso, and his arms were wrapped around me. I'd met him in London, before I'd gone on *Celebrity Big Brother*. We'd had a couple of lovely dates, but then Christmas, and me being locked in a house on TV, had cut short our courtship. Now we both happened to find ourselves on the other side of the world in the same city, the same garden, same bench.

When Asaf had messaged, I was excited to rekindle some unfinished business. Earlier that night we'd gone to get some gelato from Messina, a Sydney institution. I asked for a scoop of chocolate sorbet and he got coconut something-or-other. As we'd drifted through the lamplit streets all decked out in rainbowed regalia, I realised Asaf and I were close to where I was staying, so had asked if he wanted to come over. So far we'd only kissed – which, in my world, for two people on a third date, is a bit of an anomaly, almost cause for concern. The gay dating scene isn't known for its reserve and patience.

The garden was lit by the warm light of the full moon and the cool artificial light of a garden lamp. I couldn't see Asaf's face because I was snuggled up against him, so my gaze rested on his forearms. They belonged to a man: they were strong, hairy, masculine. I could see my forearms too: much smaller and delicate, half smooth from laser hair removal, half spiky from the hairs the laser hadn't caught yet. I thought about the fact that his arms simply were what they were, but my arms were a work in progress. His were exactly how they'd always been as an adult; mine were a creation. His limbs, to me, seemed like a lovely mature-growth forest. Mine were the manicured topiaries you'd find in the sort of gay man's garden we'd found ourselves cuddling in that night. In his arms, I felt soft and delicate. I felt safe.

Shit. Asaf is gay; he's attracted to men. Soft and delicate does not make a man.

There it was again. That voice.

It's just a matter of time before he realises you're not a real man.

In that moment with Asaf, even though I felt so physically protected by his arms, I wasn't immune from the battle of masculinity and femininity that had raged in my body and brain for most of my life. Before Asaf, I hadn't been with a gay man in years; the men I'd been involved with had been bi, pan, straight or heteroflexible. That hadn't been a conscious decision, just the path of least resistance. The LIMP phenomenon had persisted, and encounters with gay men mostly involved erectile excuses. It had been hard – or should I say challenging – not to let it affect my sense of desirability.

And so it was that the ghosts of my insecurities tried to haunt me as I lay there with Asaf. I'd never really considered myself a 'man'; the word was tinged with aggression and hostility when I applied it to myself. A boy? Yes. A girl? Sometimes. A man? It made me wince. There were many labels I identified with, many of them contradicting, but 'man' has never felt right.

My views on labels have shifted too. While my conversation with Chaz all those years ago, when he told me about gender-fluidity, was a revelatory moment about how language could affirm my sense of self and speak to me, I've since resolved to become less worried about living up to labels; I've spent my whole life doing that. While markers of gender identity can be indescribably helpful to people, and I still like to talk about labels because they serve an important purpose, these days my personal feeling is that the constructs of language can never fully capture our core selves.

Maybe we need to expand the definition of what a man is and what a woman is. Maybe we need to embrace and more fully explore non-binary identities. Maybe – definitely – both. The rigid gender binary that men cling to so desperately doesn't seem to be doing them any favours. This conversation is for more than just the sissies and the dykes, the enbies and the binary trans folk, it's also for the cisgender straight men who are so trapped in their own fucked-up creation. Instead of living as a reaction to the straight male gaze, as I did for so long, I think of all of us gender outlaws as liberators of the patriarchy. We've been made to feel wrong, but we are the ones who are trying to get it right.

In that moment in the garden with Asaf, I listened to my insecurities and recognised them for what they were. I hadn't always been aware of them in the moment; often I'd reacted based on my past experiences. But now I felt a space open up between my feelings, thoughts and actions. I was aware that they were *just* thoughts, and that they were no longer serving me.

No single thing had led me to this moment of realisation. I'm sure the introspection and self-examination had been important, as had the books I'd read, and talking to psychologists, and the hours of meditation. But more than that, life also just unfolds. All of the worry and identity angst of my late teens, 20s and 30s had ultimately helped me to arrive at this sense of peace and clarity. Perhaps if I'd just relaxed a little more into the ebbs and flows, loosened my grip on something I had no control over anyway, the ride might have been a little smoother. But I had finally arrived at a place of resolve, and I had no regrets.

I'm so grateful for how being Courtney Act has complicated my life and allowed me to know who I am outside the status quo of expectation. A beam of stark white light is actually a composite of every visible colour imaginable, yet those colours are only revealed to the eye when refracted through a prism. Courtney has been that prism for me, bending the light so I can see the full spectrum of my gender and sexuality.

Snuggled up with Asaf under the light of moon and lamp, surrounded by greenery, I realised I was with a man who I was attracted to, who was attracted to me, and who was also emotionally available (that last one is the hardest to come by). I allowed myself to feel grateful and enjoy the moment.

The original plan for January 2018 had been to rehearse my new cabaret show, *Under the Covers.* I'd written and designed it all in the previous six months, and I was going to tour during the Australian summer before heading over to the UK for summer there. The show featured famous cover songs that you might not have known were covers. For example, it opened with 'It's Oh So Quiet', which most people know as a Björk song; it's actually a cover of a song by Betty Hutton from 1951, which itself was a cover of the 1948 classic '*Und jetzt ist es still*', German for 'It's Oh So Quiet'.

I was so proud of the show, especially considering my limited budget. Marco Marco made the costumes, Dallas hand-painted the artwork for the set and Abbey built it all. I had a live pianist and some custom backing tracks to fill out the sound. I was meant to have a month of rehearsals to get the songs and choreography perfect, but *Big Brother* really shook up the timeline, and winning it even more so. Wendy and I had decided to stay in the UK for as long as possible to reap the rewards by doing lots of press, going to meetings with networks and production companies and a whistlestop club tour around the Kingdom. By the time I got back to Australia I had a week of rehearsals, which meant opening night at Adelaide Fringe was loose, chaotic and stressful.

However, by the time I got to the Seymour Centre in Sydney later that month, the show had hit its stride.

'Twas the night before Mardi Gras. The audience was packed with friends and family, and the vibe was electric.

After the show, Vanity came backstage to the dressing room. I girded my loins for one of her special-brand backhanded compliments.

'Brenda, that show was really good!' (Brenda is our term of endearment for each other.)

She sounded really impressed, but I waited for the backhanded part I knew would be coming. 'Thanks, Brenda?'

'No, seriously. It was really, really good. You looked great. You sounded great. You didn't sing like a hungry alley cat too much. But there was something else…' She paused for a moment, trying to put her finger on it. 'You're not thirsty any more. Usually there's an element of desperation, but you were just so comfortable on stage tonight. It was lovely.'

There it was.

But she was right.

Winning *Celebrity Big Brother* had profoundly validated me. People got to see the real me – the real Courtney and the real Shane – and they celebrated that. I saw this process of validation unfold as I watched back every episode after I left the house and saw the amazing response in the media. I'd been welcomed into the UK mainstream, and by proxy the Australian mainstream had opened its arms to me too. I was no longer the joke or the sideshow. I had a seat at the table. I didn't know what I had been missing all these years, but this feeling of being accepted was a full-circle moment for the 14-year-old standing near the A-block boys, wondering, *Why don't you like me?*

Vanity was right: I wasn't thirsty any more. I had finally arrived.

Closing Act

When I was born (and probably even before) my mum and dad started laying a foundation for a brand-new home. Bit by bit, piece by piece, over the next 18 years they poured thick slabs of love and drove strong beams of support deep into the earth. Once they completed a section I would start building my own little structure on top. Mum and Dad would take me around to see other homes, some brick, others wood; some tall and sleek, and others small and cosy. They showed me catalogues of carpets and wallpapers, fixtures and fittings. They took me to home decorator stores and let me wander off and bring back anything I liked.

By the age of ten I had built a gorgeous little dwelling. It was a unique and peculiar little home, like the Gaudí House in Barcelona or something you'd find in Whoville. Every surface was a different colour and a different texture. Each wall was made of a different material. There was fringe, glitter, shag walls and jewel-encrusted windows. It was eclectic but harmonious. It was self-supporting, self-sustaining and most magnificent to behold.

Then one day, sometime around the onset of puberty, some building developers turned up and declared that all of the unique little homes on my street had to look one of two ways.

All the houses with even numbers needed to look a certain way, and all of the odd-numbered houses needed to look another. Carpenters erected four big walls around my structure and painted the whole thing blue.

I could never work out which house was mine, though, so I painted its sides different colours. The front was festooned with glitter polka dots.

That decision to be different came at a cost: I got a letter in the mail telling me I had to paint it back to blue, and after I ignored it an inspector arrived on my doorstep to tell me I had to pay an on-the-spot fine. A team of men turned up with ladders and tins of blue paint, then they hurriedly slapped a coat on so it looked pretty much like all the others – but not quite. The walls were blue again but all slightly different shades, and the finish was rushed and streaky.

At Christmas I put up lights, and when New Year rolled around I decided not to take them down. People thought it was odd, but they let it slide. When I turned 18 I started making little additions here and there, mostly to the inside; I'd knock down walls and do all sorts of home renovations that were never to code. Yet still the four blue walls on the outside imposed, blocking the natural light and fresh air. Most people on my side of the street seemed content with their homes. Every now and then the outside of one would get a new coat of paint, sometimes glossy, sometimes satin, sometimes matte – but always blue.

The other houses always had the curtains drawn, so I never knew what they looked like inside, but from the outside they looked like how my house was supposed to look. I felt so much shame through my 20s 'cause everyone else's home looked uniform and mine looked slapdash. But as I got out of my neighbourhood and explored other cities and countries, I noticed the houses looked slightly different everywhere I went, and I got ideas about how my home could look.

When I turned 30 I felt the urge to renovate. I began knocking down the back wall and started to see the odd shapes of the wonderful little home I had built when I was a kid. The neighbours over the back wrote a letter to the council, but no one ever got around to following it up. As I pulled down the second wall I started to recognise in my home elements of others I had seen on my travels. I had asked some of these people why no one had sent them a letter or fined them, or come round and painted their house back to its original colour; it turned out that those things had indeed happened to them, but they had fought back. They said no. They worked together and joined the body corporate board and city councils, and they had the rules changed.

I started to meet more and more people like me. I knocked down the third wall until only the blue façade and janky white picket fence remained. I went to the local council meetings, the city council meetings, I even went on TV and started talking about how I thought we should be allowed to paint our homes whatever colour we wanted.

A couple of years ago, in the middle of the night, I demolished the final wall to reveal the peculiar, gorgeous and unique building that lay beneath, the one I'd built all those years ago. It was just as magnificent as I remembered.

I worked all through the night, clearing the last of the rubble as the sun started to rise. The sun's rays filled the house with the most perfect morning light. The architecture I'd designed so intuitively as a kid made the whole place the perfect temperature all year round. Instead of fixed rigid binaries there was now an infinite kaleidoscope of possibility.

Words can't describe how I felt when I uncovered that tiny little house – it was all I'd ever needed. The feeling was beyond the realm of right and wrong; beyond the reach of the five senses or the thinking mind. When all is stripped away, an intrinsic sense of being is all that remains. It just is.

The process of writing this book has demanded that I continually reconnect with my emotions and my younger self. I'm now able to watch and feel my past in full HD. Actually, it's more than that; I'm now capable of time travel.

These long hours, days, months I have spent going back and immersing myself in childhood memories have often been painful. I've cried, sobbed and released so much pent-up emotion I never knew existed. I would often find myself rocking back and forth with tears streaming down my face, my arms wrapped around myself. My present self would say to my younger self, *I'm sorry I wasn't there to protect you.*

But all of this time travel has also allowed me to fortify my inner child with the strength and courage and wisdom I have accumulated through my experience. I stand there with him – SPICEBOY 99 jersey, backpack, braces headgear and all – hugging him, looking him in the eye, and being the person who I needed back then.

One day in the midst of writing, I met my friend the writer Alex Leon for brunch, and our conversation turned to the subject of what it means to grow up queer in a straight-as-default world. He wrote this tweet that sums it up nicely:

> Queer people don't grow up as ourselves, we grow up playing a version of ourselves that sacrifices authenticity to minimise humiliation & prejudice. The massive task of our adult lives is to unpick which parts of ourselves are truly us & which parts we've created to protect us.

I've been unpicking all of this conditioning over the course of my life and throughout the writing process for this memoir. It's not that I've been trying to arrive at one pre-existing definition for myself. It's actually not about labels at all, because no one label fits anyone perfectly, but the labels are still important because they're like signs that guide you to the right street, at which point you have to find which house is yours. And once you've found that house, you get to decorate and redecorate it however you like to make it yours.

What if, instead of being prescribed expectations of what job we are supposed to do, who we're supposed to sleep with and what we're supposed to wear, we were shown all the available options and given the freedom to pick things up and put things down as we please; to try things on and see what works for us. I know that's not a reality yet, but given how much has changed throughout my own first few decades of life, I can see we are moving in the right direction.

And the way we get there is by hearing more than one kind of story. Not just *my* story, but more of everyone's stories. We need to hear the stories of women, First Nations people, people of colour, people with disabilities and more. Currently, people with diverse sexualities, gender identities and expressions, and sex characteristics are criminalised and persecuted in 69 countries because of who they are and who they love, and we must listen to the stories of local activists and support their efforts. This process of storytelling and listening means engaging with the worlds of people whose stories have, for so long and for so many, been pushed down and swallowed like broken glass. Their stories, both private and public, soft and loud, have let me know my story is shared by many voices. And I hope you know that yours is too.

Acknowledgements

I would like to acknowledge and pay my respects to the Gadigal people of the Eora Nation, the Traditional Owners and Custodians of the land on which I wrote parts of this book. As I look out at the salt-water harbour you have protected since time immemorial, I would like to pay my respects to Elders past and present.

Wendy Richards, you've been my friend, manager and confidante for 15 years, and I'm so glad I get to do this with you; I couldn't be in more caring and capable hands. I appreciate that you always do the right thing, not the easy thing, or the thing that will make the most money. You've always seen the best in me and you've never given up, even when times were tough and work was scarce. Thank you, and sorry I pissed the bed that one time in Tampa. (Don't worry, people: Wendy and I were in separate beds, but still, she had to share the same 3.5-star hotel room with me after that.)

At my publisher, Pantera Press, I have found people who professionally overthink every detail, which I really quite love. I never thought anyone could care as much about my story as I do, or deep-dive and drill down into the minutiae as much as I wanted to, but each of you assured me at every step that this is what writing is all about. Alison Green, I'm so glad I got to publish this book with your amazing team.

Thank you so much to Lex Hirst, my wonderful publisher. As this was my first book, I assume our daily hour-long lockdown Zooms are a normal part of the writing process? I'm still not actually sure, but I am so grateful I had you to memoir-whisper me through the birth of my first literary child. Next time you say, 'Just write everything', I'll try to not take that so literally (I lost count after 220,000 words).

Tom Langshaw, thank you for stepping in when Lex gave birth to her first human child and knowing the book better than I did by the end. You made sure I finessed every detail even when I wanted to throw my laptop out the window (which, to be fair, was only in the last few days). Thank you for caring so much about this book.

Anne Reilly: I'll be honest, I was nervous for you to read this. I know you have edited memoirs by Australian heads of state, so you probably imagined something different when you heard you'd work on a book by a queen. Thank you for your forensic editing.

Kate O'Donnell, my copyeditor: Kate, we have never met, but I feel I know you so well just from the notes we exchanged back and forth. Thank you for bringing to the edit your queer touch and your rich knowledge of the era of Sydney I grew up in. I will need to hear some of your stories one day, since you have heard all of mine.

Dustin Lance Black, thank you for reading Act I when I first wrote it. Your encouragement gave me faith that what I was doing was on the right track.

Dearest Brenda, I love you! Thank you for being my brother, sister, confidant and inspiration. I also need to acknowledge that the Courtney Act Patented Lubing Technique is actually your intellectual property that I stole.

Tim Duggan (DugDog), thank you for being such a wonderful friend, for being the trial-run Pantera author with your book *Cult*

Status, and for letting me know which emotional stage of the publishing process I would entertain ahead of time. Goodnight, Josephine.

Brad Loekle: the man who makes me funny! You told me I would love writing a book because I could spend half a page describing the light coming in through the window. As such, the first story I wrote for this (about Oscar) was 12,000 words long and only covered a seven-hour period.

Marco Marco, thank you for always making me the most beautiful dresses to wear. I truly adore you and your talent, and feel so lucky I get to wear your clothes.

Mitch and Aaron, although the story of Summer Sorbet was left on the cutting-room floor, the impact of that outfit will live on: it was pivotal for my current understanding of fashion and how that relates to my gender expression. I forever want to be dressed in a pastel rainbow of blush, peach, lemon, mint, baby blue and periwinkle.

Lucy, Toby and Zak, thank you so much for sharing your talents and writing such a beautiful song, 'In Between', with me. Now we just need Sam Smith to record it as a non-binary anthem!

Last of all, I want to thank Mum and Dad. I hope that in reading this book you see what a privileged and unique experience you've given me. I know you think it's a parent's job to love their child, but so many don't do it as unconditionally as you two have. You have inspired so many children and parents by supporting and loving me, whether it was that first show you came to at Stonewall, your appearance on *Australian Story*, or the countless other times.

Reading List

The following books are referenced in my memoir, or have more generally informed my writing and thinking:

Barker, Meg-John and Scheele, Julia, *Queer: A Graphic History*, London, Icon Books, 2016

Black, Dustin Lance, *Mama's Boy: A Story from Our Americas*, New York, Knopf, 2019

Bono, Chaz, *Transition: Becoming Who I Was Always Meant to Be* (paperback edition), New York, Plume, 2012

Bornstein, Kate, *Gender Outlaw: On Men, Women, and the Rest of Us* (updated edition), New York, Vintage, 2016

Boylan, Jennifer Finney, *She's Not There: A Life in Two Genders* (paperback edition), New York, Crown, 2013

Brown, A. J., *Michael Kirby: Paradoxes and Principles*, Sydney, Federation Press, 2011

Brown, Brené, *Daring Greatly: How the Courage to be Vulnerable Transforms the Way We Live, Love, Parent, and Lead*, London, Penguin Life, 2016

Brown, Cupcake, *A Piece of Cake*, London, Random House, 2006

Downs, Alan, *The Velvet Rage: Overcoming the Pain of Growing Up Gay in a Straight Man's World*, 2nd edn., New York, Hachette, 2012

Faye, Shon, *The Transgender Issue: An Argument for Justice*, London, Allen Lane, 2021

Harari, Yuval Noah, *Homo Deus: A Brief History of Tomorrow*, London, Harvill Secker, 2016

Harari, Yuval Noah, *Sapiens: A Brief History of Humankind*, London, Harvill Secker, 2014
Hardy, Janet W. and Easton, Dossie, *The Ethical Slut: A Practical Guide to Polyamory, Open Relationships, and Other Freedoms in Sex and Love*, 3rd edn., Berkeley, Ten Speed Press, 2017
Hari, Johann, *Chasing the Scream: The Search for the Truth About Addiction*, London, Bloomsbury, 2019
Jones, Wendy, *Grayson Perry: Portrait of the Artist as a Young Girl* (updated edition), London, Vintage, 2007
Kahneman, Daniel, *Thinking, Fast and Slow*, London, Penguin, 2011
Killermann, Sam, *A Guide to Gender: The Social Justice Advocate's Handbook*, 2nd edn., Austin, Impetus Books, 2017
Kilmer-Purcell, Josh, *I Am Not Myself These Days*, New York, Harper Perennial, 2006
Lorde, Audre, *The Master's Tools Will Never Dismantle the Master's House*, London, Penguin, 2018
Millet, Catherine, *The Sexual Life of Catherine M.*, London, Serpent's Tail, 2012
Mock, Janet, *Redefining Realness: My Path to Womanhood, Identity, Love & So Much More*, New York, Atria Books, 2014
Mock, Janet, *Surpassing Certainty: What My Twenties Taught Me*, New York, Atria Books, 2017
Molloy, Shannon, *Fourteen: My Year of Darkness, and the Light that Followed*, Sydney, Simon & Schuster, 2020
Newton, Esther, *Mother Camp: Female Impersonators in America* (updated edition), Chicago, University of Chicago Press, 1979
Obama, Barack, *A Promised Land*, New York, Crown, 2020
Palmer, Amanda, *The Art of Asking: How I Learned to Stop Worrying and Let People Help*, London, Little Brown, 2014
Perel, Esther, *Mating in Captivity: Unlocking Erotic Intelligence*, London, Hodder & Stoughton, 2007
Perry, Grayson, *The Descent of Man*, London, Allen Lane, 2016
Storr, Will, *Selfie: How We Became So Self-Obsessed and What It's Doing to Us*, London, Picador, 2017
Warhol, Andy and Hackett, Pat, *POPism*, London, Penguin, 2008

Support Services

Childline
0800 11 11

FFLAG
Families and Friends of Lesbians and Gays
fflag.org.uk

Galop
Provides helplines and other support for LGBTIQ+ adults and young people who have experienced hate crime, sexual violence or domestic violence
0207 704 2040 (LGBT+ hate crime helpline)
0800 999 5428 (national LGBT+ domestic abuse helpline)
help@galop.org.uk
galop.org.uk

Gendered Intelligence
genderedintelligence.co.uk

LGBT Foundation
Advice, support and information for people identifying as LGBTQ+
0345 3 30 30 30
lgbt.foundation

Mermaids
Supports gender-diverse young people aged 19 and under, and their families and carers
0808 801 0400

MindLine Trans+
Free, confidential listening service for people identifying as trans or non-binary, and their friends and families
0300 330 5468

Samaritans
08456 90 90 90

Saneline
0845 7678 000

Stonewall
Information and advice for LGBT people on a range of issues
08000 50 20 20
stonewall.org.uk

Switchboard
Listening services, information and support for lesbian, gay, bisexual and transgender communities
0300 330 0630
switchboard.lgbt